Baking & Desserts

This is a Parragon Publishing Book
This edition published in 2004

Parragon Publishing
Queen Street House
4 Queen Street
Bath BA1 1HE, UK

ISBN: 1-40544-383-9

Printed in China

Produced by The Bridgewater Book Company Ltd

NOTE

Cup measurements in this book are for American cups. This book also uses
imperial and metric measurements. Follow the same units of measurement
throughout; do not mix imperial and metric.
All spoon measurements are level: teaspoons are assumed to be 5 ml and
tablespoons are assumed to be 15 ml.Unless otherwise stated, milk is assumed
to be whole milk,eggs and individual vegetables such as potatoes are medium,
and pepper is freshly ground black pepper.

The nutritional information provided for each recipe is per serving or per
person. Optional ingredients, variations, or serving suggestions have not been
included in the calculations. The times given for each recipe are an
approximate guide only because the preparation times may differ according
to the techniques used by different people and the cooking times may vary as
a result of the type of oven used.

Recipes using raw or very lightly cooked eggs should be
avoided by infants, the elderly, pregnant women, convalescents, and anyone
suffering from an illness.

Baking & Desserts

p

Contents-Baking

Contents-Chocolate

Baking

Introduction

It may be a daunting prospect to bake your own bread, pastries, cookies, and cakes instead of buying them ready-made at a foodstore, but once you have acquired the basic skills—and armed yourself with a few of the "tricks"—it becomes fun, versatile, and rewarding.

There are a few points that will make sure your baking session is successful, whatever type of recipe you have chosen. So, before you start:

- Read through the recipe carefully, and make sure you have the right ingredients—using all-purpose flour when self-rising flour is specified, for example, may not produce the result you were expecting!
- Remember to preheat the oven to the right temperature.
- Make sure you are using the correct size and shape of pan or dish because the quantities given in the recipe are for the size of the pan specified.
- Prepare the cookware before you start assembling the ingredients—grease or line pans, dishes, or cookie sheets as directed in the recipe.
- Measure the ingredients accurately, and do any basic preparation, such as chopping, slicing, or grating, before you start cooking.
- Once you start cooking, follow the recipe step-by-step, in the order given. Using high-quality ingredients will give the best results—unbleached flours and unrefined sugars are available for baking; fresh vegetables, fish, and good-quality meat from a reliable supplier, and a good, extra-virgin olive oil will make all the difference to savory bakes.

Pie Dough
- Use metal pans, rather than porcelain dishes, for tarts.
- Use fat at room temperature, cut into small pieces.
- Use ice water for mixing.
- Pie dough benefits from cool ingredients and cold hands.
- Strain dry ingredients into a mixing bowl to incorporate air.
- Wrap dough in foil or plastic wrap and allow it to "rest" in the refrigerator for 30 minutes before using.

Bread
- Plan ahead—most bread recipes include one or two periods of "proving" (leaving the dough in a warm place to double its bulk).
- If the flour feels cool, warm it gently in an oven at a low temperature before using.
- Make sure the liquid is lukewarm, to activate the yeast.
- To knead dough, stretch it away from you with one hand, while pulling it toward you with the other, then fold in the edges, turn it around slightly, and repeat.
- To test whether bread is cooked, tap the base of the loaf—it should sound hollow if it is ready.

Cakes
- Using a loose-based pan will make it easier to turn out the cake.
- Bring all the ingredients to room temperature before starting to bake.
- If possible, use a hand-held electric mixer for "creaming" (beating together the butter and sugar until the mixture has a pourable consistency).
- Fold in dry ingredients very gently, using a metal spoon or spatula in a figure-eight movement. This lets the air get to the mixture and stops the cake becoming too heavy.
- When the cake is cooked, it should feel springy when pressed lightly. Alternatively, when a fine metal skewer is inserted into the center of the cake, it should come out clean if the cake is cooked.

Basic Recipes

Ragù Sauce

MAKES ABOUT 2½ CUPS

3 tbsp olive oil

3 tbsp butter

2 large onions, chopped

4 celery stalks, sliced thinly

1 cup chopped bacon

2 garlic cloves, chopped

4½ cups ground beef

2 tbsp tomato paste

1 tbsp all-purpose flour

14 oz/400 g canned chopped tomatoes

⅔ cup beef bouillon

⅔ cup red wine

2 tsp dried oregano

½ tsp freshly grated nutmeg

salt and pepper

1 Heat the oil and butter in a pan over medium heat. Add the onions, celery, and bacon and cook for 5 minutes, stirring constantly.

2 Stir in the garlic and ground beef and cook, stirring frequently, until the meat has lost its redness. Lower the heat and simmer for 10 minutes, stirring occasionally.

3 Increase the heat to medium, stir in the tomato paste and the flour, and cook for 1–2 minutes. Add the tomatoes, bouillon, and wine and bring to the boil, stirring constantly. Season to taste, then stir in the oregano and nutmeg. Lower the heat, then cover, and simmer for 45 minutes, stirring occasionally. The sauce is now ready to use.

Basic Pizza Dough

MAKES ONE 10-INCH/25-CM PIZZA

1½ cups all-purpose flour, plus extra for dusting

1 tsp salt

1 tsp active dry yeast

6 tbsp lukewarm water

1 tbsp olive oil

1 Strain the flour and salt into a large bowl and add the yeast. Pour in the water and oil and bring together to form a dough. Knead for 5 minutes, then leave in a warm place to rise until doubled in size.

2 Punch the air out from the dough, then knead lightly. Roll it out on a lightly floured counter, ready for use.

Fresh Vegetable Bouillon

This can be kept chilled for up to three days or frozen for up to three months. Salt is not added when cooking the stock: it is better to season it according to the dish in which it its to be used.

MAKES ABOUT 6¼ CUPS

9 oz/250 g shallots

1 large carrot, diced

1 celery stalk, chopped

½ fennel bulb

1 garlic clove

1 bay leaf

a few fresh parsley and

    tarragon sprigs

8 cups water

pepper

1 Place all the ingredients in a large pan and bring to a boil.

2 Skim off the surface scum with a flat spoon and reduce to a gentle simmer. Partially cover and cook for 45 minutes. Let cool.

3 Line a strainer with clean cheesecloth and place over a large pitcher or bowl. Pour the bouillon through the strainer, then discard the herbs and vegetables.

4 Cover and store in small quantities in the refrigerator for up to three days.

Pesto Sauce

MAKES ABOUT 1¼ CUPS

2 cups finely chopped fresh parsley

2 garlic cloves, crushed

½ cup pine nuts, crushed

2 tbsp chopped fresh basil leaves

⅔ cup freshly grated Parmesan cheese

⅔ cup olive oil

white pepper

1 Place all the ingredients in a food processor and process for 2 minutes. Alternatively, you can blend by hand using a pestle and mortar.

2 Season with white pepper, then transfer to a pitcher, cover with plastic wrap, and store in the refrigerator before using.

Desserts

Confirmed dessert lovers feel a meal is lacking if there isn't a tempting dessert to finish off the menu. Yet it is often possible to combine indulgence with healthy ingredients. A lot of the recipes in this chapter contain fruit, which is the perfect ingredient for healthy desserts that are still deliciously tempting, such as Hot Blackberry Sponge, Raspberry Shortcake, Paper-thin Fruit Pies, Apple Tart Tatin, and Baked Bananas. Some desserts are also packed full of protein-rich nuts, such as Pine Nut Tart and Almond Cheesecakes.

queen of desserts

serves eight

2 tbsp butter, plus extra for greasing

2½ cups milk

1¼ cups superfine sugar

finely grated rind of 1 orange

4 eggs, separated

1⅔ cups fresh bread crumbs

pinch of salt

6 tbsp orange marmalade

COOK'S TIP

If you prefer a crisper meringue, bake the dessert in the oven for an extra 5 minutes.

VARIATION

Substitute the same quantity of fine sponge cake crumbs for the bread crumbs and use raspberry, strawberry, or apricot preserve instead of orange marmalade

1 Grease a 6-cup/1.5-litre ovenproof dish with a little butter.

2 To make the custard, heat the milk in a pan with the butter, ¼ cup of the superfine sugar, and the grated orange rind, until just warm.

3 Whisk the egg yolks in a bowl. Gradually pour the warm milk over the eggs, stirring constantly.

4 Stir the bread crumbs into the pan, then transfer the mixture to the prepared dish, and let stand for about 15 minutes.

5 Bake in a preheated oven, 350°F/180°C, for 20–25 minutes, until the custard has just set. Remove the dish from the oven, but do not turn the oven off.

6 To make the meringue, whisk the egg whites with the salt until they stand in soft peaks. Whisk in the remaining sugar, a little at a time.

7 Spread the orange marmalade over the cooked custard. Top with the meringue, spreading it right to the edges of the dish.

8 Return to the oven and bake for another 20 minutes, until the meringue is crisp and golden.

bread & butter pudding

serves six

4 tbsp butter, softened

4–5 slices white or brown bread

4 tbsp chunky orange marmalade

grated rind of 1 lemon

½–¾ cup golden raisins

¼ cup chopped candied peel

1 tsp ground cinnamon or allspice

1 cooking apple, peeled, cored, and
  coarsely grated

scant ½ cup brown sugar

3 eggs

generous 2 cups milk

2 tbsp raw brown sugar

3 Add another layer of bread, cutting the slices so that they fit the dish.

4 Sprinkle over most of the remaining golden raisins and all the remaining candied peel, spice, and brown sugar, sprinkling it evenly over the bread. Top with a final layer of bread, again cutting to fit the dish.

5 Lightly beat the eggs and milk together in a large mixing bowl, then carefully strain the mixture over the bread in the ovenproof dish. If time allows, let the pudding stand for 20–30 minutes.

1 Use the softened butter to grease an ovenproof dish and to spread on 1 side of the slices of bread, then spread the bread evenly with the orange marmalade.

2 Place a layer of buttered bread in the base of the prepared dish and sprinkle with the grated lemon rind, half of the golden raisins, half of the candied peel, half of the cinnamon or allspice, all of the apple, and half of the brown sugar.

6 Sprinkle the top of the finished bread pudding with the raw brown sugar and sprinkle over the remaining golden raisins. Cook in a preheated oven , 400°F/200°C, for 50–60 minutes, until it has risen and turned golden brown. Serve hot, if you like, or let cool completely, then serve cold.

eve's dessert

serves six

6 tbsp butter, plus extra for greasing

1 lb/450 g cooking apples, peeled,
  cored, and sliced

1 tbsp lemon juice

⅓ cup granulated sugar

⅓ cup golden raisins

⅓ cup superfine sugar

1 egg, beaten

1¼ cups self-rising flour

3 tbsp milk

¼ cup sliced almonds

custard or heavy cream, to serve

COOK'S TIP

To increase the almond flavor,
add ¼ cup of ground almonds
with the flour in step 4.

1 Grease a 3½-cup/900-ml
ovenproof dish with a little butter.

2 Combine the sliced apples with
the lemon juice, granulated sugar,
and golden raisins. Spoon into the
greased dish.

3 Cream the butter and superfine
sugar together in a bowl until
pale. Add the egg, a little at a time.

4 Carefully fold in the self-rising
flour and stir in the milk to give
a pourable consistency.

5 Spread the mixture evenly over
the apples and sprinkle the top
with the sliced almonds.

6 Bake in a preheated oven,
350°F/180°C, for 40–45 minutes,
until the sponge topping has turned
golden brown.

7 Serve the dessert piping hot,
accompanied by homemade
custard or heavy cream.

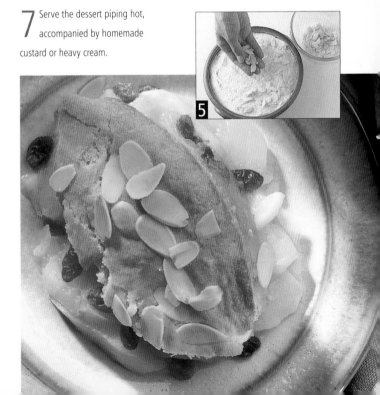

raspberry shortcake

serves eight

⅓ cup butter, diced, plus extra
    for greasing
1½ cups self-rising flour, plus extra
    for dusting
⅓ cup superfine sugar
1 egg yolk
1 tbsp rose water
2½ cups whipping cream,
    whipped lightly
1⅓ cups raspberries, plus extra
    for decoration
TO DECORATE
confectioners' sugar
fresh mint leaves (optional)

COOK'S TIP

The shortcake can be made a few
days in advance and stored in an
airtight container until required.

VARIATION

This shortcake is equally
delicious made with strawberries
or pitted and sliced peaches,
instead of raspberries.

1 Lightly grease 2 cookie sheets
with a little butter.

2 To make the shortcake, strain
the flour into a bowl.

3 Rub the butter into the flour with
your fingertips until the mixture
resembles bread crumbs.

4 Stir the sugar, egg yolk, and rose
water into the mixture and bring
together with your fingers to form a
soft dough. Divide the dough in half.

5 Roll each piece of dough into an
8-inch/20-cm circle on a lightly
floured counter. Carefully lift each one
with the rolling pin onto a prepared
cookie sheet, then crimp the edges
of the dough.

6 Bake in a preheated oven,
375°F/190°C, for 15 minutes,
until lightly golden. Transfer the
shortcakes to a wire rack and let cool.

7 Mix the whipped cream with the
raspberries and spoon on top of
one of the shortcakes. Top with the
other shortcake circle, dust with a little
confectioners' sugar, and decorate with
the extra raspberries and mint leaves,
if you like.

plum cobbler

serves six

6 tbsp butter, melted and cooled,
    plus extra for greasing
2 lb 4 oz/1 kg plums, pitted
    and sliced
½ cup superfine sugar
1 tbsp lemon juice
2¼ cups all-purpose flour
⅓ cup granulated sugar
2 tsp baking powder
1 egg, beaten
⅔ cup buttermilk
heavy cream, to serve

1 Lightly grease an 8-cup/2-litre ovenproof dish with a little butter.

2 Combine the sliced plums, superfine sugar, lemon juice, and ¼ cup of the all-purpose flour in a large bowl.

3 Spoon the coated plums into the base of the prepared ovenproof dish, spreading them out evenly.

4 Strain the remaining flour and baking powder into a bowl. Stir in the granulated sugar.

5 Add the beaten egg, buttermilk, and cooled melted butter. Mix everything gently together to form a soft dough.

6 Place spoonfuls of the dough on top of the fruit mixture until it is almost completely covered.

7 Bake in a preheated oven, 375°F/190°C, for 35–40 minutes, until the dough is golden brown and the fruit mixture is bubbling.

8 Serve the cobbler piping hot, with heavy cream.

hot blackberry sponge

serves four

6 tbsp butter, melted, plus extra
 for greasing
1 lb/450 g blackberries
⅓ cup superfine sugar
1 egg
⅓ cup brown sugar, plus extra
 for sprinkling
½ cup milk
scant 1 cup self-rising flour

1 Lightly grease a 3½-cup/900-ml
 ovenproof dish with a little butter.

2 Gently combine the blackberries
 and superfine sugar in a large
mixing bowl until well blended.

3 Transfer the blackberry and sugar
 mixture to the prepared dish,
spreading it out evenly.

4 In a separate bowl, beat the egg
 and brown sugar together. Stir in
the melted butter and milk.

5 Strain the flour into the egg and
 butter mixture and fold together
lightly, until the mixture forms a
smooth batter.

6 Carefully spread the batter over
 the blackberry and sugar mixture
in the ovenproof dish.

7 Bake the sponge in a preheated
 oven, 350°F/180°C, for about
25–30 minutes, until the topping is
firm and golden.

8 Sprinkle the sponge with a little
 brown sugar and serve hot.

treacle tart

serves eight

9 oz/250 g ready-made unsweetened
    pastry dough, thawed if frozen

1 cup light corn syrup

scant 2 cups fresh white
    bread crumbs

½ cup heavy cream

finely grated rind of ½ lemon
    or orange

2 tbsp lemon or orange juice

homemade custard, to serve

COOK'S TIP

Syrup is notoriously sticky and so
can be quite difficult to measure.
Dip the spoon in hot water first
and the syrup will slide off it
more easily and completely.

VARIATION

Use the dough trimmings to
create a lattice pattern on top of
the tart, if you wish.

1 Roll out the pie dough on a lightly floured counter and use it to line an 8-inch/20-cm loose-based tart pan, reserving the dough trimmings. Prick the bottom of the tart shell with a fork and chill in the refrigerator for 30 minutes.

2 Cut out small shapes from the reserved dough trimmings, such as leaves, stars, or hearts, to decorate the top of the tart.

3 Combine the light corn syrup, bread crumbs, heavy cream, grated lemon or orange rind, and lemon or orange juice in a bowl.

4 Pour the mixture into the tart shell and decorate the edges of the tart with the dough cut-outs.

5 Bake in a preheated oven, 375°F/190°C, for 35–40 minutes, or until the filling is just set.

6 Let the tart cool slightly in the pan Turn out and serve hot or cold with homemade custard.

apple tart tatin

serves eight

generous ½ cup butter

scant ⅔ cup superfine sugar

4 eating apples, cored and cut
into fourths

9 oz/250 g ready-made unsweetened
pastry dough, thawed if frozen

crème fraîche, to serve

1 Heat the butter and sugar in a
9-inch/23-cm ovenproof skillet
over medium heat for about 5 minutes,
until the mixture starts to caramelize.
Remove the skillet from the heat.

2 Arrange the apple fourths, skin
side down, in the skillet, taking
care as the butter and sugar will be
very hot. Place the skillet back on the
heat and simmer for 2 minutes.

3 Roll out the dough on a lightly
floured counter to form a circle
just a little larger than the skillet.

4 Place the dough over the apples,
press down, and carefully
tuck in the edges to seal the apples
underneath the layer of dough.

5 Bake in a preheated oven,
400°F/200°C, for 20–25 minutes,
until the dough is golden. Remove
from the oven and cool for about
10 minutes.

6 Place a serving plate over the
skillet and invert so that the
dough forms the base of the turned-
out tart. Serve with crème fraîche.

fruit crumble tart

serves eight

DOUGH

1¼ cups all-purpose flour, plus extra
    for dusting

2 tbsp superfine sugar

½ cup butter, diced

1 tbsp water

FILLING

1½ cups raspberries

1 lb/450 g plums, halved, pitted,
    and coarsely chopped

3 tbsp raw brown sugar

TOPPING

scant 1 cup all-purpose flour

⅓ cup raw brown sugar

⅓ cup butter, diced

⅔ cup chopped mixed nuts

1 tsp ground cinnamon

light cream or ice cream,
    to serve

1 To make the dough, place the flour, sugar, and butter in a bowl and rub in the butter with your fingertips. Add the water and bring together with your fingers to form a soft dough. Wrap in plastic wrap and chill in the refrigerator for 30 minutes.

2 Roll out the dough on a lightly floured counter and use it to line the base of a 9½-inch/24-cm loose-based tart pan. Prick the base of the tart shell with a fork and chill in the refrigerator for about 30 minutes.

3 To make the filling, toss the raspberries and plums together with the sugar and spoon into the tart shell.

4 To make the crumble topping, combine the flour, sugar, and butter in a bowl. Rub in the butter with your fingertips until the mixture resembles coarse bread crumbs. Stir in the nuts and ground cinnamon.

5 Sprinkle the crumble topping over the fruit and press down gently with the back of a spoon. Bake in a preheated oven, 400°F/200°C, for 20–25 minutes, until the topping has turned golden brown. Serve the tart with light cream or ice cream.

paper-thin fruit pies

COOK'S TIP

Keep the unused sheets of phyllo
pastry covered with a clean,
damp dish towel until you are
ready to use them, as they dry
out easily.

VARIATION

Other combinations of fruit are
equally delicious. Try peach and
apricot, raspberry, and apple, or
pineapple and mango.

1 Core and thinly slice the apple
and pear and toss them in the
lemon juice.

2 Gently melt the lowfat spread in a
small pan over low heat. Cut each
sheet of phyllo pastry into 4 and cover
with a clean, damp dish towel. Brush
4 large nonstick muffin pans,
10 cm/4 inches wide, with a little
of the lowfat spread.

3 Working on each pie separately,
brush 4 sheets of pastry with
lowfat spread. Press a small sheet
of pastry into the base of one pan.
Arrange the other sheets on top at
slightly different angles. Repeat with
the other sheets to make another
3 pies.

4 Arrange the apple and pear slices
alternately in the center of each
phyllo pastry case and lightly crimp the
edges of the pastry of each pie.

5 Combine the preserve and orange
juice until smooth and brush over
the fruit. Bake in a preheated oven,
400°F/200°C, for 12–15 minutes.

6 Sprinkle with the chopped
pistachios, dust lightly with
confectioners' sugar, and serve hot
with lowfat custard.

custard tart

serves eight

DOUGH

1¼ cups all-purpose flour, plus extra
   for dusting

2 tbsp superfine sugar

½ cup butter, diced

1 tbsp water

FILLING

3 eggs

⅔ cup light cream

⅔ cup milk

freshly grated nutmeg

1 To make the dough, place the flour and sugar in a bowl and rub in the butter with your fingertips until the mixture resembles bread crumbs.

2 Add the water and bring together with your fingers to form a soft dough. Wrap in plastic wrap and chill in the refrigerator for 30 minutes.

3 Roll out the dough to a circle on a lightly floured counter and use to line a 9½-inch/24-cm loose-based tart pan.

4 Trim the edges of the tart shell. Prick the base with a fork and chill in the refrigerator for 30 minutes.

5 Line the tart shell with foil and baking beans.

6 Bake in a preheated oven, at 375°F/190°C, for 15 minutes. Remove the foil and beans and bake for a further 15 minutes.

7 To make the filling, whisk the eggs, cream, milk, and nutmeg together. Pour the filling into the prepared tart shell. Return the tart to the oven and cook for 25–30 minutes, or until the filling is just set, then serve.

4

7

baked sweet ravioli

serves four

SWEET PASTA DOUGH

3¾ cups all-purpose flour, plus extra
    for dusting

⅔ cup butter, plus extra
    for greasing

¾ cup superfine sugar

4 eggs

1 oz/25 g yeast

½ cup lukewarm milk

FILLING

⅔ cup chestnut paste

½ cup unsweetened cocoa

generous ¼ cup superfine sugar

½ cup chopped almonds

1 cup crushed amaretti cookies

generous ½ cup orange marmalade

1 To make the sweet pasta dough, strain the flour into a large mixing bowl, then mix in the butter, sugar, and 3 of the eggs.

2 Combine the yeast and lukewarm milk in a small bowl and when thoroughly blended, mix into the dough.

3 Knead the dough for 20 minutes, then cover with a clean cloth, and let stand in a warm place for 1 hour to rise.

4 In a separate bowl, combine the chestnut paste, unsweetened cocoa, sugar, almonds, crushed amaretti cookies, and orange marmalade until blended.

5 Grease 1 or 2 cookie sheets with a little butter.

6 Roll out the pasta dough into a thin sheet on a lightly floured counter, and cut into 2-inch/5-cm circles with a plain cookie cutter.

7 Put a spoonful of filling onto each circle, then fold in half, pressing the edges firmly together to seal. Arrange the ravioli on the prepared cookie sheet, spacing them out well.

8 Beat the remaining egg and brush over the ravioli to glaze. Bake in a preheated oven, 350°F/180°C, for 20 minutes. Serve hot.

lemon tart

DOUGH

1¼ cups all-purpose flour, plus extra
  for dusting

2 tbsp superfine sugar

½ cup butter, diced

1 tbsp water

FILLING

⅔ cup heavy cream

½ cup superfine sugar

4 eggs

grated rind of 3 lemons

¾ cup lemon juice

confectioners' sugar, for dusting

COOK'S TIP

To avoid any spillage, pour half
of the filling into the tart shell,
place in the oven, then pour in
the remaining filling.

---

1 To make the dough, place the
flour and sugar in a bowl and rub
in the butter with your fingertips until
the mixture resembles bread crumbs.
Add the water and bring together to
form a dough. Wrap in plastic wrap
and chill for 30 minutes.

2 Roll out the dough on a lightly
floured counter and use it to line
a 9½-inch/24-cm loose-based tart pan.
Prick the base of the tart shell with a
fork and chill in the refrigerator for
30 minutes.

3 Line the tart shell with foil and
baking beans and bake in a
preheated oven, 375°F/190°C, for
15 minutes. Remove the foil and
baking beans and cook the tart shell
for 15 minutes more.

4 To make the filling, whisk the
cream, sugar, eggs, lemon rind,
and juice together until thoroughly
blended. Place the tart shell, still in its
pan, on a cookie sheet, and pour in the
filling (see Cook's Tip).

5 Bake the tart in the preheated
oven for about 20 minutes, or
until the filling is just set. Let cool, then
lightly dust with confectioners' sugar,
and serve.

pine nut tart

serves eight

DOUGH

1¼ cups all-purpose flour, plus extra
for dusting

2 tbsp superfine sugar

½ cup butter, diced

1 tbsp water

FILLING

1½ cups farmer's cheese

4 tbsp heavy cream

3 eggs

½ cup superfine sugar

grated rind of 1 orange

1 cup pine nuts

1 To make the dough, place the flour and sugar in a bowl and rub in the butter with your fingertips until the mixture resembles bread crumbs. Add the water and bring the mixture together with your fingers to form a soft dough. Wrap in plastic wrap and chill in the refrigerator for 30 minutes.

2 Roll out the dough on a lightly floured counter and use it to line a 9½-inch/24-cm loose-based tart pan. Prick the base of the tart shell with a fork and chill for 30 minutes.

3 Line the tart shell with foil and baking beans and bake in a preheated oven,t 375°F/190°C, for 15 minutes. Remove the foil and baking beans and cook the shell for 15 minutes more.

4 To make the filling, beat the farmer's cheese, cream, eggs, sugar, orange rind, and half of the pine nuts together in a bowl. Pour the filling into the tart shell and sprinkle with the remaining pine nuts.

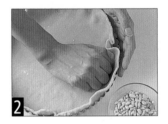

5 Reduce the oven to 325°F/160°C and bake the tart for about 35 minutes, or until the filling is just set. Let cool before removing from the pan and serving.

VARIATION

Replace the pine nuts with sliced
almonds, if you like.

---

orange tart

DOUGH

1¼ cups all-purpose flour, plus extra
 for dusting

2 tbsp superfine sugar

½ cup butter, diced

1 tbsp water

FILLING

grated rind of 2 oranges

scant ⅔ cup orange juice

scant 1 cup fresh white
 bread crumbs

2 tbsp lemon juice

⅔ cup light cream

4 tbsp butter

¼ cup superfine sugar

2 eggs, separated

salt

TO SERVE

whipped cream

grated orange rind

1 To make the dough, place the flour and sugar in a bowl and rub in the butter with your fingertips until the mixture resembles bread crumbs. Add the water and bring the mixture together with your fingers to form a soft dough. Wrap in plastic wrap and chill in the refrigerator for 30 minutes.

2 Roll out the dough on a lightly floured counter and use it to line a 9½-inch/24-cm loose-based tart pan. Prick the base of the tart shell with a fork and chill in the refrigerator for 30 minutes.

3 Line the tart shell with foil and baking beans and bake in a preheated oven, 375°F/190°C, for 15 minutes. Remove the foil and beans and cook for 15 minutes more.

4 To make the filling, combine the orange rind and juice with the bread crumbs together in a bowl. Stir in the lemon juice and light cream. Melt the butter and sugar in a small

pan over low heat. Remove the pan from the heat, add the 2 egg yolks, a pinch of salt, and the bread crumb mixture, and stir.

5 Whisk the egg whites with a pinch of salt in a mixing bowl until they form soft peaks. Fold them into the egg yolk mixture.

6 Pour the filling mixture into the tart shell. Bake in a preheated oven, 325°F/160°C, for about 45 minutes, or until just set. Let cool slightly and serve warm.

coconut cream tart

serves six—eight

DOUGH

1¼ cups all-purpose flour, plus extra
   for dusting

2 tbsp superfine sugar

½ cup butter, diced

1 tbsp water

FILLING

scant 2 cups milk

generous ½ cup coconut cream

3 egg yolks

½ cup superfine sugar

generous ⅓ cup all-purpose
   flour, sifted

¼ cup dry unsweetened coconut,
   plus extra to decorate

generous ¼ cup chopped candied
   pineapple, plus extra to decorate

2 tbsp rum or pineapple juice

1⅓ cups whipping cream, whipped

1 To make the dough, place the flour and sugar in a bowl and rub in the butter with your fingertips until the mixture resembles bread crumbs. Add the water and bring the mixture together with your fingers to form a soft dough. Wrap in plastic wrap and chill in the refrigerator for 30 minutes.

2 Roll out the dough on a lightly floured counter and use it to line a 9½-inch/24-cm loose-based tart pan. Prick the base of the tart shell with a fork and chill in the refrigerator for 30 minutes.

3 Line the tart shell with foil and baking beans and bake in a preheated oven, 375°F/190°C, for 15 minutes. Remove the foil and baking beans and cook for 15 minutes more. Let cool.

4 To make the filling, pour the milk into a small pan and add the coconut cream. Set over a low heat and bring to just below boiling point, stirring constantly until the mixture is thickened and smooth.

5 Whisk the egg yolks and the sugar together in a bowl until pale and fluffy. Whisk in the flour. Pour the hot milk over the egg mixture, stirring constantly. Return to the pan and heat gently, stirring constantly, for about 8 minutes, until thick. Let cool.

6 Stir in the coconut, pineapple, and rum or juice. Spread in the tart. Cover with cream and decorate with candied pineapple and coconut.

apricot & cranberry tart

serves eight

DOUGH

1¼ cups all-purpose flour, plus extra
for dusting

2 tbsp superfine sugar

½ cup butter, diced

1 tbsp water

FILLING

scant 1 cup sweet butter

1 cup superfine sugar

1 egg

2 egg yolks

⅓ cup all-purpose flour, sifted

1⅔ cups ground almonds

4 tbsp heavy cream

14½ oz/410 g canned apricot
halves, drained

generous 1 cup fresh cranberries

1 To make the dough, place the flour and sugar in a bowl and rub in the butter with your fingertips until the mixture resembles bread crumbs. Add the water and bring the mixture together with your fingers to form a soft dough. Wrap in plastic wrap and chill in the refrigerator for 30 minutes.

2 Roll out the dough on a lightly floured counter and use it to line a 9½-inch/24-cm loose-based tart pan. Prick the base of the tart shell with a fork and chill in the refrigerator for 30 minutes.

3 Line the tart shell with foil and baking beans and bake in a preheated oven, 375°F/190°C, for

15 minutes. Remove the foil and baking beans and cook the tart shell for 10 minutes more.

4 To make the filling, cream the butter and sugar together in a bowl until light and fluffy. Beat in the egg and egg yolks, then stir in the flour, almonds, and cream.

5 Place the apricot halves and cranberries on the base of the tart shell and spoon the filling mixture over the top.

6 Bake in the preheated oven for about 1 hour, or until the topping is just set. Let cool slightly, then serve warm or cold.

cheese & apple tart

serves eight

1 tbsp butter, for greasing

1½ cups self-rising flour

1 tsp baking powder

pinch of salt

⅓ cup brown sugar

generous 1 cup pitted
    dates, chopped

1lb 2 oz/500 g eating apples, cored
    and chopped

¼ cup chopped walnuts

¼ cup sunflower oil

2 eggs

1¾ cups grated colby cheese

COOK'S TIP

This is a deliciously moist
tart. Any leftovers should be
stored in the refrigerator and
heated through before serving.

1 Grease a 9½-inch/23-cm loose-
based tart pan with the butter
and line with baking parchment.

2 Strain the flour, baking powder,
and salt into a large bowl. Stir in
the brown sugar and the chopped
dates, apples, and walnuts. Mix
together until thoroughly blended.

3 Beat the oil and eggs together
and add the mixture to the dry
ingredients. Stir with a wooden spoon
until well blended.

4 Spoon half of the mixture into
the prepared pan and level the
surface with the back of a spoon.

5 Sprinkle with the grated cheese,
then spoon over the remaining
cake mix, spreading it to the edges
of the pan.

6 Bake in a preheated oven, 350°F/
180°C, for 45–50 minutes, or
until golden and firm to the touch.

7 Let the tart cool slightly in the
pan, then turn out of the pan,
and serve warm.

mincemeat & grape jalousie

serves four

1 tbsp butter, for greasing

1lb 2 oz/500 g ready-made puff
   pastry dough, thawed if frozen

14½ oz/410 g jar sweet mincemeat

1 cup grapes, seeded and cut
   in half

1 egg, beaten lightly

raw brown sugar, for sprinkling

COOK'S TIP

Puff pastry has a high proportion
of fat—this is what gives it its
characteristic layered appearance
and light, crisp texture. However,
this also makes it more fragile
than other types of pastry, so
handle it as lightly and as
little as possible.

VARIATION

For an enhanced festive flavor,
stir 2 tablespoons of sherry into
the mincemeat

1 Lightly grease a cookie sheet
with the butter.

2 Roll out the puff pie dough on a
lightly floured counter and cut
into 2 rectangles.

3 Place one dough rectangle on the
prepared cookie sheet and brush
the edges with water.

4 Combine the mincemeat and
grapes in a mixing bowl. Spread
the mixture evenly over the dough
rectangle on the cookie sheet, leaving
a 1-inch/2.5-cm border.

5 Fold the second pie dough
rectangle in half lengthwise,
and cut a series of parallel lines across
the folded edge with a sharp knife,
leaving a 1-inch/2.5-cm border.

6 Open out the second rectangle
and lay it over the mincemeat
filling. Press the edges of the pie
dough together to seal.

7 Flute and crimp the edges of the
dough with your fingers. Lightly
brush with the beaten egg to glaze
and sprinkle with raw brown sugar.

8 Bake in a preheated oven,
425°F/220°C, for 15 minutes.
Reduce the heat to 350°F/180°C and
cook for 30 minutes more, until the
jalousie is well risen and golden brown.

9 Transfer to a wire rack to cool
completely before serving.

lime frangipane tartlets

makes twelve

scant 1 cup all-purpose flour, plus
    extra for dusting

⅓ cup butter, softened

1 tsp grated lime rind

1 tbsp lime juice

¼ cup superfine sugar

1 egg

¼ cup ground almonds

⅓ cup confectioners' sugar, sifted

½ tbsp water

1 Reserve 5 teaspoons of the flour and 3 teaspoons of the butter and set aside until required.

2 Rub the remaining butter into the remaining flour with your fingertips until the mixture resembles fine bread crumbs. Stir in the lime rind, followed by the lime juice, then bring the mixture together with your fingers to form a soft dough.

3 Roll out the dough thinly on a lightly floured counter. Stamp out 12 circles, 3-inches/7.5-cm wide, and line a shallow muffin pan.

4 Cream the reserved butter and superfine sugar together in a bowl until pale and fluffy.

5 Mix in the egg, then the ground almonds and the reserved flour.

6 Divide the mixture among the tartlet shells and smooth the tops.

7 Bake in a preheated oven, 400°F/200°C, for 15 minutes, until set and lightly golden. Turn out onto a wire rack to cool.

8 Mix the confectioners' sugar with the water. Drizzle a little of the frosting over each tartlet and serve.

pear tarts

1 Roll out the dough on a lightly floured counter. Stamp out 6 x circles, about 4 inches/10 cm wide.

2 Place the circles on a large cookie sheet and chill in the refrigerator for 30 minutes.

3 Cream the brown sugar and butter together in a small bowl, then stir in the preserved ginger.

4 Prick the dough with a fork, then spread with the ginger mixture.

5 Slice the pear halves lengthwise, keeping them intact at the tip. Fan out the slices slightly.

6 Place a fanned-out pear half on top of each dough circle. Make small flutes around the edges of the circles. Brush the pears with butter.

7 Bake in a preheated oven, 400°F/200°C, for 15–20 minutes, until the pastry is well risen and golden. Let the tarts cool slightly before serving warm with a little cream.

> **COOK'S TIP**
>
> If you like, serve these tarts with vanilla ice cream for a delicious dessert.

crème brûlée tarts

serves six

DOUGH

1¼ cups all-purpose flour, plus extra
   for dusting

2 tbsp superfine sugar

½ cup butter, diced

1 tbsp water

FILLING

4 egg yolks

¼ cup superfine sugar

1¾ cups heavy cream

1 tsp vanilla extract

raw brown sugar, for sprinkling

1 To make the dough, place the flour and sugar in a bowl and rub in the butter with your fingertips until the mixture resembles bread crumbs. Add the water and bring the mixture together with your fingers to form a soft dough. Wrap in plastic wrap and chill in the refrigerator for 30 minutes.

2 Divide the dough into 6 pieces. Roll out the dough on a lightly floured counter and use it to line 6 tartlet pans, 4 inches/10 cm wide. Prick the base of the dough with a fork and chill in the refrigerator for 20 minutes.

3 Line the tart shells with foil and baking beans and bake in a preheated oven, 375°F/190°C, for 15 minutes. Remove the foil and beans and cook for 10 minutes more, until crisp and golden. Let cool.

4 Meanwhile, make the filling. Beat the egg yolks and sugar together in a bowl until pale. Heat the cream and vanilla extract in a pan until just below boiling point, then pour onto the egg mixture, whisking constantly.

5 Return the mixture to a clean pan and bring to just below a boil, stirring constantly until thick. Do not let the mixture boil or it will curdle.

6 Let the mixture cool slightly, then pour into the tart shells. Let cool, then chill in the refrigerator overnight.

7 Sprinkle the tarts with brown sugar. Place under a preheated hot broiler for a few minutes. Let cool, then chill for 2 hours before serving.

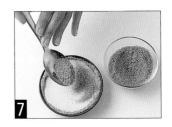

pavlova

serves six

3 egg whites

pinch of salt

¾ cup superfine sugar

1¼ cups heavy cream,
   lightly whipped

fresh fruit of your choice, such as
   raspberries, strawberries, peaches,
   passion fruit, or ground cherries

1 Line a cookie sheet with a sheet of baking parchment. Whisk the egg whites with the salt in a large bowl until they form soft peaks.

2 Whisk in the superfine sugar, a little at a time, whisking well after each addition until all of the sugar has been incorporated and the meringue is smooth and glossy.

3 Spoon three-fourths of the meringue onto the cookie sheet, forming an 8-inch/20-cm circle.

4 Place spoonfuls of the remaining meringue all around the edge of the circle to join up to make a neat nest shape.

5 Bake in a preheated oven, 275°F/140°C, for 1¼ hours.

6 Turn the heat off, but leave the pavlova in the oven until it is completely cold.

7 Place the pavlova on a serving dish. Spread with the lightly whipped cream, then arrange the fresh fruit on top. Do not add the cream and fruit too far in advance, or the pavlova will go soggy.

almond cheesecakes

serves four

12 amaretti cookies

1 egg white, beaten lightly

1 cup skim-milk soft cheese

½ tsp almond extract

½ tsp finely grated lime rind

scant ¼ cup ground almonds

2 tbsp superfine sugar

⅓ cup golden raisins

2 tsp powdered gelatin

2 tbsp boiling water

2 tbsp lime juice

TO DECORATE

2 tbsp toasted sliced almonds

strips of lime rind

1 Place the cookies in a plastic bag, seal the bag, and using a rolling pin, crush them into small pieces.

2 Place the amaretti crumbs in a bowl and stir in the egg white to bind them together.

3 Line a cookie sheet with baking parchment or use a nonstick tray. Arrange 4 nonstick pastry rings or poached egg rings, 3½ inches/9 cm wide, on top. Divide the amaretti mixture into 4 equal portions and spoon it into the rings, pressing it down well. Bake in a preheated oven, 350°F/180°C, for about 10 minutes, until crisp. Remove from the oven and let cool in the rings.

4 Place the soft cheese, almond extract, lime rind, ground almonds, sugar, and golden raisins in a bowl and beat thoroughly until well blended.

5 Dissolve the gelatin in the boiling water and stir in the lime juice. Fold into the cheese mixture and spoon over the amaretti bases. Smooth over the tops and chill in the refrigerator for 1 hour, or until set.

6 Loosen the cheesecakes from the rings using a small spatula and transfer to serving plates. Decorate with toasted sliced almonds and strips of lime rind and serve.

baked bananas

serves four

4 bananas

2 passion fruit

4 tbsp orange juice

4 tbsp orange-flavored liqueur

ORANGE-FLAVORED CREAM

⅔ cup heavy cream

3 tbsp confectioners' sugar

2 tbsp orange-flavored liqueur

VARIATION

Leave the bananas in their skins for a really quick dessert. Split the banana skins and pop in 1–2 squares of chocolate. Wrap the bananas in foil and bake for 10 minutes, or until the chocolate just melts.

---

1 To make the orange-flavored cream, pour the heavy cream into a mixing bowl and sprinkle over the confectioners' sugar. Whisk the mixture until it is standing in soft peaks. Carefully fold in the orange-flavored liqueur and chill in the refrigerator until required.

2 Peel the bananas and place each one on a sheet of foil.

3 Cut the passion fruit in half and squeeze the juice of each half over each banana. Spoon orange juice and liqueur over each banana.

4 Fold the foil sheets over the top of the bananas, tucking the ends in so they are completely enclosed.

5 Place the parcels on a cookie sheet and bake the bananas in a preheated oven, 350°F/180°C, for about 10 minutes, or until they are just tender (test by inserting a toothpick).

6 Transfer the foil parcels to warmed serving plates. Open out the banana parcels at the table, then serve immediately with the chilled orange-flavored cream.

baked apples with berries

serves four

4 medium cooking apples

1 tbsp lemon juice

1 cup prepared blackberries,
   thawed if frozen

1 tbsp sliced almonds

½ tsp ground allspice

½ tsp finely grated lemon rind

2 tbsp raw brown sugar

1¼ cups ruby port

1 cinnamon stick, broken

2 tsp cornstarch blended with
   2 tbsp cold water

lowfat custard, to serve

1 Wash and dry the apples. Make a shallow cut through the skin around the middle of each apple using a small sharp knife—this will help the apples to cook through.

2 Core the apples, brush the centers with the lemon juice to prevent them from discoloring, then stand them in an ovenproof dish.

3 Mix the blackberries, almonds, allspice, lemon rind, and sugar in a bowl Spoon the mixture into the center of each apple with a teaspoon.

4 Pour the port into the dish, add the cinnamon stick, and bake the apples in a preheated oven, 400°F/ 200°C, for 35–40 minutes, or until tender and soft.

5 Drain the cooking juices into a small pan. Keep the apples warm.

6 Remove the cinnamon and discard, then add the cornstarch mixture to the pan. Cook over medium heat, stirring constantly, until the mixture has thickened.

7 Heat the lowfat custard until piping hot. Pour the sauce over the apples and serve with the custard.

baked pears with cinnamon

serves four

4 ripe pears

2 tbsp lemon juice

¼ cup light brown sugar

1 tsp ground cinnamon

5 tbsp lowfat spread

finely grated lemon rind, to decorate

lowfat custard, to serve

1 Core and peel the pears, then slice them in half lengthwise, and brush all over with the lemon juice to prevent them from discoloring. Arrange the pear halves, cored sides down, in a small nonstick roasting pan.

2 Place the sugar, cinnamon, and lowfat spread in a small pan over low heat, stirring constantly, until the sugar has completely dissolved. Keep the heat as low as possible to prevent too much water evaporating from the lowfat spread as it starts to get hot. Spoon the sugar mixture over the pears.

3 Bake in a preheated oven, 400°F/200°C, for 20–25 minutes, or until the pears are tender and golden, occasionally spooning the sugar mixture over the fruit during the cooking time.

4 To serve, heat the lowfat custard until it is piping hot and spoon a little onto 4 warmed dessert plates, then arrange 2 pear halves on each plate.

5 Decorate the pears with a little finely grated lemon rind and serve immediately.

italian bread pudding

serves four

1 tbsp butter, for greasing

2 small eating apples, peeled,
    cored, and sliced into rings

generous ⅓ cup granulated sugar

2 tbsp white wine

3½ oz/100 g bread, sliced with
    crusts removed (slightly stale
    French baguette is ideal)

1¼ cups light cream

2 eggs, beaten

pared rind of 1 orange, cut into
    thin sticks

VARIATION

For a change, try adding
some dried fruit, such as
apricots, cherries, or dates, to
the pudding, if you like.

1 Grease a 5-cup/1.2-litre deep
ovenproof dish with the butter.

2 Arrange the apple rings across the
base of the dish, overlapping
them, then sprinkle half of the sugar
over the apples.

3 Pour the wine over the apples.
Add the bread slices, pushing
them down with your hands to flatten
them slightly.

4 Mix the cream with the eggs,
the remaining sugar, and the
orange rind and pour the mixture
over the bread. Set aside to soak
for 30 minutes.

5 Bake the pudding in a preheated
oven, 350°F/180,°C for about
25 minutes, until golden and set.
Remove from the oven and serve.

COOK'S TIP

Some varieties of eating apples
are better for cooking than
others. Among the most suitable
are Blenheim Orange, Cox's
Orange Pippin, Egremont Russet,
Granny Smith, Idared, James
Grieve, Jonagold, Jonathan
McIntosh, Northern Spy,
and Winesap.

tuscan delight

serves four

1 tbsp butter, for greasing

⅔ cup mixed dried fruit

generous 1 cup ricotta cheese

3 egg yolks

¼ cup superfine sugar

1 tsp ground cinnamon

finely grated rind of 1 orange, plus

    extra to decorate

crème fraîche, to serve (optional)

COOK'S TIP

Crème fraîche has a slightly sour, nutty taste and is very thick. It is suitable for cooking, but has the same fat content as heavy cream. It can be made by stirring cultured buttermilk into heavy cream and refrigerating it overnight.

1 Grease 4 mini ovenproof bowls or ramekin dishes with the butter.

2 Place the dried fruit in a bowl and cover with warm water. Set aside to soak for 10 minutes.

3 Beat the ricotta cheese with the egg yolks in a bowl. Stir in the superfine sugar, cinnamon, and orange rind and mix well.

4 Drain the soaked fruit in a strainer set over a bowl. Add the drained fruit to the ricotta cheese mixture and stir to blend.

5 Spoon the mixture into the prepared bowls or dishes.

6 Bake in a preheated oven, 350°F/ 180°C, for 15 minutes. The tops should just be firm to the touch, but should not have browned.

7 Decorate the desserts with grated orange rind. Serve warm or chilled with a spoonful of crème fraîche, if you like.

mascarpone cheesecake

serves eight

1½ tbsp sweet butter, plus extra
for greasing

3 cups ginger cookie crumbs

1 tablespoon chopped
preserved ginger

2¼ cups mascarpone cheese

finely grated rind and juice of 2 lemons

½ cup superfine sugar

2 extra large eggs, separated

fruit coulis (see Cook's Tip), to serve

COOK'S TIP

Fruit coulis can be made
by cooking 3½ cups
fruit, such as blueberries, for
5 minutes with 2 tablespoons of
water. Strain the mixture, then
stir in 1 tablespoon (or more to
taste) of strained confectioners'
sugar. Let cool before serving.

1 Grease the base of a 10-inch/
25-cm spring-form cake pan or
loose-based pan with butter and line
with baking parchment.

2 Melt the butter in a pan over
low heat and stir in the crushed
cookies and ginger. Use the mixture to
line the pan, pressing it about ¼ inch/
5 mm up the sides.

3 Beat the cheese, lemon rind and
juice, sugar, and egg yolks
together in a bowl until quite smooth.

4 Whisk the egg whites until stiff
and fold into the cheese mixture.

5 Pour the mixture over the cookie
shell in the prepared pan and
bake in a preheated oven, 350°F/
180°C, for 35–45 minutes, until just
set. Don't worry if it cracks or sinks—
this is quite normal.

6 Leave the cheesecake in the pan
to cool. Serve with fruit coulis
(see Cook's Tip).

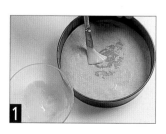

honey & nut nests

serves four

8 oz/225 g dried angel hair pasta

½ cup butter

1½ cups chopped pistachios

½ cup sugar

⅓ cup honey

⅔ cup water

2 tsp lemon juice

salt

strained plain yogurt, to serve

COOK'S TIP

Angel hair pasta is also known as capelli d'angelo. It is long and very fine, and is usually sold in small bunches that resemble nests.

1 Bring a large pan of lightly salted water to a boil. Add the pasta, bring back to a boil, and cook for 8–10 minutes, or until tender but still firm to the bite. Drain and return to the pan. Add the butter and toss to coat the pasta thoroughly. Let cool.

2 Arrange 4 small tart or poaching rings on a cookie sheet. Divide the angel hair pasta into 8 equal portions and spoon 1 portion into each ring. Press down lightly. Top the pasta with half of the nuts, then add the remaining pasta portions.

3 Bake in a preheated oven, 350°F/180°C, for 45 minutes, or until golden brown.

4 Meanwhile, put the sugar, honey, and water in a pan and bring to a boil over low heat, stirring constantly, until the sugar has dissolved. Simmer for 10 minutes, add the lemon juice and simmer for 5 minutes more.

5 Carefully transfer the angel hair nests to a serving dish using a spatula. Pour the honey syrup over them, sprinkle with the remaining pistachios, and let cool completely before serving. Hand the strained plain yogurt separately.

banana pies

serves four

DOUGH

3½ cups all-purpose flour, plus extra
    for dusting

4 tbsp shortening

4 tbsp sweet butter

½ cup water

FILLING

2 large bananas

⅓ cup finely chopped no-need-
    to-soak dried apricots

pinch of nutmeg

dash of orange juice

1 egg yolk, beaten

confectioners' sugar, for dusting

1 To make the dough, strain the
flour into a large mixing bowl.
Add the shortening and butter and rub
into the flour with your fingertips until
the mixture resembles bread crumbs.
Gradually blend in the water and bring
together with your fingers to form a
soft dough. Wrap in plastic wrap and
chill in the refrigerator for 30 minutes.

2 To make the filling, mash the
bananas in a bowl with a fork
and stir in the apricots, nutmeg, and
orange juice, mixing well.

3 Roll the dough out on a lightly
floured counter and stamp out
16 circles, 4 inches/10 cm wide.

4 Spoon a little banana filling onto
one half of each circle and fold
the dough over the filling to make
semicircles. Pinch the edges together
and seal by pressing with a fork.

5 Arrange the pies on a large
nonstick cookie sheet and brush
them with the beaten egg yolk. Cut a
small slit in the top of each pie, then
cook in a preheated oven, 350°F/
180°C, for about 25 minutes, or until
golden brown.

6 Dust the banana pies with
confectioners' sugar and serve.

chinese custard tarts

makes fifteen

DOUGH

1¼ cups all-purpose flour, plus extra
   for dusting

scant ¼ cup superfine sugar

4 tbsp sweet butter

2 tbsp shortening

2 tbsp water

CUSTARD

2 medium eggs

generous ¼ cup superfine sugar

¾ cup milk

½ tsp ground nutmeg, plus extra
   for sprinkling

cream, to serve

1 To make the dough, strain the flour into a bowl. Add the sugar and rub in the butter and shortening with your fingertips until the mixture resembles bread crumbs. Add the water and mix to form a firm dough.

2 Transfer the dough to a lightly floured counter and knead for 5 minutes, until smooth. Cover with plastic wrap and chill in the refrigerator while you are preparing the filling.

3 To make the custard, beat the eggs and sugar together. Gradually add the milk and ground nutmeg and beat until well blended.

4 Separate the dough into 15 even-size pieces. Flatten the dough pieces into circles and press into shallow muffin pans.

5 Spoon the custard into the tart shells and cook the tarts in a preheated oven, 300°F/150°C, for 25–30 minutes.

6 Transfer the Chinese custard tarts to a wire rack, let cool slightly, then sprinkle with nutmeg. Serve warm or cold with cream.

Cakes & Bread

There is nothing more traditional than morning coffee and cakes and this chapter gives a wickedly extravagant twist to some of those  delicious classics—full of chocolate, spice, and all things nice, these recipes are a treat to enjoy. The chapter includes a variety of different cakes depending on the time you have and the effort you want to spend. Small cakes include Cranberry Muffins, Almond Slices, and Dark Biscuits. These cakes are easier to prepare and cook than larger ones and are particular favorites.

cinnamon & currant loaf

makes one loaf

⅔ cup butter, diced, plus extra
   for greasing

2¾ cups all-purpose flour

pinch of salt

1 tbsp baking powder

1 tbsp ground cinnamon

¾ cup brown sugar

¾ cup currants

finely grated rind of 1 orange

5–6 tbsp orange juice

6 tbsp milk

2 eggs, beaten lightly

1 Grease a 2-lb/900-g loaf pan with butter and line the base with baking parchment.

2 Strain the flour, salt, baking powder, and ground cinnamon into a bowl. Rub in the butter with your fingertips until the mixture resembles bread crumbs.

3 Stir in the sugar, currants, and orange rind. Beat the orange juice, milk, and eggs together and add to the dry ingredients. Mix well.

4 Spoon the mixture into the prepared pan. Make a dip in the center to help the loaf rise evenly.

5 Bake the loaf in a preheated oven, 350°F/180°C, for about 1–1 hour 10 minutes, or until a fine metal skewer inserted into the center of the loaf comes out clean.

6 Let the loaf cool before turning it out of the pan. Transfer to a wire rack and let cool completely before slicing.

COOK'S TIP

Once you have added the liquid to the dry ingredients, work as quickly as possible because the baking powder is activated by the liquid.

banana & cranberry loaf

makes one loaf

1 tbsp butter, for greasing

1¼ cups self-rising flour

½ tsp baking powder

¾ cup brown sugar

2 bananas, mashed

⅓ cup chopped candied peel

2 tbsp chopped mixed nuts

¼ cup dried cranberries

5–6 tbsp orange juice

2 eggs, beaten lightly

⅔ cup sunflower oil

¾ cup confectioners' sugar, strained

grated rind of 1 orange

COOK'S TIP

This tea bread will keep for a couple of days. Wrap it carefully and store in a cool, dry place.

1 Grease a 2-lb/900-g loaf pan with the butter and line the base with baking parchment.

2 Strain the flour and baking powder into a mixing bowl. Stir in the sugar, bananas, chopped candied peel, nuts, and cranberries.

3 Stir the orange juice, eggs, and oil together, until thoroughly blended. Add the mixture to the dry ingredients and mix well. Pour the mixture into the prepared pan and level the surface with a spatula.

4 Bake in a preheated oven, 350°F/180°C, for about 1 hour, until firm to the touch or until a fine metal skewer inserted into the center of the loaf comes out clean.

5 Turn out the loaf onto a wire rack and let cool completely.

6 Mix the confectioners' sugar with a little water and drizzle the frosting over the loaf. Sprinkle orange rind over the top. Let the frosting set before serving the loaf in slices.

banana & date loaf

makes one loaf

⅓ cup butter, diced, plus extra
  for greasing
generous 1½ cups self-rising flour
⅓ cup superfine sugar
⅔ cup chopped pitted dried dates
2 bananas, mashed coarsely
2 eggs, beaten lightly
2 tbsp honey

COOK'S TIP

This tea bread will keep for
several days if stored in an
airtight container and kept
in a cool, dry place.

VARIATION

Substitute other dried fruit, such
as prunes or apricots, for the
dates. Use no-soak varieties for
the best results.

1 Grease a 2-lb/900-g loaf pan and
line with baking parchment.

2 Strain the flour into a mixing
bowl. Rub the butter into the flour
with your fingertips until the mixture
resembles fine bread crumbs.

3 Add the sugar, chopped dates,
bananas, beaten eggs, and honey
to the dry ingredients. Mix together to
form a pourable consistency.

4 Spoon the mixture into the
prepared loaf pan and level the
surface with a spatula.

5 Bake the loaf in a preheated
oven, 325°F/160°C for about,
1 hour, or until golden brown and a
fine metal skewer inserted into the
center of the loaf comes out clean.

6 Let the loaf cool for 10 minutes
before turning out of the pan,
then transfer to a wire rack to cool.

7 Serve the loaf warm or cold, cut
into thick slices.

fruit loaf with apple spread

makes one loaf

1 tbsp butter, for greasing

2 cups rolled oats

1 tsp ground cinnamon

½ cup light brown sugar

⅔ cup golden raisins

1 cup seedless raisins

2 tbsp malt extract

1¼ cups unsweetened apple juice

1¼ cups whole-wheat flour

3 tsp baking powder

FRUIT SPREAD

1½ cups strawberries, washed
    and hulled

2 eating apples, cored, chopped,
    and mixed with 1 tbsp
    lemon juice

1¼ cups unsweetened
    apple juice

TO SERVE

strawberries

apple wedges

1 Grease and line a 2-lb/900-g loaf pan. Place the oats, sugar, cinnamon, raisins, and malt extract in a bowl. Pour in the apple juice, stir, and let soak for 30 minutes.

2 Strain in the flour and baking powder, adding any bran that remains in the strainer, and fold in using a metal spoon.

3 Spoon the mixture into the pan and bake in a preheated oven, 350°F/180°C, for 1½ hours, until a fine metal skewer inserted into the center of the loaf comes out clean.

4 Let the loaf stand for 10 minutes, then turn out onto a wire rack and let cool completely.

5 Meanwhile, to make the fruit spread, place the strawberries and apples in a pan and pour in the apple juice. Bring the mixture to a boil,

cover, and simmer gently for 30 minutes. Beat the sauce well, then spoon into a sterilized, warmed jar. Let the sauce cool completely, then seal and label the jar.

6 Serve the fruit loaf cut into slices with 1–2 tablespoons of the fruit spread and an assortment of strawberries and apple wedges.

cranberry muffins

makes eighteen

1 tbsp butter, for greasing

generous 1½ cups all-purpose flour

2 tsp baking powder

½ tsp salt

¼ cup superfine sugar

4 tbsp butter, melted

2 eggs, beaten lightly

generous ¾ cup milk

1 cup fresh cranberries

scant ½ cup freshly grated
   Parmesan cheese

1 Lightly grease 2 muffin pans with a little butter. Strain the flour, baking powder, and salt into a mixing bowl. Stir in the superfine sugar.

2 In a separate bowl, combine the butter, beaten eggs, and milk, then pour into the bowl of dry ingredients. Mix lightly together until all of the ingredients are evenly blended, then stir in the cranberries.

3 Divide the mixture among the prepared pans.

4 Sprinkle the grated Parmesan cheese over the top of each portion of the muffin mixture.

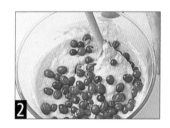

5 Bake in a preheated oven, 400°F/200°C, for 20 minutes, or until the muffins are well risen and golden brown.

6 Let the muffins cool slightly in the pans for 10 minutes, then transfer them to a wire rack, and let cool completely.

date & honey loaf

makes one loaf

1 tbsp butter, for greasing

1¾ cups strong white bread flour

½ cup brown bread flour

½ tsp salt

1 envelope active dry yeast

generous ¾ cup lukewarm water

3 tbsp sunflower oil

3 tbsp honey

½ cup chopped pitted dates

2 tbsp sesame seeds

COOK'S TIP

If you cannot find a warm place, sit a bowl with the dough in it over a pan of warm water and cover.

1 Grease a 2-lb/900-g loaf pan with the butter.

2 Strain both types of flour into a large mixing bowl, and stir in the salt and dry yeast. Pour in the lukewarm water, sunflower oil, and honey. Bring together to form a dough.

3 Place the dough on a lightly floured counter and knead for about 5 minutes, until smooth.

4 Place the dough in a greased bowl, cover, and let rise in a warm place for about 1 hour, or until doubled in size.

5 Knead in the dates and sesame seeds. Shape the dough and place in the pan.

6 Cover and stand in a warm place for a further 30 minutes, or until springy to the touch.

7 Bake in a preheated oven, 425°F/220°C, for 30 minutes. When the loaf is cooked, it should sound hollow when tapped.

8 Transfer the loaf to a wire rack and let cool completely. Serve cut into thick slices.

mango twist bread

makes one loaf

3 tbsp butter, diced, plus extra
   for greasing

3½ cups strong white bread flour,
   plus extra for dusting

1 tsp salt

1 envelope active dry yeast

1 tsp ground ginger

¼ cup brown sugar

1 small mango, peeled, pitted, and
   blended to a paste

1 cup lukewarm water

2 tbsp honey

⅔ cup golden raisins

1 egg, beaten lightly

confectioners' sugar, for dusting

1 Grease a cookie sheet with a little butter. Strain the flour and salt into a mixing bowl, stir in the dry yeast, ginger, and brown sugar and rub in the butter with your fingertips until the mixture resembles bread crumbs.

2 Stir in the mango paste, lukewarm water, and honey and bring together to form a dough.

3 Place the dough on a lightly floured counter. Knead for about 5 minutes, until smooth. Alternatively, use an electric mixer with a dough hook. Place the dough in a greased bowl, cover, and let rise in a warm place for about 1 hour, until it has doubled in size.

4 Knead in the golden raisins and shape the dough into 2 sausage shapes, each 10 inches/25 cm long. Carefully twist the 2 pieces together and pinch the ends to seal. Place the dough on the cookie sheet, cover, and leave in a warm place for another 40 minutes.

5 Brush the loaf with the egg and bake in a preheated oven, 425°F/220°C, for 30 minutes, or until golden. Let cool on a wire rack. Dust with confectioners' sugar before serving.

COOK'S TIP

You can tell when the bread is cooked because it will sound hollow when tapped.

citrus bread

makes one loaf

4 tbsp butter, diced, plus extra
    for greasing

3½ cups strong white bread flour,
    plus extra for dusting

½ tsp salt

¼ cup superfine sugar

1 envelope active dry yeast

5–6 tbsp orange juice

4 tbsp lemon juice

3–4 tbsp lime juice

⅔ cup lukewarm water

1 orange

1 lemon

1 lime

2 tbsp honey, for glazing

1 Lightly grease a cookie sheet with a little butter.

2 Strain the flour and salt into a large mixing bowl. Stir in the sugar and dry yeast.

3 Rub in the butter with your fingertips until the mixture resembles bread crumbs. Add all of the fruit juices and the water and bring together with your fingers to form a dough.

4 Place the dough on a lightly floured counter and knead for 5 minutes. Alternatively, use an electric mixer with a dough hook. Place the dough in a greased bowl, cover, and let rise in a warm place for 1 hour, until doubled in size.

5 Meanwhile, grate the rind of the orange, lemon, and lime. Knead the fruit rinds into the dough.

6 Divide the dough into 2 balls, making one slightly bigger than the other.

7 Place the larger ball on the cookie sheet and set the smaller one on top.

8 Push a floured finger through the center of the dough. Cover and let rise for about 40 minutes, or until springy to the touch.

9 Bake in a preheated oven, 425°F/220°C, for 35 minutes. Remove from the oven and transfer to a wire rack. Glaze with the honey and let cool completely.

crown loaf

makes one loaf

2 tbsp butter, diced, plus extra
for greasing

generous 1½ cups strong white
bread flour, plus extra for dusting

½ tsp salt

1 envelope active dry yeast

½ cup lukewarm milk

1 egg, beaten lightly

FILLING

4 tbsp butter, softened

¼ cup brown sugar

2 tbsp chopped hazelnuts

1 tbsp chopped preserved ginger

⅓ cup candied peel

1 tbsp rum or brandy

1 cup confectioners' sugar

2 tbsp lemon juice

1 Grease a cookie sheet with a little
butter. Strain the flour and salt
into a large mixing bowl. Stir in the
yeast. Rub in the butter with your
fingertips. Add the milk and egg and
bring together with your fingers to
form a dough.

2 Place the dough in a greased
bowl, cover, and stand in a warm
place for about 40 minutes, until
doubled in size. Punch down the
dough lightly for 1 minute, then roll
out into a rectangle measuring
12 x 9 inches/30 x 23 cm.

3 To make the filling, cream the
butter and sugar together in a
large bowl until light and fluffy. Stir in
the hazelnuts, ginger, candied peel,
and rum or brandy. Spread the filling
over the dough, leaving a 1-inch/
2.5-cm border around the edges.

4 Roll up the dough, starting
from one of the long edges, into
a sausage shape. Cut into slices at
2-inch/5-cm intervals and place the
slices in a circle on the cookie sheet,
sides just touching. Cover and stand in
a warm place to rise for 30 minutes.

5 Bake in a preheated oven,
325°F/190°C, for 20–30 minutes
or until golden. Meanwhile, mix the
confectioners' sugar with enough
lemon juice to form a thin frosting.

6 Let the loaf cool slightly before
drizzling with frosting. Let the
frosting set slightly before serving.

chocolate bread

makes one loaf

1 tbsp butter, for greasing

3½ cups strong white bread flour,
    plus extra for dusting

¼ cup unsweetened cocoa

1 tsp salt

1 envelope active dry yeast

2 tbsp brown sugar

1 tbsp oil

1¼ cups lukewarm water

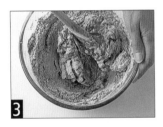

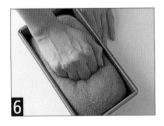

1 Lightly grease a 2-lb/900-g loaf pan with the butter.

2 Strain the flour and unsweetened cocoa into a mixing bowl. Stir in the salt, dry yeast, and sugar.

3 Pour in the oil with the water and mix the ingredients together to form a dough.

4 Place the dough on a lightly floured counter and knead for 5 minutes. Alternatively, use an electric mixer with a dough hook.

5 Place the dough in a greased bowl, cover, and let rise in a warm place for about 1 hour, or until it has doubled in size.

6 Punch down the dough lightly for 1 minute, then shape it into a loaf. Place in the prepared pan, cover, and let rise in a warm place for another 30 minutes.

7 Bake in a preheated oven, 400°F/200°C, for 25–30 minutes. When the loaf is cooked, it should sound hollow when tapped on the base.

8 Transfer the bread to a wire rack and let cool completely. Cut into slices and serve .

cinnamon swirls

makes twelve

2 tbsp butter, diced, plus extra
    for greasing
generous 1½ cups strong white
    bread flour, plus extra for dusting
½ tsp salt
1 envelope active dry yeast
1 egg, beaten lightly
½ cup lukewarm milk
2 tbsp maple syrup

FILLING
4 tbsp butter, softened
2 tsp ground cinnamon
¼ cup brown sugar
⅓ cup currants

1 Grease a 9-inch/23-cm square baking pan with a little butter.

2 Strain the flour and salt into a mixing bowl. Stir in the dry yeast. Rub in the butter with your fingertips until the mixture resembles bread crumbs. Add the egg and milk and bring together with your fingers to form a dough.

3 Form the dough into a ball, place in a greased bowl, cover, and let stand in a warm place for about 40 minutes, or until doubled in size.

4 Punch down the dough lightly for 1 minute, then roll out to a rectangle measuring 12 x 9 inches/ 30 x 23 cm.

5 To make the filling, cream the softened butter, cinnamon, and brown sugar together in a bowl until light and fluffy. Spread the filling evenly over the dough rectangle, leaving a 1-inch/2.5-cm border around the edges. Sprinkle the currants evenly over the top.

6 Roll up the dough from one of the long edges, and press down to seal. Cut the roll into 12 slices. Place them in the pan, cover, and let rise in a warm place for 30 minutes.

7 Bake in a preheated oven, 375°F/190°C, for 20–30 minutes, or until well risen. Brush with the syrup and let cool slightly before serving.

crunchy fruit cake

serves eight

⅓ cup butter, softened, plus extra
    for greasing

½ cup superfine sugar

2 eggs, beaten lightly

generous ⅓ cup self-rising
    flour, strained

1 tsp baking powder

⅔ cup cornmeal

1⅓ cups mixed dried fruit

¼ cup pine nuts

grated rind of 1 lemon

4 tbsp lemon juice

2 tbsp milk

VARIATION

To give a crumblier, lighter fruit
cake, omit the cornmeal and use
a generous 1 cup of self-rising
flour instead.

1 Grease a 7-inch/18-cm cake pan
with a little butter and line the
base with baking parchment.

2 Whisk the butter and sugar
together in a bowl until light
and fluffy.

3 Whisk in the beaten eggs, a little
at a time, whisking thoroughly
after each addition.

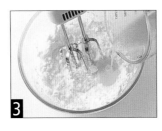

4 Gently fold the flour, baking
powder, and cornmeal into the
mixture until well blended.

5 Stir in the mixed dried fruit, pine
nuts, grated lemon rind, lemon
juice, and milk.

6 Spoon the mixture into the pan
and level the surface.

7 Bake in a preheated oven,
350°F/180°C, for about 1 hour, or
until a fine metal skewer inserted into
the center of the cake comes out clean.

8 Let the cake cool in the pan
before turning out.

clementine cake

serves eight

¾ cup butter, softened, plus extra
   for greasing

2 clementines

¾ cup superfine sugar

3 eggs, beaten lightly

1¼ cups self-rising flour

3 tbsp ground almonds

3 tbsp light cream

GLAZE AND TOPPING

6 tbsp clementine juice

2 tbsp superfine sugar

3 white sugar lumps, crushed

COOK'S TIP

If you like, chop the rind
from the clementines in a
food processor or blender
with the sugar in step 2. Tip
the mixture into a bowl
with the butter and begin
to cream the mixture.

1 Grease a 7-inch/18-cm round pan
with a little butter and line the
base with baking parchment.

2 Pare the rind from the clementines
and chop it finely. Cream the
butter, sugar, and clementine rind
together in a bowl until pale and fluffy.

3 Gradually add the beaten eggs to
the mixture, beating thoroughly
after each addition.

4 Gently fold in the flour, ground
almonds, and light cream. Spoon
the mixture into the prepared pan.

5 Bake in a preheated oven,
350°F/180°C, for 55–60 minutes,
or until a fine metal skewer inserted
into the center comes out clean. Let
cool for 10 minutes.

6 Meanwhile, to make the glaze,
put the clementine juice into a
small pan with the superfine sugar.
Bring to a boil over low heat and
simmer for 5 minutes.

7 Turn out the cake onto a wire
rack. Drizzle the glaze over the
cake until it has been absorbed and
sprinkle with the crushed sugar lumps.
Let cool completely before serving.

caraway madeira

serves eight

1 cup butter, softened, plus extra
   for greasing

scant 1 cup brown sugar

3 eggs, beaten lightly

2½ cups self-rising flour

1 tbsp caraway seeds

grated rind of 1 lemon

6 tbsp milk

1 or 2 strips of citron peel

1 Grease a 2-lb/900-g loaf pan and line with baking parchment.

2 Cream the butter and brown sugar together in a bowl until pale and fluffy.

3 Gradually add the beaten eggs to the creamed mixture, beating well after each addition.

4 Strain the flour into the bowl and gently fold into the creamed mixture with a figure-eight movement.

5 Add the caraway seeds, lemon rind, and milk, and gently fold in until thoroughly blended.

6 Spoon the mixture into the prepared pan and level the surface with a spatula.

7 Bake in a preheated oven, 325°F/160°C, for 20 minutes.

8 Remove the cake from the oven and gently place the pieces of citron peel on top. Return to the oven and bake for 40 minutes more, or until the cake is well risen, golden, and a fine skewer inserted into the center comes out clean.

9 Let the cake cool in the pan for 10 minutes before turning out, then transfer it to a wire rack to let it cool completely.

COOK'S TIP

Citron peel is available in the baking section of large stores. If it is unavailable, you can substitute chopped mixed peel.

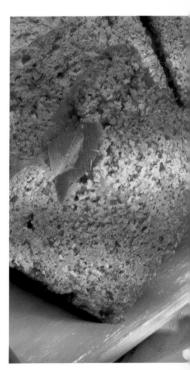

orange kugelhopf cake

serves four

1 cup butter, softened, plus extra
for greasing
generous 1 cup superfine sugar
4 eggs, separated
scant 3½ cups all-purpose flour
pinch of salt
3 tsp baking powder
1¼ cups fresh orange juice
1 tbsp orange flower water
1 tsp grated orange rind
SYRUP
¾ cup orange juice
1 cup granulated sugar

1 Grease and flour a 10-inch/25-cm
kugelhopf pan or deep ring mold.

2 Cream the butter and superfine
sugar together in a bowl until
light and fluffy, then add the egg
yolks, 1 at a time, whisking well after
each addition.

3 Strain the flour, salt, and baking
powder into a separate bowl.
Fold the dry ingredients and the
orange juice alternately into the
creamed mixture with a metal spoon,
working as lightly as possible. Gently
stir in the orange flower water and
orange rind.

4 Whisk the egg whites until they
form soft peaks, then gently fold
them into the mixture using a figure-
eight movement.

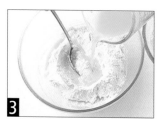

5 Pour into the prepared pan or
mold. Bake in a preheated oven,
350°F/180°C, for 50–55 minutes, or
until a fine metal skewer inserted into
the center of the cake comes out clean.

6 To make the syrup, bring the
orange juice and sugar to a boil
in a small pan over low heat, then
simmer gently for 5 minutes, until the
sugar has dissolved.

7 Remove the cake from the
oven and let cool in the pan for
10 minutes. Prick the top of the cake
with a fine metal skewer and brush
over half of the syrup. Let the cake
cool, still in the pan, for another
10 minutes, then invert the cake
onto a wire rack placed over a deep
plate and brush the syrup over the
cake until it is completely covered.
Serve warm or cold.

lemon syrup cake

serves eight

1 tbsp butter, for greasing

scant 1½ cups all-purpose flour

2 tsp baking powder

1 cup superfine sugar

4 eggs

⅔ cup sour cream

grated rind of 1 large lemon

4 tbsp lemon juice

⅔ cup sunflower oil

SYRUP

4 tbsp confectioners' sugar

3 tbsp lemon juice

1 Lightly grease an 8-inch/20-cm loose-based round cake pan with a little butter and line the base with baking parchment.

2 Strain the flour and baking powder into a large mixing bowl and stir in the sugar.

3 In a bowl or pitcher, whisk the eggs, sour cream, lemon rind, lemon juice, and oil together.

4 Pour the egg mixture into the dry ingredients and mix well until evenly blended.

5 Pour the mixture into the prepared pan and bake in a preheated oven, 350°F/180°C, for 45–60 minutes, until risen and golden on top.

6 To make the syrup, mix the confectioners' sugar and lemon juice together in a small pan. Stir over low heat until just starting to bubble and turn syrupy.

7 As soon as the cake comes out of the oven prick the surface with a fine metal skewer, then brush the syrup over the top. Let cool completely in the pan before turning out and serving.

COOK'S TIP

Pricking the surface of the hot cake with a skewer insures that the syrup seeps into the cake and the flavor is absorbed.

apple cake with cider

serves eight

6 tbsp butter, diced, plus extra
  for greasing

generous 1½ cups self-rising flour

1 tsp baking powder

⅓ cup superfine sugar

3½ cups chopped dried apple

generous ½ cup raisins

⅔ cup sweet cider

1 egg, beaten lightly

1 cup raspberries

1 Grease an 8-inch/20-cm cake pan with a little butter and line with baking parchment.

2 Strain the flour and baking powder into a large mixing bowl and rub in the butter with your fingertips until the mixture resembles fine bread crumbs.

3 Stir in the superfine sugar, dried apple, and raisins.

4 Pour in the sweet cider and egg and mix together until thoroughly blended. Stir in the raspberries very gently so that they do not break up.

5 Pour the mixture into the prepared cake pan.

6 Bake in a preheated oven, 375°F/190°C, for 40 minutes, or until risen and lightly golden.

7 Let the cake cool in the pan for 10 minutes, then turn out onto a wire rack, and let cool completely before serving

rich fruit cake

serves four

1 tbsp butter, for greasing

generous ½ cup no-soak prunes

1 cup chopped pitted dates

generous ¾ cup unsweetened
   orange juice

2 tbsp molasses

1 tsp finely grated lemon rind

1 tsp finely grated orange rind

generous 1½ cups whole-
   wheat flour

2 tsp baking powder

1 tsp allspice

⅔ cup seedless raisins

⅔ cup golden raisins

⅔ cup currants

generous 1 cup dried cranberries

3 extra large eggs, separated

TO DECORATE

1 tbsp apricot preserve, warmed

confectioners' sugar, for dusting

generous 1 cup sugarpaste

strips of orange rind

strips of lemon rind

1 Grease a deep round 8-inch/
20-cm cake pan and line with
baking parchment. Chop the prunes,
place in a pan with the dates, pour
over the orange juice, and simmer over
low heat for 10 minutes. Remove from
the heat and beat to a paste. Stir in the
molasses and rinds. Let cool.

2 Strain the flour, baking powder
and allspice into a bowl, adding
any bran from the strainer. Add the
dried fruits. When the prune mixture
is cool, whisk in the egg yolks. In a
separate bowl, whisk the egg whites
until stiff. Spoon the fruit mixture into
the dry ingredients and mix together.

3 Gently fold in the egg whites
using a metal spoon. Transfer
to the prepared cake pan and bake
in a preheated oven, 325°F/170°C,
for 1½ hours. Let cool in the pan

4 Turn the cake out and brush the
top with apricot preserve. Dust
the counter with confectioners' sugar
and roll out the sugarpaste thinly.
Lay the sugarpaste over the top of the
cake and trim the edges. Decorate
with citrus rind.

carrot & ginger cake

serves ten

1 tbsp butter, for greasing

generous 1½ cups all-purpose flour

1 tsp baking powder

1 tsp baking soda

2 tsp ground ginger

½ tsp salt

scant 1 cup light brown sugar

generous 1 cup grated carrots

2 pieces of preserved
    ginger, chopped

1 tbsp grated fresh gingerroot

⅓ cup seedless raisins

2 eggs, beaten lightly

3 tbsp corn oil

juice of 1 orange

FROSTING

1 cup lowfat soft cheese

4 tbsp confectioners' sugar

1 tsp vanilla extract

TO DECORATE

grated carrot

finely chopped preserved ginger

ground ginger

1 Grease an 8-inch/20-cm round cake pan with butter and line with baking parchment.

2 Strain the flour, baking powder, baking soda, ground ginger, and salt into a bowl. Stir in the sugar, carrots, preserved ginger, fresh ginger, and raisins. In a separate bowl, beat together the eggs, oil, and orange juice, then stir into the dry ingredients.

3 Spoon the mixture into the prepared pan and bake in a preheated oven, 350°F/180°C, for 1–1¼ hours, until firm to the touch, or until a fine metal skewer inserted into the center of the cake comes out clean. Let cool in the pan

4 To make the frosting, place the soft cheese in a bowl and beat to soften. Sift in the confectioners' sugar and add the vanilla extract. Mix well.

5 Turn the cake out and smooth the frosting over the top. Decorate with grated carrot and preserved and ground ginger and serve.

strawberry roulade

serves eight

3 extra large eggs

⅔ cup superfine sugar

scant 1 cup all-purpose flour

1 tbsp hot water

FILLING

¾ cup mascarpone

1 tsp almond extract

1½ cups small strawberries

TO DECORATE

1 tbsp toasted sliced almonds

1 tsp confectioners' sugar

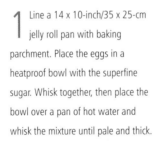

1 Line a 14 x 10-inch/35 x 25-cm jelly roll pan with baking parchment. Place the eggs in a heatproof bowl with the superfine sugar. Whisk together, then place the bowl over a pan of hot water and whisk the mixture until pale and thick.

2 Remove the bowl from the pan. Strain in the flour and fold into the egg mixture with the hot water. Pour the mixture into the prepared pan and bake in a preheated oven, 425°F/220°C, for 8–10 minutes, until golden and set.

3 Remove from the oven and turn out the roulade onto a sheet of baking parchment. Peel off the lining paper and roll up the sponge cake tightly along with the baking parchment. Wrap in a dish towel and let cool.

4 To make the filling, mix together the mascarpone and almond extract. Reserve a few strawberries for decoration, then wash, hull, and slice the rest. Chill the mascarpone mixture and the strawberries in the refrigerator until required.

5 Unroll the cake, spread the mascarpone mixture over the surface, and sprinkle with sliced strawberries. Roll the cake up again and transfer to a serving plate. Sprinkle with almonds and lightly dust with confectioners' sugar. Decorate with the reserved strawberries.

orange & almond cake

serves eight

1 tbsp butter, for greasing

4 eggs, separated

scant ¾ cup superfine sugar

finely grated rind and juice
    of 2 oranges

finely grated rind and juice
    of 1 lemon

generous 1 cup ground almonds

2½ tbsp self-rising flour

ORANGE-CINNAMON CREAM

generous ¾ cup whipping cream

1 tsp ground cinnamon

2 tsp caster sugar

TO DECORATE

1 tbsp toasted sliced almonds

confectioners' sugar, for dusting

VARIATION

You could serve this cake with a
syrup. Boil the juice and grated
rind of 2 oranges with scant
⅓ cup superfine sugar and
2 tablespoons of water for
5–6 minutes until slightly
thickened. Stir in 1 tablespoon
orange liqueur before serving.

1 Grease a deep 7-inch/18-cm round cake pan with butter. Line the base with baking parchment.

2 Cream the egg yolks and sugar in a bowl until the mixture is pale and thick. Whisk half of the orange rind and all of the lemon rind into the egg yolk mixture.

COOK'S TIP

When whipping cream, chill the
bowl, whisk, and cream before
starting. Whisk briskly until it
starts to thicken and then more
slowly until soft peaks form.

3 Mix the juice from the oranges and lemon with the ground almonds and stir into the egg yolk mixture. Gently fold in the flour.

4 Whisk the egg whites until stiff, then gently fold them into the egg yolk mixture.

5 Pour the mixture into the prepared pan and bake in a preheated oven, 350°F/180°C, for 35–40 minutes, or until golden and springy to the touch. Let cool in the pan for 10 minutes, then turn out and leave to cool completely.

6 Whip the cream until soft peaks form. Stir in the remaining orange rind, cinnamon and sugar. Cover the cooled cake with the sliced almonds, dust with confectioners' sugar, and serve immediately with the orange and cinnamon cream.

coconut cake

½ cup butter, diced, plus extra
   for greasing

generous 1½ cups self-rising flour

pinch of salt

½ cup raw brown sugar

1 cup dry unsweetened coconut,
   plus extra for sprinkling

2 eggs, beaten lightly

4 tbsp milk

2 Strain the flour and salt into a
mixing bowl and rub in the butter
with your fingertips until the mixture
resembles fine bread crumbs.

1 Lightly grease a 2-lb/900-g loaf
pan with butter and line with
baking parchment.

3 Stir in the sugar, coconut, eggs,
and milk and mix to a soft
pourable consistency.

4 Spoon the mixture into the
prepared loaf pan and level the
surface with a spatula. Bake in a
preheated oven, 325°F/160°C, for
30 minutes.

5 Remove the cake from the
oven and sprinkle with the extra
coconut. Return to the oven and bake
for 30 minutes more, until risen and
golden and a metal skewer inserted
into the center comes out clean.

6 Let the cake cool slightly in the
pan, then turn out, and transfer
to a wire rack, and let cool completely
before serving.

almond slices

makes eight

3 eggs

⅔ cup ground almonds

1½ cups dry milk

1 cup granulated sugar

½ tsp saffron threads

scant ½ cup sweet butter

1 tbsp sliced almonds, to decorate

1 Beat the eggs together in a bowl and set aside.

2 Place the ground almonds, dry milk, sugar, and saffron in a large mixing bowl and mix well.

3 Melt the butter in a small pan over low heat. Pour the melted butter over the dry ingredients and mix well until thoroughly blended.

4 Add the reserved beaten eggs to the mixture and mix well.

5 Spread the cake mixture evenly in a shallow 7–9-inch/15–20-cm ovenproof dish and bake in a preheated oven, 325°F/160°C, for

COOK'S TIP
These almond slices are best eaten hot, but they may also be served cold. They can be made a day or even a week in advance and reheated. They also freeze beautifully.

45 minutes, or until a fine metal skewer inserted into the center of the cake comes out clean.

6 Cut the almond cake into 8 slices. Decorate the almond slices with sliced almonds, and transfer to serving plates. Serve hot or cold.

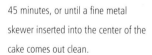

pear & ginger cake

serves six

scant 1 cup sweet butter, softened,
plus extra for greasing
generous ¾ cup superfine sugar
1¼ cups self-rising flour, strained
1 tbsp ground ginger
3 eggs, beaten lightly
1 lb/450 g pears, peeled, cored,
and thinly sliced, then brushed
with lemon juice
1 tbsp brown sugar
ice cream or heavy cream, lightly
whipped, to serve (optional)

COOK'S TIP

Store brown sugar in an airtight
container, rather than in its
package, where it can absorb
water from the air. If the sugar
becomes hard, do not throw it
away. Wrap the package in a
clean, damp dish towel and heat
in the microwave on Medium
for 1–2 minutes, until it begins
to soften.

---

1 Lightly grease a deep 8-inch/
20-cm cake pan with butter and
line the base with baking parchment.

2 Mix all but 2 tablespoons of the
butter with the superfine sugar,
flour, ginger, and eggs in a bowl. Beat
with a whisk until the mixture forms a
smooth consistency.

3 Spoon the cake batter into the
prepared pan and level out the
surface with a spatula.

4 Arrange the pear slices over
the cake batter. Sprinkle with
the brown sugar and dot with the
remaining butter.

5 Bake in a preheated oven,
350°F/180°C, for 35–40 minutes,
or until the cake is golden on top and
feels springy to the touch.

6 Serve the pear and ginger cake
warm, with ice cream or whipped
cream, if you like.

VARIATION

For a different flavor, substitute 2
teaspoons ground cinnamon for
the ground ginger and use
vanilla sugar instead of plain.

coffee streusel cake

serves eight

½ cup butter, melted and cooled,
    plus extra for greasing

2 cups all-purpose flour

1 tbsp baking powder

⅓ cup superfine sugar

⅔ cup milk

2 eggs

2 tbsp instant coffee mixed with
    1 tbsp boiling water

⅓ cup chopped almonds

confectioners' sugar, for dusting

TOPPING

½ cup self-rising flour

⅓ cup raw brown sugar

2 tbsp butter, diced

1 tsp ground allspice

1 tbsp water

1 Grease a 9-inch/23-cm loose-based round cake pan with butter and line with baking parchment. Strain the flour and baking powder into a mixing bowl, then stir in the superfine sugar.

2 Whisk the milk, eggs, melted butter, and coffee mixture together and pour onto the dry ingredients. Add the chopped almonds and mix lightly together. Spoon the mixture into the prepared pan.

3 To make the topping, combine the flour and raw brown sugar in a bowl.

4 Rub in the butter with your fingertips until the mixture resembles bread crumbs. Sprinkle in the allspice and water and bring the mixture together into loose crumbs. Sprinkle evenly over the cake batter.

5 Bake the cake in a preheated oven, 375°F/190°C, for about 50 minutes–1 hour. Cover loosely with foil if the topping starts to brown too quickly. Let the cake cool in the pan, then turn out, dust with confectioners' sugar, and serve.

gingerbread

makes twelve

⅔ cup butter, plus extra
    for greasing

scant 1 cup brown sugar

2 tbsp molasses

generous 1½ cups all-
    purpose flour

1 tsp baking powder

2 tsp baking soda

2 tsp ground ginger

⅔ cup milk

1 egg, beaten lightly

2 eating apples, peeled, chopped,
    and coated with lemon juice

VARIATION

If you enjoy the flavor of
ginger, try adding 1 tablespoon
finely chopped preserved ginger
to the mixture in step 3.

1 Grease a 9-inch/23-cm square
cake pan with a little butter and
line with baking parchment.

2 Melt the butter, sugar, and
molasses in a pan over low heat.
Remove from the heat and let cool.

3 Strain the flour, baking powder,
baking soda, and ground ginger
together into a mixing bowl.

4 Stir in the milk, egg, and cooled
butter and molasses mixture,
followed by the chopped apples.

5 Stir gently, then pour the mixture
into the prepared pan, and level
the surface with a spatula.

6 Bake in a preheated oven,
325°F/160°C, for 30–35 minutes,
until the cake has risen and a fine
metal skewer inserted into the center
comes out clean.

7 Let the ginger cake cool in
the pan, then turn out, and cut
into 12 bars.

cherry biscuits

makes eight

6 tbsp butter, diced, plus extra
  for greasing
generous 1½ cups self-rising flour,
  plus extra for dusting
1 tbsp superfine sugar
pinch of salt
3 tbsp candied cherries, chopped
3 tbsp golden raisins
1 egg, beaten lightly
scant ¼ cup milk

COOK'S TIP
These biscuits will freeze
very successfully, but they
are best thawed and eaten
within 1 month.

---

1 Lightly grease a cookie sheet with a little butter.

2 Strain the flour, sugar, and salt into a mixing bowl and rub in the butter with your fingertips until the mixture resembles bread crumbs.

3 Stir in the candied cherries and golden raisins. Add the egg.

4 Reserve 1 tablespoon of the milk for glazing, then add the remainder to the mixture. Bring together to form a soft dough.

5 Roll out the dough on a lightly floured counter to a thickness of ¾ inch/2 cm and cut out 8 circles, using a 2-inch/5-cm cutter.

6 Place the biscuits on the prepared cookie sheet and brush the tops with the reserved milk.

7 Bake in a preheated oven, 425°F/220°C, for 8–10 minutes, or until the biscuits are golden brown.

8 Transfer the biscuits to a wire rack and let cool. Serve split in half and spread with butter.

dark biscuits

makes eight

6 tbsp butter, diced, plus extra
  for greasing

generous 1½ cups self-rising flour,
  plus extra for dusting

pinch of salt

1 tbsp superfine sugar

1 eating apple, peeled, cored,
  and chopped

1 egg, beaten lightly

2 tbsp molasses

5 tbsp milk

1 Lightly grease a cookie sheet with a little butter.

2 Strain the flour, sugar, and salt into a mixing bowl.

3 Add the butter and rub it in with your fingertips until the mixture resembles fine bread crumbs.

4 Stir the apple into the mixture until thoroughly combined.

5 Combine the beaten egg, molasses, and milk in a pitcher. Add to the dry ingredients and bring together to form a soft dough.

6 Roll out the dough on a lightly floured counter to a thickness of ¾ inch/2 cm and stamp out 8 circles, using a 2-inch/5-cm cutter.

7 Arrange the biscuits on the prepared cookie sheet and bake in a preheated oven, 425°F/220°C, for about 8–10 minutes.

8 Transfer the biscuits to a wire rack and let cool slightly. Serve split in half and spread with butter

apple shortcakes

serves four

2 tbsp butter, diced, plus extra
    for greasing

1¼ cups all-purpose flour, plus extra
    for dusting

½ tsp salt

1 tsp baking powder

1 tbsp superfine sugar

¼ cup milk

confectioners' sugar, for
    dusting (optional)

FILLING

3 eating apples, peeled, cored,
    and sliced

½ cup superfine sugar

1 tbsp lemon juice

1 tsp ground cinnamon

1¼ cups water

⅔ cup heavy cream, whipped lightly

1 Lightly grease a cookie sheet with a little butter. Strain the flour, salt, and baking powder into a mixing bowl. Stir in the sugar, then rub in the butter with your fingertips until the mixture resembles fine bread crumbs.

2 Pour in the milk and bring together to form a soft dough. Knead the dough lightly on a lightly

floured counter, then roll out to ½ inch/ 1 cm thick. Stamp out 4 circles, using a 2-inch/5-cm cutter. Transfer the circles to the prepared cookie sheet.

3 Bake in a preheated oven, 425°F/220°C, for 15 minutes, until risen and browned. Let cool.

4 To make the filling, place the apple slices, sugar, lemon juice, and cinnamon in a pan. Add the water, bring to a boil, and simmer, uncovered, for 5–10 minutes, until the apples are tender. Let cool a little, then remove the apples.

5 Split the shortcakes in half. Place each lower half on a serving plate and spoon a fourth of the apple slices onto each, and top with cream. Place the other half of the shortcake on top. Serve dusted with confectioners' sugar if you like.

sugar-topped blackberry & apple cake

serves ten

1 tbsp butter, for greasing

12 oz/350 g cooking apples

3 tbsp lemon juice

generous 2 cups whole-
wheat flour

2½ tsp baking powder

1 tsp ground cinnamon, plus extra
for dusting

1 cup prepared blackberries,
thawed if frozen, plus extra
to decorate

scant 1 cup light brown sugar

1 egg, beaten lightly

¾ cup lowfat plain yogurt

2 oz/55 g white or brown sugar
lumps, crushed lightly

sliced eating apple, to decorate

VARIATION

Try replacing the blackberries
with blueberries. Use the canned
or frozen variety if fresh
blueberries are unavailable.

1 Grease a 2-lb/900-g loaf pan with a little butter and line with baking parchment. Core, peel, and finely dice the cooking apples. Place them in a pan with the lemon juice, bring to a boil, cover, and simmer for 10 minutes, until soft. Beat well. Set aside to cool.

2 Strain the flour, baking powder, and cinnamon into a bowl, adding any bran that remains in the strainer. Stir in ⅔ cup of the blackberries and the sugar.

3 Make a well in the center of the ingredients and add the egg, yogurt, and cooled apple paste. Mix until thoroughly blended. Spoon the mixture into the prepared loaf pan and level over the top with a spatula.

4 Sprinkle with the remaining blackberries, pressing them down into the cake batter, and top the batter with the crushed sugar lumps. Bake in a preheated oven, 375°F/190°C, for 40–45 minutes, then let cool in the pan.

5 Turn the cake out and peel away the baking parchment. Serve dusted with cinnamon and decorated with blackberries and apple slices.

spicy bread

makes one loaf

2 tbsp butter, diced, plus extra
for greasing
generous 1½ cups self-rising flour
¾ cup all-purpose flour, plus extra
for dusting
1 tsp baking powder
¼ tsp salt
¼ tsp cayenne pepper
2 tsp curry powder
2 tsp poppy seeds
⅔ cup milk
1 egg, beaten lightly

1 Lightly grease a cookie sheet with a little butter.

2 Strain the self-rising flour and the all-purpose flour into a mixing bowl with the baking powder, salt, cayenne, curry powder, and poppy seeds.

3 Rub in the butter with your fingertips until the mixture resembles bread crumbs.

4 Add the milk and beaten egg and bring together with your fingers to form a soft dough.

5 Turn the dough out onto a lightly floured counter, then knead lightly for a few minutes.

6 Shape the dough into a circle about 2 inches/5 cm deep and mark a cross shape on the top with a sharp knife.

7 Bake in a preheated oven, 375°F/190°C, for 45 minutes.

8 Remove the bread from the oven, transfer to a wire rack, and let cool. Serve the bread cut into chunks or slices.

COOK'S TIP

If the bread looks as though it is browning too much, cover it with foil for the remainder of the cooking time.

cheese & ham loaf

makes one loaf

6 tbsp butter, diced, plus extra
  for greasing

generous 1½ cups self-rising flour

1 tsp salt

2 tsp baking powder

1 tsp paprika

1¼ cups grated sharp cheese

scant ½ cup chopped smoked ham

2 eggs, beaten lightly

⅔ cup milk

COOK'S TIP

This tasty bread is best eaten on
the day it is made, as it does not
keep for very long.

1 Grease a 1-lb/450-g loaf pan
with a little butter and line the
base with baking parchment.

2 Strain the flour, salt, baking
powder, and paprika into a large
mixing bowl.

3 Rub in the butter with your
fingertips until the mixture
resembles fine bread crumbs. Stir
in the cheese and ham.

4 Add the beaten eggs and milk
to the dry ingredients in the
bowl and mix well.

5 Spoon the cheese and ham
mixture into the prepared pan.

6 Bake in a preheated oven,
350°F/180°C, for about 1 hour,
or until the loaf is well risen.

7 Let the bread cool in the pan,
then turn out, and transfer to
a wire rack to cool completely.

8 Cut the bread into thick slices
to serve.

101

sun-dried tomato rolls

makes eight

⅓ cup butter, melted and cooled
  slightly, plus extra for greasing
generous 1½ cups strong white
  bread flour, plus extra
  for dusting
½ tsp salt
1 envelope active dry yeast
3 tbsp lukewarm milk
2 eggs, beaten lightly
1¾ oz/50 g sun-dried tomatoes in
  oil, drained and finely chopped
milk, for brushing

VARIATION
Add some finely chopped
anchovies or olives to the dough
in step 5 for extra flavor,
if you wish.

---

1 Lightly grease a cookie sheet
with a little butter.

2 Strain the flour and salt into a
large mixing bowl. Stir in the dry
yeast, then pour in the melted butter,
milk, and eggs. Bring together to form
a dough.

3 Turn the dough out onto a
lightly floured counter and knead
for about 5 minutes, until smooth.
Alternatively, use an electric mixer with
a dough hook.

4 Place the dough in a greased
bowl, cover, and let rise in a
warm place for 1–1½ hours, or until
the dough has doubled in size.

5 Punch down the dough for
2–3 minutes. Knead the sun-dried
tomatoes into the dough, sprinkling
the counter with extra flour, because
the tomatoes are quite oily.

6 Divide the dough into 8 even-size
balls and place them on the
prepared cookie sheet. Cover and let
rise for about 30 minutes, or until the
rolls have doubled in size.

7 Brush the rolls with milk and
bake in a preheated oven,
450°F/230°C, for 10–15 minutes,
or until they are golden brown.

8 Transfer the tomato rolls to a
wire rack and let cool slightly
before serving.

garlic bread rolls

makes eight

1 tbsp butter, for greasing

12 garlic cloves

1½ cups milk, plus extra
  for brushing

3½ cups strong white bread flour,
  plus extra for dusting

1 tsp salt

1 envelope active dry yeast

1 tbsp dried mixed herbs

2 tbsp sunflower oil

1 egg, beaten lightly

rock salt, for sprinkling

1 Lightly grease a cookie sheet with
the butter.

2 Peel the garlic cloves and place
them in a pan with the milk.
Bring to a boil over low heat and
simmer gently for 15 minutes. Let cool
slightly, then place in a blender or food
processor, and process into a paste.

3 Strain the flour and salt into a
large mixing bowl and stir in
the dry yeast and mixed herbs.

4 Add the garlic-flavored milk,
sunflower oil, and beaten egg
to the dry ingredients, mix well, and
bring together with your fingers to
form a dough.

5 Turn the dough out onto a
lightly floured counter and knead
lightly for a few minutes until smooth
and soft.

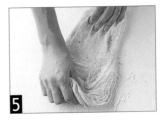

6 Place the dough in a greased
bowl, cover, and let rise in a
warm place for about 1 hour, or until
doubled in size.

7 Punch down the dough for
2 minutes. Divide into 8, shape
into rolls, and place on the cookie
sheet. Score the top of each roll with a
knife, cover, and leave for 15 minutes.

8 Brush the rolls with milk and
sprinkle rock salt over the top.

9 Bake in a preheated oven,
425°F/220°C, for 15–20 minutes.
Transfer the rolls to a wire rack to cool
before serving.

mini focaccia

serves four

2 tbsp olive oil, plus extra
    for brushing

2½ cups strong white bread flour,
    plus extra for dusting

½ tsp salt

1 envelope active dry yeast

1 cup lukewarm water

1 cup pitted green or black olives,
    cut in half

TOPPING

2 red onions, sliced

2 tbsp olive oil

1 tsp sea salt

1 tbsp fresh thyme leaves

1 Lightly brush several cookie sheets with olive oil. Strain the flour and salt into a large bowl, then stir in the yeast. Pour in the olive oil and water and bring together with your fingers to form a dough.

2 Turn the dough out onto a lightly floured counter and knead for about 5 minutes. Alternatively, use an electric mixer with a dough hook and knead for 7–8 minutes.

3 Place the dough in a greased bowl, cover, and let stand in a warm place for about 1–1½ hours, or until it has doubled in size.

4 Punch down the dough for 1–2 minutes. Knead half of the olives into the dough. Divide the dough into fourths and then shape the fourths into circles. Place them on the cookie sheets and push your fingers into them to achieve a dimpled effect.

5 To make the topping, sprinkle the red onions and remaining olives over the dough circles. Drizzle the olive oil over the top of the onions and olives, then sprinkle with the sea salt and thyme leaves. Cover and let rise for 30 minutes.

6 Bake in a preheated oven, 375°F/190°C, for 20–25 minutes, or until the focaccia are golden.

7 Transfer to a wire rack and let cool before serving.

VARIATION

Use this quantity of dough
to make 1 large focaccia,
if you like.

soda bread

makes one loaf

1 tbsp butter, for greasing

generous 2 cups all-purpose flour,
plus extra for dusting

generous 2 cups whole-wheat flour

2 tsp baking powder

1 tsp baking soda

2 tbsp superfine sugar

1 tsp salt

1 egg, beaten lightly

generous 1¾ cups plain yogurt

VARIATION

For a fruity version of this soda
bread, add ¾ cup of raisins to the
dry ingredients in step 2.

---

1 Grease a cookie sheet with the
butter and dust lightly with flour.

2 Strain both types of flour, the
baking powder, baking soda,
sugar, and salt into a large bowl, and
add any bran remaining in the strainer.

3 In a pitcher, beat together the egg
and yogurt and pour the mixture
into the dry ingredients. Mix well,
bringing together to form a soft and
sticky dough.

4 Knead the dough for a few
minutes on a lightly floured
counter until smooth, then shape it
into a large round about 2 inches/
5 cm deep.

5 Transfer the dough to the prepared
cookie sheet. Mark a cross shape
on top with a sharp knife.

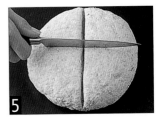

6 Bake in a preheated oven,
375°F/190°C, for 40 minutes, or
until the bread is golden brown.

7 Transfer the loaf to a wire rack
and let cool completely. Cut into
slices to serve.

Cookies

Nothing can compare with a homemade cookie for bringing a touch of pleasure to a coffee break or tea-time. This selection of delicious cookies and after-dinner treats will tantalize your taste buds and keep you coming back for more.

Tempting cookies, such as Citrus Crescents, Meringues, Rock Drops, and Gingersnaps, are quick, easy, and satisfying to make. You can easily vary the ingredients to suit your taste—the possibilities for inventiveness when making cookies are endless and this chapter shows you how.

savory curried crackers

makes forty

scant ½ cup butter, softened, plus
    extra for greasing
¾ cup all-purpose flour, plus extra
    for dusting
1 tsp salt
2 tsp curry powder
1 cup grated mellow
    semihard cheese
1 cup freshly grated
    Parmesan cheese

COOK'S TIP

These crackers can be
stored for several days in an
airtight container.

---

1 Lightly grease about 4 cookie
sheets with a little butter.

2 Strain the flour and salt into a
mixing bowl.

3 Stir in the curry powder and both
the grated cheeses. Rub in the
softened butter with your fingertips,
then bring the mixture together to form
a soft dough.

4 Roll out the dough thinly on a
lightly floured counter to form
a rectangle.

5 Cut out 40 crackers using a
2-inch/5-cm cookie cutter.

6 Arrange the crackers on the
cookie sheets.

7 Bake in a preheated oven,
350°F/180°C, for 10–15 minutes,
until golden brown.

8 Let the crackers cool slightly on
the cookie sheets. Transfer them
to a wire rack to cool completely and
crispen, then serve.

rosemary cookies

makes twenty-five

1¾ oz/50g butter, softened, plus
   extra for greasing

1¾ oz/50g superfine sugar

grated rind of 1 lemon

4 tbsp lemon juice

1 egg, separated

2 tsp finely chopped fresh rosemary

scant 1½ cups all-purpose flour,
   strained, plus extra for dusting

superfine sugar,
   for sprinkling

VARIATION

In place of the fresh rosemary,
use 1½ teaspoons of dried
rosemary, if you like.

---

1 Lightly grease 2 cookie sheets
with a little butter.

2 Cream the butter and sugar
together in a large mixing bowl
until pale and fluffy.

3 Add the lemon rind and juice,
then the egg yolk, and beat until
the mixture is thoroughly blended. Stir
in the chopped fresh rosemary.

4 Mix in the strained flour and
bring together with your fingers
to form a soft dough. Wrap in plastic
wrap and place in the refrigerator to
chill for 30 minutes.

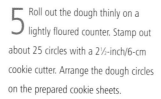

5 Roll out the dough thinly on a
lightly floured counter. Stamp out
about 25 circles with a 2½-inch/6-cm
cookie cutter. Arrange the dough circles
on the prepared cookie sheets.

6 Lightly whisk the egg white
in a small bowl. Gently brush
the egg white over the surface of each
cookie, then sprinkle with a little
superfine sugar.

7 Bake in a preheated oven,
350°F/180°C, for 15 minutes.

8 Transfer the cookies to a wire rack
and let cool before serving.

cheese sablés

makes thirty-five

⅔ cup butter, diced, plus extra
    for greasing
generous 1 cup all-purpose flour,
    plus extra for dusting
1½ cups grated sharp cheese
1 egg yolk
sesame seeds, for sprinkling

COOK'S TIP

Cut out any shape you like for your savory sablés. Children will enjoy them cut into animal shapes or other fun designs.

1 Lightly grease several cookie sheets with a little butter.

2 Combine the flour and grated cheese in a bowl.

3 Add the butter to the cheese and flour mixture and rub in with your fingertips until the mixture resembles bread crumbs.

4 Stir in the egg yolk. Bring together to form a dough. Wrap in plastic wrap and chill for 30 minutes.

5 Roll out the cheese dough thinly on a lightly floured counter. Stamp out circles with a 2½-inch/6-cm cookie cutter, re-rolling the trimmings to make about 35 crackers.

6 Carefully transfer the dough circles onto the prepared cookie sheets and sprinkle the sesame seeds evenly over the top of them.

7 Bake in a preheated oven, 200°C/400°F, for 20 minutes, until lightly golden.

8 Carefully transfer the cheese sablés to a wire rack and let cool slightly before serving.

VARIATION

For a sweet variation of these traditional French cookies, substitute the grated rind of 1 lemon for the cheese and stir in 125 g/4½ oz superfine sugar at the end of step 2. Beat the egg yolk with 1 tablespoon brandy before adding it to the mixture. Roll out the dough, stamp out circles, and bake as above.

cheese & chive biscuits

makes ten

generous 1½ cups self-rising flour,
    plus extra for dusting

1 tsp mustard powder

½ tsp cayenne pepper

½ tsp salt

½ cup lowfat soft cheese with
    added herbs

2 tbsp chopped fresh chives, plus
    extra to garnish

scant ½ cup skim milk, plus 2 tbsp
    for brushing

generous ½ cup grated reduced-fat
    sharp colby cheese

- lowfat soft cheese, to serve

1 Strain the flour, mustard, cayenne, and salt into a mixing bowl.

2 Add the soft cheese to the flour mixture and stir together until well blended, then stir in the chopped chives.

3 Make a well in the center of the ingredients and gradually pour in the skim milk, stirring as you pour, bringing together with your fingers to form a soft dough.

4 Turn the dough out onto a floured counter and knead lightly. Roll out to a thickness of ¾ inch/2 cm. Stamp out as many circles as you can using a 2-inch/5-cm plain cookie cutter. Transfer the circles to a cookie sheet.

5 Knead the dough trimmings together and roll out again. Stamp out more circles—you should be able to make 10 biscuits in total.

6 Brush the biscuits with the remaining milk and sprinkle with the grated cheese. Bake in a preheated oven, 400°F/200°C, for 15–20 minutes, until risen and golden. Transfer to a wire rack to cool. Serve warm with lowfat soft cheese, garnished with chopped chives.

cheese & mustard biscuits

makes eight

4 tbsp butter, diced, plus extra
    for greasing

generous 1½ cups self-rising flour,
    plus extra for dusting

1 tsp baking powder

pinch of salt

1¼ cups grated sharp cheese

1 tsp mustard powder

⅔ cup milk, plus extra for brushing

pepper

1 Lightly grease a cookie sheet with a little butter.

2 Strain the flour, baking powder, and salt into a mixing bowl. Rub in the butter with your fingertips until the mixture resembles bread crumbs.

3 Stir in the grated cheese, mustard powder, and enough milk to form a soft dough.

4 Knead the dough very lightly on a lightly floured counter. Flatten it out with the palm of your hand to a depth of about 1 inch/2.5 cm.

5 Cut the dough into 8 wedges with a knife. Brush the wedges with a little milk and sprinkle with pepper to taste.

6 Bake in a preheated oven, 425°F/220°C, for 10–15 minutes, until the biscuits are golden brown.

7 Transfer the biscuits to a wire rack and let cool slightly before serving.

gingersnaps

makes thirty

½ cup butter, plus extra for greasing

2½ cups self-rising flour

pinch of salt

1 cup superfine sugar

1 tbsp ground ginger

1 tsp baking soda

¼ cup light corn syrup

1 egg, beaten lightly

1 tsp grated orange rind

COOK'S TIP

Store these cookies in an airtight container and eat them within 1 week.

VARIATION

For less traditional, but equally delicious cookies, substitute 1 tablespoon apple pie spice for the ground ginger and 1 teaspoon finely grated lemon rind for the orange rind.

---

1 Lightly grease several cookie sheets with a little butter.

2 Strain the flour, salt, sugar, ground ginger, and baking soda into a large mixing bowl.

3 Put the butter and light corn syrup into a pan and place the pan over very low heat until the butter has melted.

4 Remove the pan from the heat and let the butter mixture cool slightly, then pour the mixture onto the dry ingredients.

5 Add the egg and orange rind and bring together to form a dough.

6 Using your hands, carefully shape the dough into 30 even-size balls.

7 Place the balls well apart on the prepared cookie sheets, then flatten them slightly with your fingers.

8 Bake in a preheated oven, 325°F/160°C, for 15–20 minutes. Transfer the cookies to a wire rack to cool and crispen before serving.

lemon jumbles

makes fifty

⅓ cup butter, softened, plus extra
    for greasing
generous ½ cup superfine sugar
grated rind of 1 lemon
1 egg, beaten lightly
4 tbsp lemon juice
2½ cups all-purpose flour, plus extra
    for dusting
1 tsp baking powder
1 tbsp milk
confectioners' sugar, for dredging

VARIATION

If you prefer, form the dough into
other shapes—letters of the
alphabet or geometric designs.

1 Lightly grease several cookie sheets with a little butter.

2 Cream the butter, superfine sugar, and lemon rind together in a mixing bowl until pale and fluffy.

3 Add the beaten egg and lemon juice, a little at a time, beating thoroughly after each addition.

4 Strain the flour and baking powder into the mixture and mix until blended. Add the milk and bring together with your fingers to form a soft dough.

5 Turn the dough out onto a lightly floured counter and divide into about 50 equal-size pieces.

6 Roll each piece into a sausage shape with your hands and bend into an "S" shape.

7 Place the dough shapes on the prepared cookie sheets and bake in a preheated oven, 325°F/160°C, for 15–20 minutes. Transfer to a wire rack and let cool completely. Dredge generously with confectioners' sugar before serving.

cinnamon & seed squares

makes twelve

generous 1 cup butter, softened,
    plus extra for greasing
1¼ cups superfine sugar
3 eggs, beaten lightly
1¾ cups self-rising flour
½ tsp baking soda
1 tbsp ground cinnamon
⅔ cup sour cream
3½ oz/100 g sunflower seeds

COOK'S TIP

These moist squares will
freeze well and will keep for
up to 1 month.

1 Grease a 9-inch/23-cm square
cake pan with a little butter and
line the base with baking parchment.

2 Cream together the butter and
superfine sugar in a large
mixing bowl until the mixture is light
and fluffy.

3 Gradually add the beaten eggs to
the mixture, beating thoroughly
after each addition.

4 Strain the self-rising flour, baking
soda, and ground cinnamon
into the creamed mixture, then fold
in gently, using a metal spoon in a
figure-eight movement.

5 Spoon in the sour cream and
sunflower seeds and mix gently
until well blended.

6 Spoon the cake batter into the
prepared cake pan, then level
the surface with the back of a spoon
or a spatula.

7 Bake in a preheated oven,
350°F/180°C, for 45 minutes,
until the surface is firm to the touch
when pressed with a finger.

8 Loosen the edges with a round-
bladed knife, then turn out onto a
wire rack to cool completely. Slice into
12 squares before serving.

oat & raisin cookies

makes ten

4 tbsp butter, plus extra for greasing

generous ½ cup superfine sugar

1 egg, lightly beaten

generous ⅓ cup all-purpose flour

½ tsp salt

½ tsp baking powder

2 cups rolled oats

¾ cup raisins

2 tbsp sesame seeds

COOK'S TIP

To enjoy these cookies at
their best, store them in an
airtight container.

1 Lightly grease 2 cookie sheets with a little butter.

2 Cream the butter and sugar together in a large mixing bowl until light and fluffy.

3 Gradually add the beaten egg, beating well after each addition until thoroughly blended.

4 Strain the flour, salt, and baking powder into the creamed mixture. Mix together gently. Add the oats, raisins, and sesame seeds, and mix together thoroughly.

5 Place 10 spoonfuls of the mixture on the prepared cookie sheets, spaced well apart to allow room to expand during cooking, and flatten them slightly with the back of a spoon.

6 Bake in a preheated oven, 350°F/180°C, for 15 minutes.

7 Let the cookies cool slightly on the cookie sheets.

8 Carefully transfer the cookies to a wire rack and let cool completely before serving.

hazelnut squares

makes sixteen

⅓ cup butter, diced, plus extra
   for greasing
generous 1 cup all-purpose flour
pinch of salt
1 tsp baking powder
¾ cup brown sugar
1 egg, beaten lightly
4 tbsp milk
1 cup hazelnuts, cut into halves
raw brown sugar, for
   sprinkling (optional)

1 Grease a 9-inch/23-cm square cake pan with a little butter and line the base with baking parchment.

2 Strain the flour, salt, and the baking powder into a large mixing bowl.

3 Rub in the butter with your fingertips until the mixture resembles fine bread crumbs. Add the brown sugar to the mixture and stir to blend.

4 Add the beaten egg, milk, and nuts to the mixture and stir well until thoroughly blended and the mixture has a soft consistency.

5 Spoon the mixture into the prepared cake pan and level the surface with a spatula. Sprinkle with raw brown sugar, if you like.

VARIATION

For a coffee time cookie, replace the milk with the same amount of cold strong black coffee—the stronger the better.

6 Bake in a preheated oven, 350°F/180°C, for 25 minutes, or until the surface is firm to the touch when pressed with a finger.

7 Let cool in the pan for about 10 minutes, then loosen the edges with a round-bladed knife, and turn out onto a wire rack. Cut into 16 squares to serve.

rock drops

makes eight

⅓ cup butter, diced, plus extra
　　for greasing

scant 1½ cups all-purpose flour

2 tsp baking powder

⅓ cup raw brown sugar

½ cup golden raisins

2 tbsp candied cherries,
　　chopped finely

1 egg, beaten lightly

2 tbsp milk

COOK'S TIP

For convenience, prepare the dry
ingredients in advance and just
before cooking, stir in the liquid.

---

1 Lightly grease a cookie sheet
with a little butter.

2 Strain the flour and baking
powder into a mixing bowl. Rub
in the butter with your fingertips until
the mixture resembles bread crumbs.

3 Stir in the raw brown sugar,
raisins, and candied cherries.

4 Add the beaten egg and milk to
the mixture and bring together to
form a soft dough.

5 Spoon 8 mounds of the mixture
onto the prepared cookie sheet,
spacing them well apart to allow room
to expand during cooking.

6 Bake in a preheated oven,
400°F/200°C, for 15–20 minutes,
until firm to the touch when pressed
with a finger.

7 Remove the rock drops from the
cookie sheet. Serve piping hot
from the oven, or transfer to a wire
rack and let cool before serving.

coconut flapjacks

makes sixteen

1 cup butter, plus extra
  for greasing
1 cup raw brown sugar
2 tbsp light corn syrup
3½ cups rolled oats
1 cup dry unsweetened coconut
⅓ cup chopped candied cherries

COOK'S TIP

The flapjacks are best stored in
an airtight container and eaten
within 1 week. They can also be
frozen for up to 1 month.

VARIATION

For plain flapjacks, heat
3 tablespoons superfine sugar,
3 tablespoons light corn syrup,
and ½ cup butter in a pan over
low heat until the butter has
melted. Stir in 1¾ cups rolled
oats or oat flakes until combined,
then transfer to a greased cookie
sheet, and bake as above.

1 Lightly grease a 12 x 9-inch/
30 x 23-cm cookie sheet with
a little butter.

2 Heat the butter, raw brown sugar,
and light corn syrup in a large
pan over low heat until just melted.

3 Stir in the oats, shredded coconut,
and candied cherries and mix well
until evenly combined.

4 Place the mixture on the prepared
cookie sheet. Spread evenly
across the cookie sheet and level the
surface by pressing with a spatula.

5 Bake the flapjack in a preheated
oven, 325°F/170°C, for about
30 minutes, until golden.

6 Remove from the oven and
let cool on the cookie sheet for
10 minutes.

7 Cut the mixture into 16 pieces
using a sharp knife.

8 Carefully transfer the flapjack
squares to a wire rack and let
cool completely.

citrus crescents

makes twenty-five

⅓ cup butter, softened, plus extra
    for greasing

⅓ cup superfine sugar, plus extra
    for dusting (optional)

1 egg, separated

scant 1½ cups all-purpose flour, plus
    extra for dusting

grated rind of 1 orange

grated rind of 1 lemon

grated rind of 1 lime

2–3 tbsp orange juice

1 Lightly grease 2 cookie sheets with a little butter.

2 Cream the butter and sugar together in a mixing bowl until light and fluffy, then gradually beat in the egg yolk.

3 Strain the flour into the creamed mixture and mix until evenly blended. Add the orange, lemon, and lime rinds to the mixture, with enough orange juice to form a soft dough.

4 Roll out the dough on a lightly floured counter. Stamp out circles using a 3-inch/7.5-cm cookie cutter. Make crescent shapes by cutting away a fourth of each circle. Re-roll the trimmings to make about 25 crescents.

5 Place the crescents on the prepared cookie sheets. Prick the surface of each crescent with a fork.

6 Lightly whisk the egg white in a small bowl and brush it over the cookies. Dust with extra superfine sugar, if you like.

7 Bake in a preheated oven, 400°F/200°C, for 12–15 minutes. Transfer the cookies to a wire rack to cool and crispen before serving.

spiced cookies

makes twelve

¾ cup sweet butter, plus extra
    for greasing
scant 1 cup dark brown sugar
generous 1½ cups all-purpose flour
pinch of salt
½ tsp baking soda
1 tsp ground cinnamon
½ tsp ground coriander
½ tsp ground nutmeg
¼ tsp ground cloves
2 tbsp dark rum

1 Lightly grease 2 cookie sheets with a little butter.

2 Cream the butter and sugar together in a mixing bowl and whisk until light and fluffy.

3 Strain the flour, salt and baking soda into the butter and sugar mixture, then stir in the cinnamon, coriander, nutmeg, and cloves.

4 Add the dark rum and stir it into the creamed mixture.

5 Place small mounds of the mixture on the prepared cookie sheets using 2 teaspoons. Space the mounds well apart to allow room to expand during cooking. Flatten each one slightly with the back of a spoon.

6 Bake in a preheated oven at 350°F/180°C for 10–12 minutes, until golden brown in color.

7 Carefully transfer the cookies to wire racks to cool completely and crispen before serving.

COOK'S TIP

Use the back of a fork to flatten
the cookies instead of a spoon,
to give them a textured surface.

peanut butter cookies

COOK'S TIP

For a crunchy bite and
sparkling appearance, sprinkle
the cookies with raw brown
sugar before baking.

VARIATION

For a change, use light molasses
sugar instead of granulated and
add 1 teaspoon apple pie
spice with the flour and
baking powder.

1 Lightly grease 2 cookie sheets
with a little butter.

2 Beat the softened butter and
peanut butter together in a large
mixing bowl.

3 Gradually add the granulated
sugar and beat well.

4 Add the beaten egg, a little at a
time, beating after each addition
until thoroughly blended.

5 Strain the flour, baking powder,
and salt into the creamed peanut
butter mixture.

6 Add the chopped peanuts
and bring the mixture together
with your fingers to form a soft, sticky
dough. Wrap the cookie dough in
plastic wrap and chill in the refrigerator
for 30 minutes.

7 Form the dough into 20 balls
and place them on the prepared
cookie sheets, spaced well apart to
allow room to expand during cooking,
and flatten slightly with your hand.

8 Bake in a preheated oven,
375°F/190°C, for 15 minutes,
until golden brown. Transfer the
cookies to a wire rack and let cool
before serving.

shortbread fantails

makes eight

½ cup butter, softened, plus extra
   for greasing
scant ¼ cup granulated sugar
2 tbsp confectioners' sugar
generous 1½ cups all-purpose flour,
   plus extra for dusting
pinch of salt
2 tsp orange flower water
superfine sugar, for sprinkling

1 Grease a shallow 8-inch/20-cm
   round cake pan with butter.

2 Cream the butter, granulated
   sugar, and confectioners' sugar
together in a large mixing bowl until
light and fluffy.

3 Strain the flour and salt into the
   creamed mixture. Add the orange
flower water and bring together with
your fingers to form a soft dough.

4 Roll out the dough on a lightly
   floured counter into an 8-inch/
20-cm circle and place in the prepared
pan. Prick well and score into
8 triangles with a round-bladed knife.

5 Bake the shortbread in a
   preheated oven, 325°F/160°C, for
30–35 minutes, or until it is crisp and
the top is pale golden.

6 Sprinkle with superfine sugar,
   then cut along the marked lines
to make the fantails.

7 Let the shortbread cool in the pan
   before serving.

meringues

makes thirteen

4 egg whites

pinch of salt

generous ½ cup granulated sugar

generous ½ cup superfine sugar

1¼ cups heavy cream,
   whipped lightly

VARIATION

For a finer texture, replace
the granulated sugar with
superfine sugar.

1 Line 3 large cookie sheets with baking parchment.

2 Whisk the egg whites and salt in a large clean bowl until stiff, using an electric whisk or a balloon whisk. (You should be able to turn the bowl upside down without any movement from the egg whites.)

3 Whisk in the granulated sugar, a little at a time; the meringue should start to look glossy.

4 Whisk in the superfine sugar, a little at a time, whisking well after each addition until all the sugar has been incorporated and the meringue is thick, white, and forms peaks.

5 Transfer the meringue mixture into a pastry bag fitted with a ¾-inch/2-cm star tip. Pipe about 26 small whirls of meringue onto the prepared cookie sheets.

6 Bake in a preheated oven, 250°F/120°C, for 1½ hours, or until the meringues are pale golden and can be easily lifted off the parchment. Turn off the heat and let cool in the oven overnight.

7 Just before serving, sandwich the meringue whirls together in pairs with the whipped cream and arrange on a serving plate.

131

vanilla hearts

makes twelve

⅔ cup butter, diced, plus extra
   for greasing

2 cups all-purpose flour, plus extra
   for dusting

½ cup superfine sugar, plus extra
   for dusting

1 tsp vanilla extract

COOK'S TIP

Place a fresh vanilla bean in
your superfine sugar and keep
it in a storage jar for several
weeks to give the sugar a
delicious vanilla flavor.

VARIATION

If you like, you could add a few
drops of red or pink food
coloring with the vanilla
extract and decorate the the
hearts with tiny silver, gold, or
pink balls.

1 Lightly grease a cookie sheet
with a little butter.

2 Strain the flour into a large mixing
bowl and rub in the butter with
your fingertips until the mixture
resembles fine bread crumbs.

3 Stir in the superfine sugar and
vanilla extract and bring the
mixture together with your hands
to form a firm dough.

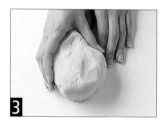

4 Roll out the dough on a lightly
floured surface to a thickness of
1 inch/2.5 cm. Stamp out 12 hearts
with a heart-shaped cookie cutter
measuring about 2 inches/5 cm
across and 1 inch/2.5 cm deep.

5 Arrange the hearts on the
prepared cookie sheet. Bake in
a preheated oven, 350°F/180°C, for
15–20 minutes, until light golden.

6 Transfer the vanilla hearts to a
wire rack and let cool completely.
Dust the cookies with a little superfine
sugar just before serving.

Appetizers & Snacks

With so many fresh ingredients readily available, it is very easy to create some deliciously different appetizers to make the perfect introduction to any meal. The ideas in this chapter are an inspiration to cook and a treat to eat, and they give an edge to the appetite that makes the main course even more enjoyable. When choosing an appetizer, make sure that you provide a good balance of flavors, colors, and textures that offer variety and contrast. Balance the nature of the recipes too—a rich entrée is best preceded by a light appetizer to stimulate the taste buds.

onion & mozzarella tarts

serves four

9 oz/250 g puff pastry dough,
   thawed if frozen

2 red onions

1 red bell pepper

8 cherry tomatoes, halved

3½ oz/100 g mozzarella cheese,
   cut into chunks

8 fresh thyme sprigs

1 Roll out the pie dough on a lightly floured counter to make 4 squares, 3 inches/7.5 cm wide. Trim the edges of the dough, reserving the trimmings. Chill the dough in the refrigerator for 30 minutes.

2 Place the dough squares on a cookie sheet. Brush a little water around the edges of each square and use the reserved dough trimmings to make a rim around each tart.

3 Cut the red onions into thin wedges and halve and seed the red bell pepper.

4 Place the onions and red bell pepper on a broiler rack. Cook under a preheated medium broiler for 15 minutes, or until the bell pepper skin is charred.

5 Place the roasted bell pepper halves in a plastic bag and set aside to sweat for 10 minutes. When the bell pepper is cool enough to handle, peel off the skin and cut the flesh into strips.

6 Line the dough squares with squares of foil. Bake in a preheated oven, 400°F/200°C, for 10 minutes. Remove and discard the foil, then bake the pastry squares for 5 minutes more.

7 Divide the onions, bell pepper strips, tomatoes, and cheese among the tarts and sprinkle with the fresh thyme.

8 Bake the tarts for 15 minutes more, or until they are golden. Transfer to warmed serving plates if serving hot, or to a wire rack to cool if serving cold.

baked eggplant

serves four

3–4 tbsp olive oil

2 garlic cloves, crushed

2 large eggplant

3½ oz/100 g mozzarella cheese

generous ¾ cup bottled
  strained tomatoes

scant ⅔ cup freshly grated
  Parmesan cheese

1 Heat 2 tablespoons of the olive oil in a large skillet. Add the garlic and sauté over a low heat for 30 seconds.

2 Slice the eggplant lengthwise. Add the slices to the skillet and cook in the oil for 3–4 minutes on each side, or until tender (you may have to do this in batches, so add the remaining oil as necessary.)

3 Remove the eggplant with a slotted spoon and drain on paper towels.

4 Place a layer of eggplant slices in a shallow ovenproof dish. Thinly slice the mozzarella, then place a layer of cheese slices over the eggplant. Pour

over a third of the tomatoes. Continue layering in the same order, finishing with a layer of tomatoes.

5 Generously sprinkle the grated Parmesan cheese over the top of the dish. Bake in a preheated oven, 400°F/200°C, for 25–30 minutes, or until the top is golden and bubbling.

6 Transfer the baked eggplant to serving plates and serve warm, or let cool, then chill and serve cold.

baked fennel

serves four

2 fennel bulbs

2 celery stalks, cut into 3-inch/
   7.5-cm pieces

6 sun-dried tomatoes, cut in half

generous ¾ cup bottled
   strained tomatoes

2 tsp dried oregano

scant ⅔ cup freshly grated
   Parmesan cheese

1 Trim the fennel using a sharp knife, discard any tough outer leaves, and cut the bulbs into fourths.

2 Bring a large pan of water to a boil, add the fennel and celery, and cook for 8–10 minutes, or until just tender. Remove with a slotted spoon and drain.

3 Place the fennel pieces, celery, and sun-dried tomatoes in a large ovenproof dish.

4 Mix the tomatoes and oregano in a bowl and pour the mixture over the vegetables in the dish.

5 Sprinkle with the Parmesan cheese and bake in a preheated oven, 375°F/190°C, for 20 minutes, or until hot. Serve as an appetizer or as a vegetable side dish.

cheese & onion pies

serves four

FILLING

3 tbsp vegetable oil

4 onions, thinly sliced

4 garlic cloves, crushed

4 tbsp finely chopped fresh parsley

¾ cup grated sharp cheese

salt and pepper

DOUGH

1¼ cups all-purpose flour, plus extra
    for dusting

½ tsp salt

⅓ cup butter, diced

3–4 tbsp water

COOK'S TIP

You can prepare the filling in
advance and store it in the
refrigerator until required.

1 Heat the oil in a skillet over low heat. Add the onions and garlic and cook for 10–15 minutes, or until the onions are soft. Remove the skillet from the heat, stir in the parsley and cheese, and season to taste.

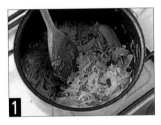

2 To make the dough, strain the flour and salt into a bowl. Rub in the butter with your fingertips until the mixture resembles bread crumbs. Gradually stir in the water and bring together to form a dough.

3 Roll out the dough on a lightly floured counter and divide it into 8 portions.

4 Roll out each portion into a circle 4 inches/10 cm wide and use 4 of the circles to line individual tartlet pans. Fill each pie shell with a fourth of the cheese and onion mixture.

5 Cover the pies with the remaining 4 dough circles. Make a slit in the top of each pie with the point of a sharp knife to allow steam to escape during cooking, then press the edges of the pies firmly with the back of a teaspoon to seal.

6 Bake in a preheated oven, 425°F/220°C, for 20 minutes. Transfer the cheese and onion pies to warmed plates and serve.

stuffed tomato

serves six

6 large, firm tomatoes, rinsed

4 tbsp sweet butter

5 tbsp vegetable oil

1 onion, chopped finely

1 tsp finely chopped fresh
  gingerroot

1 tsp crushed garlic

1 tsp pepper

1 tsp salt

½ tsp garam masala

4 cups ground lamb

1 fresh green chile, seeded and
  finely chopped

fresh cilantro leaves

1 Slice the tops off the tomatoes
  and reserve, then scoop out the
pulp. Grease an ovenproof dish with all
of the butter and place the tomatoes
in the dish.

2 Heat the oil in a pan over medium
  heat, add the onion, and cook,
stirring frequently, until golden.

3 Reduce the heat and add the
  ginger, garlic, pepper, salt, and
garam masala. Cook for 3–5 minutes.

4 Add the ground lamb and cook
  for 15 minutes, until browned.

5 Add the green chile and fresh
  cilantro leaves and cook for
3–5 minutes more.

6 Spoon the lamb mixture into the
  tomatoes and replace the tops.
Bake in a preheated oven, 350°F/
180°C, for 15–20 minutes.

7 Transfer the tomatoes to serving
  plates and serve hot.

pasta-stuffed tomatoes

serves eight

5 tbsp extra virgin olive oil, plus
    extra for greasing
8 beefsteak tomatoes or large round
    tomatoes, rinsed
1 cup dried ditalini or other very
    small pasta shapes
8 black olives, pitted and
    finely chopped
2 tbsp finely chopped fresh basil
1 tbsp finely chopped fresh parsley
⅔ cup freshly grated
    Parmesan cheese
salt and pepper
fresh basil sprigs, to garnish

1 Brush a cookie sheet with olive oil. Slice the tops off the tomatoes and reserve to use as lids. If the tomatoes will not stand up, cut a thin slice off the base of each of them.

2 Scoop out the tomato pulp into a strainer using a teaspoon, and leave the pulp to drain. Invert the tomato shells on paper towels, pat dry, and let drain.

3 Bring a large pan of lightly salted water to a boil. Add the pasta and 1 tablespoon of the remaining olive oil, bring back to a boil, and cook for 8–10 minutes, or until tender but still firm to the bite. Drain and set aside.

4 Put the olives, basil, parsley, and Parmesan cheese into a large mixing bowl and stir in the drained tomato pulp. Add the pasta to the bowl. Stir in the remaining oil, mix together well, and season to taste.

5 Spoon the pasta mixture into the tomato shells and replace the lids. Arrange on the prepared cookie sheet and bake in a preheated oven, 375°F/190°C, for 15–20 minutes.

6 Remove the tomatoes from the oven and let cool until just warm.

7 Arrange the tomatoes on a serving dish, garnish with basil sprigs, and serve.

mexican-style pizzas

serves four

4 ready-made, pre-cooked
   individual pizza bases

1 tbsp olive oil

7 oz/200 g canned chopped
   tomatoes with garlic and herbs

2 tbsp tomato paste

7 oz/200 g canned kidney beans,
   drained and rinsed

⅔ cup corn kernels, thawed
   if frozen

1–2 tsp chili sauce

1 large red onion, shredded

1 cup grated sharp colby cheese

1 large fresh green chile, seeded
   and sliced into rings

salt and pepper

COOK'S TIP

Serve a Mexican-style salad
with this pizza. Arrange sliced
tomatoes, fresh cilantro leaves,
and a few slices of a small, ripe
avocado on a platter. Sprinkle
with fresh lime juice and
coarse sea salt.

1 Arrange the ready-made pizza bases on a large cookie sheet and brush the surfaces lightly with the olive oil.

2 Combine the chopped tomatoes, tomato paste, kidney beans, and corn in a large bowl and add chili sauce to taste. Season to taste with salt and pepper.

3 Spread the tomato and kidney bean mixture evenly over each of the pizza bases.

4 Top each pizza with shredded onion and sprinkle with some grated cheese and a few slices of fresh green chile to taste.

5 Bake in a preheated oven, 425°F/220°C, for 20 minutes, until the vegetables are tender, the cheese has melted, and the pizza dough is crisp and golden.

6 Remove the pizzas from the cookie sheet and transfer to serving plates. Serve hot.

mini pizzas

serves eight

BASIC PIZZA DOUGH

2 tsp dry yeast

1 tsp sugar

1 cup warm water

2½ cups strong white bread flour,
    plus extra for dusting

1 tsp salt

1 tbsp olive oil, plus extra
    for brushing

TOPPING

2 zucchini

generous ⅓ cup bottled
    strained tomatoes

½ cup diced pancetta

½ cup pitted black olives, chopped

1 tbsp mixed dried herbs

2 tbsp olive oil

salt and pepper

1 To make the dough, combine the yeast, sugar, and 4 tablespoons of the water. Set the mixture aside in a warm place for 15 minutes, until frothy.

2 In a separate bowl, combine the flour and salt and make a well in the center. Add the oil, yeast mixture, and remaining water. Mix into a smooth dough using a wooden spoon.

3 Turn the dough out onto a floured counter and knead for 4–5 minutes, or until smooth. Return the dough to the bowl, cover with an oiled sheet of plastic wrap, and let rise for 30 minutes, or until the dough has doubled in size.

4 Knead the dough for 2 minutes, then divide it into 8 balls. Roll out each portion thinly to form a circle about 4 inches/10 cm wide, then carefully transfer all of the dough circles to an oiled cookie sheet and push out the edges until the circles are even. The pizza doughs should be no more than ¼ inch/5 mm thick because they will rise during cooking.

5 To make the topping, grate the zucchini finely. Cover with paper towels and let stand for 10 minutes to soak up some of the juices.

6 Spread 2–3 teaspoons of the tomatoes over each pizza base and top with the grated zucchini, pancetta, and olives. Season with pepper, then add a sprinkling of mixed dried herbs to taste, and drizzle over the top with olive oil.

7 Bake in a preheated oven, 400°F/200°C, for 15 minutes, or until crispy. Season with salt and pepper to taste and serve hot.

creamy ham pizzas

serves four

9 oz/250 g flaky pastry dough,
  well chilled

3 tbsp butter

1 red onion, chopped

1 garlic clove, chopped

⅓ cup white bread flour

1¼ cups milk

scant ⅔ cup finely grated Parmesan
  cheese, plus extra for sprinkling

2 eggs, hard-cooked, cut
  into fourths

3½ oz/100 g Italian pork sausage,
  such as feline salame, cut
  into strips

salt and pepper

fresh thyme sprigs, to garnish

1 Fold the pastry dough in half and evenly grate it into 4 individual tart pans measuring 4 inches/10 cm wide. Using a floured fork, gently press the dough flakes down, making sure that there are no holes, and that the dough comes up the sides of the pans.

2 Line with foil and bake blind in a preheated oven, 425°F/220°C, for 10 minutes. Reduce the heat to 400°F/200°C, remove the foil from the pizza shells, and cook for 15 minutes, or until golden and set.

3 Heat the butter in a skillet. Add the onion and garlic and cook for 5–6 minutes, or until softened.

4 Add the flour, stirring well to coat the onion. Gradually stir in the milk to make a thick sauce.

5 Season the sauce with salt and pepper to taste and then stir in the Parmesan cheese. Do not reheat once the cheese has been added or the sauce will become too stringy.

6 Spread the sauce evenly over the cooked pizza shells. Decorate with the eggs and strips of sausage.

7 Sprinkle with a little extra Parmesan cheese, return to the oven, and bake for 5 minutes just to heat through.

8 Serve immediately, garnished with sprigs of fresh thyme.

gnocchi romana

serves four

scant 4 cups milk

pinch of freshly grated nutmeg

6 tbsp butter, plus extra
    for greasing

1¼ cups semolina

generous 1 cup freshly grated
    Parmesan cheese

2 eggs, beaten

½ cup grated Swiss cheese

salt and pepper

fresh basil sprigs, to garnish

1 Pour the milk into a pan and bring to a boil. Remove the pan from the heat and stir in the nutmeg and 2 tablespoons of the butter. Season to taste with salt and pepper.

2 Gradually stir the semolina into the milk, whisking to prevent lumps forming, then return to the stove over low heat. Simmer, stirring constantly, for about 10 minutes, or until very thick.

3 Beat ⅔ cup of the Parmesan cheese into the semolina mixture, then beat in the eggs. Continue beating the mixture until smooth. Let the mixture cool slightly.

4 Spread out the cooled semolina mixture in an even layer across a sheet of baking parchment, smoothing the surface with a damp spatula until it is about ½ inch/1 cm thick. Let cool completely, then chill the mixture in the refrigerator for 1 hour.

5 Remove the mixture from the refrigerator. Stamp out circles of gnocchi, about 1½ inches/4 cm wide, using a plain, greased cookie cutter.

6 Grease a shallow ovenproof dish or 4 individual ovenproof dishes. Lay the gnocchi trimmings in the base of the dish or dishes and arrange the circles of gnocchi on top, slightly overlapping each other.

7 Melt the remaining butter and drizzle it over the gnocchi. Sprinkle over the remaining grated Parmesan cheese, then sprinkle over the Swiss cheese.

8 Bake in a preheated oven, 400°F/200°C, for 25–30 minutes, until the top is crisp, golden brown, and bubbling. Serve immediately, garnished with fresh sprigs of basil.

spinach & ricotta shells

serves four

14 oz/400 g dried lumache rigate
 grande pasta

5 tbsp olive oil

1 cup fresh white bread crumbs

½ cup milk

10½ oz/300 g frozen spinach,
 thawed and drained

1 cup ricotta cheese

pinch of freshly grated nutmeg

14 oz/400 g canned chopped
 tomatoes, drained

1 garlic clove, crushed

salt and pepper

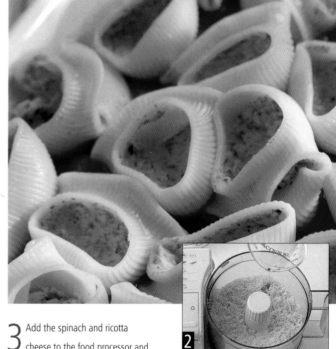

1 Bring a large pan of lightly salted water to a boil. Add the pasta and 1 tablespoon of the oil, bring back to a boil, and cook for 8–10 minutes, until just tender but still firm to the bite. Drain the pasta, refresh under cold water, and set aside until required.

2 Put the bread crumbs, milk, and 3 tablespoons of the remaining olive oil in a food processor and process until blended.

3 Add the spinach and ricotta cheese to the food processor and process to a smooth mixture. Transfer the mixture to a bowl, stir in the nutmeg, and season to taste.

4 Mix the tomatoes, garlic, and remaining oil together in a bowl and spoon the mixture into the base of a large ovenproof dish.

5 Fill the lumache with the spinach and ricotta mixture using a teaspoon, then arrange the pasta shells on top of the tomato mixture in the ovenproof dish. Cover and bake in a preheated oven, 350°F/180°C, for 20 minutes. Serve the lumache hot, straight from the oven.

tricolor timballini

serves four

1 tbsp butter, for greasing

1 cup dried white bread crumbs

6 oz/175 g dried tricolor spaghetti,
  broken into 2-inch/5-cm lengths

3 tbsp olive oil

1 egg yolk

1 cup grated Swiss cheese

1¼ cups Béchamel Sauce
  (see page 210)

1 onion, chopped finely

1 bay leaf

⅔ cup dry white wine

⅔ cup bottled strained tomatoes

1 tbsp tomato paste

salt and pepper

fresh basil leaves, to garnish

1 Grease four ¾-cup molds or ramekins with the butter, then evenly coat the insides with half of the bread crumbs.

2 Bring a pan of lightly salted water to a boil. Add the spaghetti and 1 tablespoon of oil, bring back to a boil, and cook for 8–10 minutes, or until just tender but still firm to the bite. Drain and transfer to a mixing bowl. Add the egg yolk and cheese to the pasta and season to taste.

3 Pour the béchamel sauce into the bowl containing the pasta and mix. Spoon the mixture into the ramekins and sprinkle over the remaining bread crumbs.

4 Stand the ramekins on a cookie sheet and bake in a preheated oven, 425°F/220°C, for 20 minutes. Remove from the oven and let stand for 10 minutes.

5 Meanwhile, heat the remaining oil in a pan, add the onion and bay leaf, and cook over low heat for 2–3 minutes.

6 Stir in the wine, tomatoes, and tomato paste, and season with salt and pepper to taste. Simmer gently for 20 minutes, until thickened. Remove and discard the bay leaf.

7 Turn the timballini out onto serving plates, garnish with basil, and serve with the tomato sauce.

pasta baked with three cheeses

serves four

1 tbsp butter, for greasing

14 oz/400 g dried penne pasta

1 tbsp olive oil

2 eggs, beaten

1½ cups ricotta cheese

generous ½ cup basil leaves, plus
   extra to garnish

1 cup grated mozzarella or
   halloumi cheese

⅔ cup freshly grated
   Parmesan cheese

salt and pepper

VARIATION

Try substituting smoked Bavarian
cheese for the mozzarella or
halloumi and grated colby
cheese for the Parmesan, for a
slightly different, but just as
delicious flavor.

---

1 Lightly grease a large ovenproof dish with the butter.

2 Bring a large pan of lightly salted water to a boil. Add the penne and olive oil, bring back to a boil, and cook for 8–10 minutes, until just tender but still firm to the bite. Drain the pasta, set aside, and keep warm.

3 Beat the eggs into the ricotta cheese and season to taste.

4 Spoon half of the penne into the base of the prepared dish and cover with half of the basil leaves.

5 Spoon half of the ricotta cheese mixture over the pasta. Sprinkle over the grated mozzarella or halloumi cheese and top with the remaining basil leaves. Cover with the remaining penne, then spoon over the remaining ricotta cheese mixture. Lightly sprinkle the freshly grated Parmesan cheese over the top.

6 Bake in a preheated oven, 375°F/190°C, for 30–40 minutes, until golden brown and the cheese topping is bubbling. Garnish with fresh basil leaves, if you like, and serve hot straight from the dish.

baked macaroni

serves four

4 cups dried short-cut macaroni

1 tbsp olive oil

4 tbsp beef drippings

1 lb/450 g potatoes, sliced thinly

1 lb/450 g onions, sliced

2 cups grated mozzarella cheese

⅔ cup heavy cream

salt and pepper

crusty brown bread and butter,
   to serve

VARIATION

For a stronger flavor, use
mozzarella affumicata, a
smoked version of this cheese,
or Swiss cheese, instead of
the normal mozzarella.

1 Bring a large pan of lightly salted water to a boil. Add the macaroni and olive oil, bring back to a boil, and cook for about 12 minutes, or until tender but still firm to the bite. Drain thoroughly and set aside.

2 Melt the beef drippings in a large flameproof casserole over a low heat, then remove the casserole from the heat.

3 Make alternate layers of potatoes, onions, macaroni, and grated mozzarella in the casserole, seasoning well with salt and pepper between each layer and finishing with a layer of cheese on top. Finally, pour the cream over the top layer of cheese.

4 Bake in a preheated oven, 400°F/200°C, for 25 minutes. Remove the casserole from the oven and carefully brown the top under a preheated hot broiler.

5 Serve the macaroni straight from the casserole with crusty brown bread and butter as a filling snack or as a vegetable accompaniment with your favorite entrée.

pancetta & romano cakes

serves four

2 tbsp butter, plus extra
for greasing

3 ½ oz/100 g pancetta,
rind removed

scant 2 cups self-rising flour

¾ cup grated romano cheese

⅔ cup milk, plus extra for glazing

1 tsp Worcestershire sauce

1 tbsp tomato catsup

14 oz/400 g dried farfalle pasta

1 tbsp olive oil

salt

TO SERVE

3 tbsp Pesto Sauce (see page 11)
or anchovy sauce, optional

salad greens, to serve

1 Grease a cookie sheet with a little butter. Cook the pancetta under a preheated broiler until it is cooked. Let cool, then chop finely.

2 Strain the flour and a pinch of salt into a mixing bowl. Add the butter and rub in with your fingertips until the mixture resembles bread crumbs, then add the pancetta and ¼ cup of the grated romano cheese, and stir to blend.

3 In a separate bowl, combine the milk, Worcestershire sauce, and tomato catsup, then add to the dry ingredients. Bring together with your fingers to form a soft dough.

4 Roll out the dough on a lightly floured counter to make a 7-inch/18-cm circle. Brush with a little milk to glaze and cut into 8 wedges.

5 Arrange the dough wedges on the prepared cookie sheet and sprinkle over the remaining cheese. Bake in a preheated oven, 400°F/ 200°C, for 20 minutes.

6 Meanwhile, bring a pan of lightly salted water to a boil. Add the farfalle and the oil, bring back to a boil, and cook for 8–10 minutes, until just tender, but still firm to the bite. Drain and transfer to a large serving dish. Top with the pancetta and romano cakes. Serve with the sauce of your choice and salad greens.

garlic & pine nut tarts

serves four

4 slices of whole-wheat or
   multigrain bread

½ cup pine nuts

¾ cup butter

5 garlic cloves, cut in half

2 tbsp chopped fresh oregano

4 pitted black olives, cut in half

fresh oregano leaves, to garnish

VARIATION

Puff pastry dough can be used
for the tarts. Use 7 oz/200 g
dough to line 4 tartlet pans. Chill
in the refrigerator for 20 minutes.
Line with foil and bake blind for
10 minutes. Remove the foil and
bake for 3–4 minutes, or until
the dough is set. Cool, then
continue from step 2, adding
2 tablespoons fresh bread
crumbs to the mixture instead
of the bread trimmings.

---

1 Flatten the bread slightly using a
rolling pin, then stamp out
4 circles of bread to fit your individual
tartlet pans, using a cookie cutter
about 4 inches/10 cm wide. Reserve
the bread trimmings and chill them in
the refrigerator for 10 minutes, or
until required.

2 Meanwhile, place the pine nuts
on a cookie sheet and toast them
under a preheated medium broiler for
2–3 minutes, or until golden.

3 Place the bread trimmings, pine
nuts, butter, garlic, and oregano
in a food processor and process for
about 20 seconds. Alternatively, pound
the ingredients by hand in a mortar
with a pestle. The mixture should have
a coarse texture.

4 Spoon the mixture into the bread-
lined pans and top with the olive
halves. Bake in a preheated oven,
400°F/200°C, for 10–15 minutes, or
until golden.

5 Transfer the tarts to serving plates
and serve warm, garnished with
fresh oregano leaves.

provencal tart

serves six

9 oz/250 g ready-made puff pastry
 dough, thawed if frozen

3 tbsp olive oil

2 red bell peppers, seeded and diced

2 green bell peppers, seeded
 and diced

⅔ cup heavy cream

1 egg

2 zucchini, sliced

salt and pepper

1 Roll out the pie dough on a lightly floured counter and use it to line an 8-inch/20-cm loose-based tart pan. Chill the dough in the refrigerator for 20 minutes.

2 Meanwhile, heat 2 tablespoons of the olive oil in a large skillet. Add the diced red and green bell peppers and cook over low heat, stirring frequently, for about 8 minutes, until softened.

3 Whisk the heavy cream and egg together in a bowl and season to taste with salt and pepper. Stir in the cooked bell peppers.

4 Heat the remaining oil in a separate skillet and cook the zucchini slices over medium heat for 4–5 minutes, stirring frequently, until lightly browned.

5 Pour the egg and bell pepper mixture into the tart shell.

6 Arrange the zucchini slices around the edge of the tart.

7 Bake in a preheated oven, 350°F/180°C, for 35–40 minutes, or until just set and golden brown. Serve hot or cold.

fresh tomato tarts

serves six

9 oz/250 g ready-made puff pastry
    dough, thawed if frozen
1 egg, beaten
2 tbsp Pesto Sauce (see page 11)
6 plum tomatoes, sliced
salt and pepper
fresh thyme leaves,
    to garnish (optional)

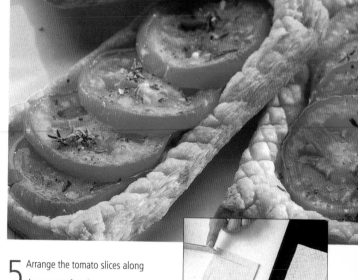

1 Roll out the pie dough on a lightly floured counter into a rectangle measuring 12 x 10 inches/30 x 25 cm.

2 Cut the rectangle in half and divide each half into 3 pieces to make 6 even-size rectangles. Chill in the refrigerator for 20 minutes.

3 Lightly score the edges of the pie dough rectangles and brush with the beaten egg.

4 Spread the pesto sauce over the rectangles, dividing it equally among them, leaving 1-inch/2.5-cm borders around the edges.

5 Arrange the tomato slices along the center of each rectangle, on top of the pesto sauce.

6 Season with salt and pepper to taste and lightly sprinkle with fresh thyme leaves, if you like.

7 Bake in a preheated oven, 400°F/200°C, for 15–20 minutes, until well risen and golden brown.

8 Transfer the tomato tarts to warmed serving plates straight from the oven, and serve while they are still piping hot.

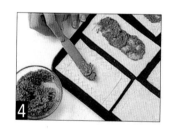

vegetable pasta nests

serves four

6 oz/175 g dried spaghetti

1 eggplant, cut in half lengthwise, then sliced

1 zucchini, diced

1 red bell pepper, seeded and chopped diagonally

6 tbsp olive oil

2 garlic cloves, crushed

butter, for greasing

4 tbsp butter or margarine, melted

1 tbsp dry white bread crumbs

salt and pepper

fresh parsley sprigs, to garnish

COOK'S TIP

The Italian term *al dente* means "to the bite" and describes cooked pasta that is not too soft and still has a "bite" to it. Start timing the pasta from the moment the water comes back to a boil. Begin testing, by biting a small piece of pasta between your front teeth, about 2 minutes before the specified cooking time is up. Drain as soon as it is ready, or it will become soggy.

1 Bring a pan of water to a boil. Add the spaghetti, bring back to a boil, and cook for 8–10 minutes, until tender but still firm to the bite. Drain and set aside.

2 Place the eggplant, zucchini, and bell pepper on a cookie sheet.

3 Combine the oil and garlic and pour over the vegetables, tossing them to coat well.

4 Cook the vegetables under a preheated hot broiler for about 10 minutes, turning occasionally, until tender and lightly charred. Set aside and keep warm.

5 Lightly grease 4 large, shallow muffin pans and divide the spaghetti between them. Curl the spaghetti to form nests using 2 forks.

6 Brush the pasta nests with melted butter or margarine and sprinkle with the bread crumbs. Bake in a preheated oven, 400°F/200°C, for 15 minutes, or until lightly golden. Remove the pasta nests from the pans and transfer to warmed individual serving plates. Divide the broiled vegetables among the pasta nests, season to taste with salt and pepper, and garnish with sprigs of parsley.

mini cheese & onion tarts

makes twelve

DOUGH

¾ cup all-purpose flour, plus extra
  for dusting

¼ tsp salt

5½ tbsp butter, diced

1–2 tbsp water

FILLING

1 egg, beaten

generous ⅓ cup light cream

½ cup grated Dry Jack or
  colby cheese

3 scallions, chopped finely

salt

cayenne pepper

1 To make the dough, strain the flour and salt into a mixing bowl. Add the butter and rub it in with your fingertips until the mixture resembles bread crumbs. Stir in the water, bring together to form a dough, and shape into a ball. Cover with plastic wrap and chill in the refrigerator for 30 minutes.

2 Roll out the dough on a lightly floured counter. Stamp out 12 circles from the dough using a 3-inch/7.5-cm cookie cutter and use them to line a shallow muffin pan.

3 To make the filling, whisk the beaten egg, cream, grated cheese, and scallions together in a pitcher. Season to taste with salt and cayenne pepper.

4 Pour the filling mixture into the tart shells and bake in a preheated oven, 350°F/180°C, for about 20–25 minutes, or until the filling is just set. Serve hot, or transfer to a wire rack to cool.

ham & cheese lattice pies

serves six

1 tbsp butter, for greasing

9 oz/250 g ready-made puff pastry
   dough, thawed if frozen

generous ⅓ cup finely chopped ham

½ cup soft cheese

2 tbsp chopped fresh chives

1 egg, beaten

scant ½ cup freshly grated
   Parmesan cheese

pepper

1 Lightly grease 2 large cookie
sheets with the butter. Roll out
the pastry dough on a lightly floured
counter, then cut out 12 rectangles
of dough measuring 6 x 2 inches/
15 x 5 cm.

2 Place the rectangles on the
prepared cookie sheets and chill
in the refrigerator for 30 minutes.

3 Meanwhile, combine the ham,
cheese, and chives in a small
bowl. Season with pepper to taste.

4 Divide the ham and cheese
mixture along the center of 6 of
the rectangles, leaving a 1-inch/2.5-cm
border around the edges. Brush the
borders with the beaten egg.

5 To make the lattice pattern,
fold the remaining rectangles
lengthwise. Leaving a 1-inch/2.5-cm
border, cut vertical lines across the
folded edge of the rectangles.

6 Unfold the latticed rectangles and
place them over the rectangles
topped with the ham and cheese
mixture. Press the dough edges to seal
them and lightly sprinkle with the
grated Parmesan cheese.

7 Bake in a preheated oven, 350°F/
180°C, for 15–20 minutes. Serve
immediately or transfer to a wire rack
to cool and serve cold.

pissaladière

serves eight

1 tbsp butter, for greasing

4 tbsp olive oil

1 lb 9 oz/700 g red onions,
    sliced thinly

2 garlic cloves, crushed

2 tsp superfine sugar

2 tbsp red wine vinegar

12 oz/350 g ready-made puff pastry
    dough, thawed if frozen

salt and pepper

TOPPING

3½ oz/100 g canned anchovy fillets

12 pitted green olives

1 tsp dried marjoram

VARIATION

Cut the pissaladière into squares
or triangles for easy finger food
at a party or barbecue grill.

1 Lightly grease an edged cookie
sheet. Heat the olive oil in a
large pan. Cook the onions and garlic
over low heat for about 30 minutes,
stirring occasionally.

2 Add the sugar and red wine
vinegar to the pan and season
with plenty of salt and pepper.

3 Roll out the dough on a lightly
floured counter into a rectangle
measuring 13 x 9 inches/33 x 23 cm.
Carefully transfer the dough rectangle
to the prepared cookie sheet, pushing
the dough well into the corners.

4 Spread the onion mixture evenly
over the dough.

5 To make the decorative topping,
arrange the anchovy fillets in a
criss-cross pattern over the top of the
onion mixture, then dot with the green
olives, and sprinkle the dried marjoram
over the top.

6 Bake in a preheated oven, 425°F/
220°C, for 20–25 minutes, until
lightly golden. Serve the pissaladière
piping hot, straight from the oven.

tuna-stuffed tomatoes

serves four

4 plum tomatoes

2 tbsp sun-dried tomato paste

2 egg yolks

2 tsp lemon juice

finely grated rind of 1 lemon

4 tbsp olive oil

4 oz/115 g canned tuna, drained

2 tbsp capers, rinsed

salt and pepper

TO GARNISH

2 sun-dried tomatoes in oil, drained
    and cut into strips

fresh basil leaves

1 Halve the tomatoes and scoop out the seeds. Divide the sun-dried tomato paste among the tomato halves and spread around the inside of the skins.

2 Place on a cookie sheet and roast in a preheated oven, 400°F/200°C, for 12–15 minutes. Let cool slightly.

3 To make the mayonnaise, place the egg yolks and lemon juice in a food processor with the lemon rind and process until a smooth mixture forms. With the motor running, gradually add the olive oil. Stop the processor as soon as the mayonnaise has thickened. Alternatively, use a hand whisk to beat the mixture constantly until it thickens.

4 Add the tuna and capers to the mayonnaise, season, and stir.

5 Spoon the tuna mixture into the tomato shells and garnish with sun-dried tomato strips and basil. Return to the oven for a few minutes to warm through, or serve chilled.

baked tuna & ricotta rigatoni

serves four

1 tbsp butter, for greasing

1 lb/450 g dried rigatoni pasta

1 tbsp olive oil

7 oz/200 g canned flaked
tuna, drained

1 cup ricotta cheese

½ cup heavy cream

2 cups freshly grated
Parmesan cheese

4½ oz/125 g sun-dried tomatoes in
oil, drained and sliced

salt and pepper

VARIATION

For a vegetarian alternative to
this recipe, simply substitute a
mixture of pitted and chopped
black olives and chopped
walnuts for the tuna.

1 Lightly grease a large ovenproof
dish with the butter.

2 Bring a large pan of lightly
salted water to a boil. Add the
rigatoni and olive oil, bring back to a
boil, and cook for 8–10 minutes, until
just tender but still firm to the bite.
Drain the pasta and set aside until cool
enough to handle.

3 Meanwhile, combine the flaked
tuna and ricotta cheese in a bowl
until thoroughly blended into a soft
paste. Spoon the mixture into a pastry
bag and use it to fill the rigatoni.
Arrange the filled pasta tubes side by
side in a single layer in the prepared
ovenproof dish.

4 Combine the cream and Parmesan
cheese and season with salt and
pepper to taste.

5 Spoon the cream mixture over
the rigatoni and top with the
sun-dried tomatoes, arranged in a
criss-cross pattern. Bake in a preheated
oven, 400°F/200°C, for 20 minutes.
Serve hot straight from the dish.

roasted seafood & vegetables

serves four

1 lb 5 oz/600 g new potatoes

3 red onions, cut into wedges

2 zucchini, cut into chunks

8 garlic cloves

2 lemons, cut into wedges

4 fresh rosemary sprigs

4 tbsp olive oil

12 oz/350 g shell-on shrimp,
  preferably raw

2 small prepared squid, chopped
  into rings

4 tomatoes, quartered

VARIATION

Most vegetables are suitable for roasting in the oven. Try adding 1 lb/450 g pumpkin, squash, or eggplant, if you like.

1 Scrub the potatoes to remove any dirt. Cut any large potatoes in half. Place the potatoes in a large roasting pan, together with the onions, zucchini, garlic, lemon wedges, and rosemary sprigs.

2 Pour the oil into the roasting pan and toss well to coat the vegetables. Cook in a preheated oven, 400°F/200°C, for about 40 minutes, turning occasionally, until the potatoes are cooked and tender.

3 Once the potatoes are tender, add the shrimp, squid, and tomatoes, tossing to coat them in the oil, and roast for 10 minutes more. All of the vegetables should be cooked through and slightly charred for full flavor, and the shrimp should have turned pink.

4 Transfer the roasted seafood and vegetables to warmed serving plates using a slotted spoon, and serve immediately.

Savory Entrées

This chapter presents a mouthwatering array of savory dishes to tempt any palate, including pies, pastries, tarts, and flans, as well as a variety of delicious savory bakes. The choice is wide, including Baked Cheese Cream, Red Onion Tart Tatin, and Asparagus & Cheese Tart. Fish fans can choose from a wide menu, including Smoky Fish Pie, Fresh Baked Sardines, and Fillets of Red Snapper & Pasta. Meat and poultry dishes include Red Roast Pork in Soy Sauce, Fruity Lamb Casserole, and Italian Chicken Parcels.

vermicelli & vegetable tart

serves four

6 tbsp butter, plus extra for greasing

8 oz/225 g dried vermicelli
 or spaghetti

1 tbsp olive oil

1 onion, chopped

5 oz/140 g white mushrooms

1 green bell pepper, seeded, and
 sliced into thin rings

⅔ cup milk

3 eggs, beaten lightly

2 tbsp heavy cream

1 tsp dried oregano

freshly grated nutmeg

¼ cup freshly grated
 Parmesan cheese

salt and pepper

tomato and basil salad,
 to serve (optional)

1 Generously grease an 8-inch/20-cm loose-based tart pan with a little butter.

2 Bring a large pan of lightly salted water to a boil. Add the vermicelli or spaghetti and olive oil, bring back to a boil, and cook for 8–10 minutes, until tender but still firm to the bite. Drain, return to the pan, add 2 tablespoons of the butter, and shake the pan to coat the pasta.

3 Press the pasta onto the base and around the sides of the tart pan to make a tart shell, pressing the center down to make a hollow.

4 Melt the remaining butter in a large skillet over medium heat. Add the chopped onion and cook until it is translucent.

5 Add the mushrooms and bell pepper rings to the skillet. Cook, stirring constantly, for 2–3 minutes. Spoon the onion, mushroom, and bell pepper mixture into the pasta tart shell and press it evenly into the base.

6 Beat together the milk, eggs, and cream, stir in the oregano, and season to taste with nutmeg and pepper. Carefully pour the mixture over the vegetables, then sprinkle with the Parmesan cheese.

7 Bake in a preheated oven, 350°F/180°C, for 40–45 minutes, or until the filling has set.

8 Carefully slide the tart out of the pan onto a serving platter and serve warm with a tomato and basil salad, if you like.

asparagus & cheese tart

serves six

9 oz/250 g ready-made pie dough,
  thawed if frozen

9 oz/250 g asparagus

1 tbsp vegetable oil

1 red onion, chopped finely

2 tbsp chopped hazelnuts

7 oz/200 g goat cheese

2 eggs, beaten

4 tbsp light cream

salt and pepper

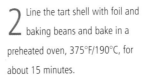

1 Roll out the pie dough on a lightly floured counter and use it to line a 9½-inch/24-cm loose-based tart pan. Prick the base of the tart shell with a fork and chill in the refrigerator for 30 minutes.

2 Line the tart shell with foil and baking beans and bake in a preheated oven, 375°F/190°C, for about 15 minutes.

3 Remove the foil and baking beans and bake for 15 minutes more.

4 Cook the asparagus in boiling water for 2–3 minutes, drain, and cut into bite-size pieces.

5 Heat the oil in a small skillet. Add the onion and cook over low heat, stirring occasionally, until soft and lightly golden. Spoon the asparagus, onion, and hazelnuts into the prepared tart shell.

6 Beat the cheese, eggs, and cream together in a bowl until smooth, or place in a food processor and process until smooth. Season well with salt and pepper, then pour over the mixture in the tart shell.

7 Bake in the preheated oven for 15–20 minutes, or until the filling is just set. Serve warm or cold.

VARIATION
Omit the hazelnuts and sprinkle Parmesan cheese over the top of the tart just before cooking, if you like.

baked cheese cream

serves four

1 tbsp butter, for greasing

2½ cups fresh white bread crumbs

1 cup grated Swiss cheese

⅔ cup lukewarm milk

½ cup butter, melted

2 eggs, separated

2 tbsp chopped fresh parsley

salt and pepper

salad greens, to serve

1 Grease a 4-cup/1-litre ovenproof dish with the butter.

2 Combine the bread crumbs and cheese in a bowl. Pour the milk over the cheese and bread crumb mixture and stir to blend. Add the melted butter, egg yolks, parsley, and salt and pepper to taste and mix.

3 In a separate bowl, whisk the egg whites until they form soft peaks. Gently fold the cheese mixture into the egg whites, using a figure-eight movement.

4 Transfer the mixture to the prepared ovenproof dish and smooth the surface with a spatula.

5 Bake in a preheated oven, 375°F/ 190°C, for 45 minutes, or until golden and slightly risen, and a fine metal skewer inserted into the middle of the dish comes out clean.

6 Serve the baked cheese cream piping hot, straight from the dish, with salad greens.

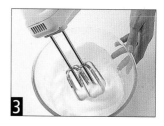

red onion tart tatin

serves four

4 tbsp butter

2 tbsp sugar

1 lb 2 oz/500 g red onions, cut
into fourths

3 tbsp red wine vinegar

2 tbsp fresh thyme leaves

9 oz/250 g ready-made puff pastry
dough, thawed if frozen

salt and pepper

VARIATION

Replace the red onions with
shallots, leaving them whole,
if you like.

COOK'S TIP

A heavy, cast iron skillet is best
for making this classic upside-
down tart, as it distributes the
heat evenly so that the onions
will not stick.

1 Place the butter and sugar in a
9-inch/23-cm ovenproof skillet and
cook over medium heat until the butter
has melted and the sugar has dissolved.

2 Add the red onion fourths and
sweat over low heat for about
10–15 minutes, stirring occasionally,
until golden and caramelized.

3 Add the red wine vinegar and
thyme leaves to the skillet.
Season to taste, then simmer over
medium heat until the liquid has
reduced and the red onion pieces
are coated in the buttery sauce.

4 Roll out the dough on a lightly
floured counter into a circle
slightly larger than the skillet.

5 Place the dough over the onion
mixture in the skillet and press
down, tucking in the edges to seal.

6 Bake in a preheated oven, 350°F/
180°C, for 20–25 minutes, until
the dough is firm and golden Remove
the skillet from the oven and let the
tart stand for 10 minutes.

7 To turn out, place a serving plate
over the skillet and, holding them
firmly together, carefully invert so that
the pastry becomes the base of the
tart. Serve the tart warm.

celery & onion pies

makes twelve

DOUGH

1 cup all-purpose flour, plus extra
   for dusting

½ tsp salt

2 tbsp butter, diced

¼ cup grated sharp cheese

3–4 tbsp water

FILLING

2 tbsp butter

1 cup finely chopped celery

2 garlic cloves, crushed

1 small onion, chopped finely

1 tbsp all-purpose flour

¼ cup milk

salt

pinch of cayenne pepper

1 To make the filling, melt the butter in a large skillet. Add the celery, garlic, and onion and cook over low heat, stirring occasionally, for about 5 minutes, or until softened.

2 Reduce the heat and stir in the flour, then the milk. Bring back to a simmer, then cook gently over low heat until the mixture is thick, stirring frequently. Season with salt and cayenne pepper to taste and let cool.

3 To make the dough, strain the flour and salt into a bowl and rub in the butter with your fingertips. Stir in the cheese and the cold water, and bring together to form a dough.

4 Roll out three-fourths of the dough on a lightly floured counter. Stamp out 12 circles using a 2½-inch/6-cm cookie cutter. Line a patty pan with the dough circles.

5 Divide the filling between the dough circles. Roll out the remaining dough and, using a 2-inch/5-cm cutter, stamp out 12 circles. Place the smaller circles on top of the pie filling and press to seal. Make a slit in each pie and chill in the refrigerator for 30 minutes.

6 Bake in a preheated oven, 425°F/220°C, for 15–20 minutes. Let cool in the pan for 10 minutes before turning out. Serve warm.

onion tart

serves four

9 oz/250 g ready-made pie dough,
    thawed if frozen

3 tbsp butter

generous ⅓ cup chopped bacon

1 lb 9 oz/700 g onions,
    thinly sliced

2 eggs, beaten

scant ⅔ cup freshly grated
    Parmesan cheese

1 tsp dried sage

salt and pepper

VARIATION

To make a vegetarian version
of this tart, replace the bacon
with the same amount of
chopped mushrooms.

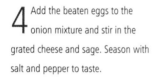

1 Roll out the pie dough on a lightly floured counter and use it to line a 9½-inch/24-cm loose-based tart pan.

2 Prick the base of the tart shell with a fork and chill in the refrigerator for 30 minutes.

3 Meanwhile, heat the butter in a pan, add the bacon and onions, and sweat over low heat for about 25 minutes, or until tender. If the onion slices start to brown, add 1 tablespoon of water to the pan.

4 Add the beaten eggs to the onion mixture and stir in the grated cheese and sage. Season with salt and pepper to taste.

5 Spoon the onion mixture into the prepared tart shell, spreading it out evenly over the base.

6 Bake in a preheated oven, 350°F/ 180°C, for 20–30 minutes, or until the filling has just set and the pastry is crisp and golden.

7 Let the tart cool slightly in the pan. Serve warm or cold.

gorgonzola & pumpkin pizza

serves four

PIZZA DOUGH

¼ oz/10 g active dry yeast

1 tsp sugar

1 cup lukewarm water

1¼ cups whole-wheat all-purpose
  flour, plus extra for dusting

1¼ cups white bread flour

1 tsp salt

1 tbsp olive oil, plus extra
  for brushing

1 fresh rosemary sprig, to garnish

TOPPING

14 oz/400 g pumpkin or squash,
  peeled and cubed

1 tbsp olive oil

1 pear, cored, peeled, and sliced

3½ oz/100 g Gorgonzola cheese

1 Place the yeast and sugar in a medium pitcher and mix with 4 tablespoons of the lukewarm water. Let the yeast mixture stand in a warm place for 15 minutes, or until frothy.

2 Combine both of the flours with the salt and make a well in the center. Add the oil, yeast mixture, and remaining water. Bring together using a wooden spoon to form a dough.

3 Turn the dough out onto a floured counter and knead for 4–5 minutes, or until smooth.

4 Return the dough to the bowl and cover with an oiled sheet of plastic wrap. Let rise for 30 minutes or until doubled in size.

5 Brush a cookie sheet with oil. Punch down the dough for 2 minutes. Roll out the dough into a long oval shape, then place it on the cookie sheet, and push out the edges until even. The dough should be no more than ¼ inch/5 mm thick because it will rise during cooking.

6 To make the topping, place the pumpkin in a shallow roasting pan. Drizzle with the olive oil and cook under a preheated medium broiler for 20 minutes, or until lightly golden.

7 Arrange the pear and pumpkin on top of the dough, brushing with the oil from the roasting pan. Crumble over the Gorgonzola. Bake in a preheated oven, 400°F/200°C, for 15 minutes, or until the base is golden. Garnish with a sprig of rosemary.

stuffed eggplant

serves four

8 oz/225 g dried penne pasta

4 tbsp olive oil, plus extra
for brushing

2 eggplant

1 large onion, chopped

2 garlic cloves, crushed

14 oz/400 g canned
chopped tomatoes

2 tsp dried oregano

2 oz/55 g mozzarella cheese,
sliced thinly

⅓ cup freshly grated
Parmesan cheese

2 tbsp dry white or whole-wheat
bread crumbs

salt and pepper

salad greens, to serve

1 Bring a pan of lightly salted
water to a boil. Add the pasta
and 1 tablespoon of the olive oil,
bring back to a boil, and cook for
8–10 minutes, or until tender but still
firm to the bite. Drain, return to the
pan, cover, and keep warm.

2 Cut the eggplant in half
lengthwise and score around
the inside with a sharp knife, being
careful not to pierce the shells. Scoop
out the pulp with a spoon. Brush the
insides of the shells with olive oil.
Chop the pulp and set aside.

3 Heat the remaining oil in a skillet.
Cook the onion until translucent.
Add the garlic and cook for 1 minute.
Add the chopped eggplant pulp and
cook, stirring frequently, for 5 minutes.
Add the tomatoes and oregano
and season to taste. Bring to a boil
and simmer for 10 minutes, or until
thickened. Remove the skillet from the
heat and stir in the pasta.

4 Brush a cookie sheet with oil and
arrange the eggplant shells on
the sheet in a single layer. Divide half
of the tomato and pasta mixture

among them. Sprinkle over the
mozzarella, then pile the remaining
tomato and pasta mixture on top. Mix
the Parmesan cheese and bread
crumbs in a small bowl and sprinkle
over the top, patting lightly into the
stuffing mixture.

5 Bake the stuffed eggplant in a
preheated oven, 400°F/200°C,
for 25 minutes, or until the topping
is golden brown. Serve hot with a
selection of salad greens.

smoky fish pie

serves four

2 lb/900 g smoked haddock or
cod fillets

2½ cups skim milk

2 bay leaves

4 oz/115 g white mushrooms, cut
into fourths

1 cup frozen peas

⅔ cup frozen corn kernels

4 cups diced potatoes

5 tbsp lowfat plain yogurt

4 tbsp chopped fresh parsley

2 oz/60 g smoked salmon, sliced
into thin strips

3 tbsp cornstarch

¼ cup grated smoked cheese

salt and pepper

1 Place the fish in a large pan and add the milk and bay leaves. Bring to a boil, cover, then reduce the heat, and simmer for 5 minutes. Add the mushrooms, peas, and corn, bring back to a simmer, cover, and cook for 5–7 minutes. Let cool.

2 Place the potatoes in a pan, cover with water, bring to a boil, and cook for 8 minutes. Drain well and mash with a fork or potato masher. Stir in the yogurt, parsley and seasoning and set aside.

3 Using a slotted spoon, remove the fish from the pan. Flake the cooked fish away from the skin and place in a gratin dish.

4 Drain the mushrooms, peas, and corn, reserving the cooking liquid. Gently stir into the fish with the salmon strips.

5 Blend a little cooking liquid into the cornstarch to make a paste. Transfer the rest of the cooking liquid to a pan and add the paste. Heat through, stirring, until thickened. Discard the bay leaves and season to taste with salt and pepper. Pour the sauce over the fish and vegetables and stir to mix. Spoon the mashed potato on top and spread to cover the fish, sprinkle with cheese, and bake in a preheated oven, 400°F/200°C, for 25–30 minutes.

pasta & shrimp parcels

serves four

1 lb/450 g dried fettuccine pasta

⅔ cup Pesto Sauce (see page 11)

4 tsp extra virgin olive oil

1 lb 10 oz/750 g jumbo shrimp,
   peeled and deveined

2 garlic cloves, crushed

½ cup dry white wine

salt and pepper

wedges of lemon, to garnish

COOK'S TIP

Traditionally, these parcels are
designed to look like money
bags. The resemblance is more
effective with waxed paper
rather than with foil.

---

1 Cut 4 squares, 12 inches/30 cm wide, out of waxed paper.

2 Bring a large pan of lightly salted water to a boil. Add the fettuccine and cook for 2–3 minutes, until just softened. Drain thoroughly.

3 Mix the fettuccine with half of the pesto sauce. Spread out the paper squares and place 1 teaspoon of olive oil in the center of each. Divide the fettuccine among the squares, then divide the shrimp, and place on top of the fettuccine.

4 Mix the remaining pesto sauce with the garlic in a small bowl and spoon it over the shrimp. Season each parcel with salt and pepper and sprinkle with the white wine.

5 Dampen the edges of the waxed paper and bring them together to wrap the parcels loosely, twisting the edges to seal.

6 Place the parcels on a cookie sheet and bake in a preheated oven, 400°F/200°C, for 10–15 minutes, until piping hot and the shrimp have changed color. Transfer the parcels to serving plates, garnish with lemon wedges, and serve.

baked macaroni & shrimp

serves four

12 oz/350 g short pasta, such as
    short-cut macaroni
1 tbsp olive oil, plus extra
    for brushing
6 tbsp butter, plus extra for greasing
2 small fennel bulbs, thinly sliced,
    leaves reserved
2½ cups thinly sliced mushrooms
6 oz/175 g shelled, cooked shrimp
2½ cups Béchamel Sauce
    (see page 210)
pinch of cayenne pepper
⅔ cup freshly grated
    Parmesan cheese
2 large tomatoes, sliced
1 tsp dried oregano
salt

1 Bring a large pan of lightly salted water to a boil. Add the pasta and olive oil, bring back to a boil, and cook for 8–10 minutes, or until tender but still firm to the bite. Drain the pasta, return to the pan, and dot with 2 tablespoons of the butter. Shake the pan well to coat the pasta, cover, and keep warm.

2 Melt the remaining butter in a large skillet over medium heat, add the fennel, and cook for about 3–4 minutes, until it begins to soften. Stir in the mushrooms and cook, stirring, for 2 minutes. Stir in the cooked shrimp, remove the pan from the heat, and set aside until required.

3 Season the hot béchamel sauce to taste with a pinch of cayenne. Stir the reserved fennel, mushroom, and shrimp mixture into the sauce, then stir in the pasta.

4 Grease a round, shallow ovenproof dish with a little butter. Pour in the pasta mixture and spread evenly over the base of the dish. Sprinkle with the Parmesan cheese and arrange the tomato slices in a ring around the edge of the dish. Brush the tomato with olive oil and sprinkle with the dried oregano.

5 Bake in a preheated oven, 350°F/ 180°C, for 25 minutes, or until golden. Serve hot.

seafood lasagna

serves four

1 lb/450 g smoked haddock fillets
  skin removed and flesh flaked

4 oz/115 g shrimp

4 oz/115 g sole fillet, skin removed
  and flesh sliced

juice of 1 lemon

4 tbsp butter

3 leeks, sliced very thinly

scant ½ cup all-purpose flour

2⅓ cups milk

2 tbsp honey

2 cups grated mozzarella cheese

1 lb/450 g pre-cooked lasagna

⅔ cup freshly grated
  Parmesan cheese

pepper

1 Put the haddock, shrimp, and sole into a large mixing bowl and season with pepper and lemon juice according to taste. Set aside while you make the sauce.

2 Melt the butter in a large pan over low heat. Add the leeks and cook, stirring occasionally, for about 8 minutes, until softened. Add the flour and cook, stirring constantly, for 1 minute. Gradually stir in enough milk to make a thick, creamy sauce.

3 Thoroughly blend in the honey and mozzarella cheese and cook the sauce for 3 minutes more, then remove the pan from the heat, and mix in the seasoned haddock, sole, and shrimp mixture.

4 Place a layer of fish sauce in an ovenproof dish, followed by a layer of lasagna, and continue with alternate layers, finishing with a layer of fish sauce on top. Generously sprinkle over the grated Parmesan cheese and bake the lasagna in a preheated oven, 350°F/180°C, for 30 minutes. Serve immediately.

VARIATION

For a hard cider sauce, substitute 1 finely chopped shallot for the leeks, 1½ cups of hard cider and 1½ cups of heavy cream for the milk, and 1 teaspoon of mustard for the honey. For a Tuscan sauce, substitute 1 chopped fennel bulb for the leeks and omit the honey.

smoked haddock casserole

serves four

2 tbsp butter, plus extra for greasing

1 lb/450 g smoked haddock fillets,
    cut into 4 portions

2½ cups milk

scant ¼ cup all-purpose flour

pinch of freshly grated nutmeg

3 tbsp heavy cream

1 tbsp chopped fresh parsley

2 eggs, hard-cooked and mashed
    to a pulp

1 lb/450 g dried fusilli pasta

1 tbsp lemon juice

salt and pepper

fresh flatleaf parsley, to garnish

TO SERVE

boiled new potatoes

beets

VARIATION

Try using penne, conchiglie, or
rigatoni for this casserole.

---

1 Generously grease a casserole with butter. Put the haddock in the casserole and pour over the milk. Bake in a preheated oven, 400°F/200°C, for about 15 minutes, until tender and the flesh flakes easily.

2 Carefully pour off the cooking liquid into a pitcher without breaking up the fish and reserve. The fish should remain in the casserole.

3 Melt the butter in a pan and stir in the flour. Gradually whisk in the cooking liquid. Season with salt, pepper, and nutmeg. Stir in the cream, chopped parsley, and mashed eggs and cook, stirring, for 2 minutes.

4 Meanwhile, bring a large pan of lightly salted water to a boil. Add the fusilli and lemon juice, bring back to a boil, and cook for 8–10 minutes, until tender but still firm to the bite.

5 Drain the pasta and spoon or tip it over the fish. Top with the egg sauce and return the casserole to the oven for 10 minutes.

6 Transfer the haddock casserole to serving plates, garnish with flatleaf parsley, and serve piping hot with boiled new potatoes and beets.

fresh baked sardines

serves four

2 tbsp olive oil

2 large onions, sliced into rings

3 garlic cloves, chopped

2 large zucchini, cut into sticks

3 tbsp fresh thyme leaves

8 sardine fillets or about

    2 lb 4 oz/1 kg sardines, filleted

1 cup freshly grated

    Parmesan cheese

4 eggs, beaten

1¼ cups milk

salt and pepper.

VARIATION

If you cannot find sardines that are large enough to fillet, use small mackerel instead.

1 Heat 1 tablespoon of the olive oil in a skillet. Add the onions and garlic and cook over low heat, stirring occasionally, for 2–3 minutes, until soft and translucent.

2 Add the zucchini to the skillet and cook, stirring occasionally, for about 5 minutes, or until turning golden. Stir 2 tablespoons of the thyme leaves into the mixture and remove from the heat.

3 Place half of the onion and zucchini mixture in the base of a large ovenproof dish. Top with the sardine fillets and half of the Parmesan cheese. Place the remaining onions and zucchini on top and sprinkle with the remaining thyme.

4 Combine the eggs and milk in a bowl and season to taste with salt and pepper. Pour the mixture into the dish and sprinkle the remaining Parmesan cheese over the top.

5 Bake in a preheated oven, 350°F/ 180°C, for about 20–25 minutes, or until golden and set. Serve the sardines hot.

trout with smoked bacon

serves four

1 tbsp butter, for greasing

4 whole trout, about 9½ oz/275 g
   each, gutted and cleaned

12 anchovies in oil, drained
   and chopped

2 apples, peeled, cored, and sliced

4 fresh mint sprigs

juice of 1 lemon

12 strips of smoked lean bacon

1 lb/450 g dried tagliatelle

1 tbsp olive oil

salt and pepper

TO GARNISH

2 apples, cored and sliced

4 fresh mint sprigs

1 Grease a deep cookie sheet with the butter.

2 Open up the cavities of each trout and rinse with warm salt water.

3 Season each cavity with salt and pepper. Divide the anchovies, sliced apples, and mint sprigs among the cavities. Sprinkle the lemon juice into each cavity.

4 Carefully wrap 3 strips of smoked bacon around the whole of each trout, except the head and tail, in a spiral. Tuck the loose ends of bacon underneath to secure them.

5 Arrange the trout on the prepared cookie sheet. Season with pepper. Bake in a preheated oven, 400°F/ 200°C, for 20 minutes, turning the trout over after 10 minutes.

6 Meanwhile, bring a large pan of lightly salted water to a boil. Add the tagliatelle and olive oil, bring back to a boil, and cook for about 12 minutes, until tender but still firm to the bite. Drain and transfer to a warmed serving dish.

7 Remove the trout from the oven and arrange on the tagliatelle. Garnish with sliced apples and fresh mint sprigs and serve immediately.

spaghetti alla bucaniera

serves four

¾ cup all-purpose flour

1 lb/450 g flounder or sole fillets, skinned and chopped

1 lb/450 g hake fillets, skinned and chopped

6 tbsp butter

4 shallots, chopped finely

2 garlic cloves, crushed

1 carrot, diced

1 leek, chopped finely

1¼ cups hard cider

1¼ cups medium sweet cider

2 tsp anchovy paste

1 tbsp tarragon vinegar

1 lb/450 g dried spaghetti

1 tbsp olive oil

salt and pepper

chopped fresh parsley, to garnish

crusty brown bread, to serve

1 Season the flour with salt and pepper. Sprinkle ¼ cup of the seasoned flour onto a shallow plate. Press the fish pieces into the seasoned flour to coat thoroughly all over. Alternatively, put the flour in a plastic bag, add the fish pieces, a few at a time, and shake gently.

2 Melt the butter in a flameproof casserole. Add the fish fillets, shallots, garlic, carrot, and leek and cook over low heat, stirring frequently, for about 10 minutes.

3 Sprinkle over the remaining seasoned flour and cook, stirring constantly, for 2 minutes. Gradually stir in the cider, anchovy paste, and tarragon vinegar and bring to a boil. Cover the casserole, transfer to a preheated oven, 350°F/180°C, and bake for 30 minutes.

4 About 15 minutes before the end of the cooking time, bring a large pan of lightly salted water to a boil. Add the spaghetti and olive oil, bring back to a boil, and cook for about 12 minutes, until tender but still firm to the bite. Drain the pasta and transfer to a large, warmed serving dish.

5 Arrange the baked fish mixture on top of the spaghetti in the serving dish and pour over any remaining sauce. Garnish with chopped parsley and serve immediately with warm, crusty brown bread.

cannelloni filetti di sogliola

serves six

12 small fillets of sole, about
    4 oz/115 g each

⅔ cup red wine

6 tbsp butter

1⅓ cups sliced white mushrooms

4 shallots, chopped finely

4 oz/115 g tomatoes, chopped

2 tbsp tomato paste

scant ½ cup all-purpose
    flour, strained

⅔ cup warm milk

2 tbsp heavy cream

6 dried cannelloni tubes

6 oz/175 g cooked, peeled
    freshwater shrimp

salt and pepper

1 fresh fennel frond, to garnish

1 Brush the sole fillets with a little wine, season with salt and pepper, and roll up, skin side inward. Secure with a toothpick or skewer.

2 Arrange the fish rolls in a single layer in a large skillet, add the remaining red wine, and poach for 4 minutes. Remove the fish from the pan and reserve the liquid.

3 Melt the butter in a separate pan, add the mushrooms and shallots, and cook for 2 minutes, then add the tomatoes and tomato paste. Season the flour and stir it into the pan. Stir in the reserved cooking liquid and half of the milk. Cook over low heat, stirring, for 4 minutes. Remove from the heat and stir in the cream.

4 Bring a large pan of lightly salted water to a boil. Add the cannelloni, bring back to a boil, and cook for 8 minutes, until tender but still firm to the bite. Drain and let cool.

5 Remove the toothpicks or skewers from the fish rolls. Put 2 fish rolls into each cannelloni tube with 2 or 3 shrimp and a little red wine sauce. Arrange the cannelloni in a single layer in an ovenproof dish, pour over the red wine sauce, and bake in a preheated oven, 400°F/200°C, for 20 minutes, until cooked through and piping hot.

6 Serve the cannelloni with the red wine sauce, garnished with the remaining shrimp and a fennel frond.

orange mackerel

serves four

2 tbsp vegetable oil

4 scallions, chopped

2 oranges

scant ½ cup ground almonds

1 tbsp oats

½ cup mixed pitted green and black
   olives, chopped

8 mackerel fillets

salt and pepper

salad greens, to serve

1 Heat the oil in a skillet. Add the scallions and cook over low heat for 2 minutes, stirring frequently, then set aside.

2 Finely grate the rind of the oranges, then, using a sharp knife, cut away the remaining skin and the white pith.

3 Using a sharp knife, segment the oranges by cutting down either side of the membranes to loosen each segment. Do this over a plate so that you can catch and reserve any juices. Cut each orange segment in half.

4 Lightly toast the almonds under a preheated medium broiler for 2–3 minutes, or until golden; watch them carefully as they brown quickly.

5 Combine the scallions, orange rind and segments, ground almonds, oats, and olives in a bowl and season with salt and pepper.

6 Lay the mackerel fillets in an ovenproof dish. Spoon the orange mixture along the center of each, then roll up and secure with toothpicks.

7 Bake in a preheated oven, 375°F/190°C for 25 minutes, until the fish is tender and cooked through.

8 Transfer the mackerel to warmed serving plates and remove and discard the toothpicks. Serve warm with salad greens.

italian cod

serves four

2 tbsp butter

1 cup fresh whole-wheat
    bread crumbs

2 tbsp chopped walnuts

grated rind and juice of 2 lemons

2 fresh rosemary sprigs,
    stems removed

2 tbsp chopped fresh parsley

4 cod fillets, about 5½ oz/150 g each

1 garlic clove, crushed

1 small fresh red chile, seeded
    and diced

3 tbsp walnut oil

salad greens, to serve

VARIATION

If you like, the walnuts may
be omitted from the crust. In
addition, extra virgin olive oil
can be used instead of walnut
oil, if you like.

---

1 Melt the butter in a large pan over low heat.

2 Remove the pan from the heat and stir in the bread crumbs and walnuts, the rind and juice of 1 lemon, half of the fresh rosemary, and half of the fresh parsley.

3 Line a roasting pan with foil and place the cod fillets in the pan in a single layer. Gently press the bread crumb mixture over the top of the cod fillets with your fingers.

4 Bake in a preheated oven, 400°F/200°C, for 25–30 minutes.

5 Place the garlic, the remaining lemon rind and juice, rosemary and parsley in a bowl with the chile and mix. Beat in the walnut oil. Drizzle the dressing over the cod steaks as soon as they are cooked.

6 Transfer the fish to warmed serving plates and serve hot with salad greens.

seafood pizza

serves four

5 oz/140 g standard pizza dough mix

4 tbsp chopped fresh dill, plus extra
   to garnish

SAUCE

1 large red bell pepper

14 oz/400 g canned chopped
   tomatoes with onion and herbs

3 tbsp tomato paste

salt and pepper

TOPPING

12 oz/350 g assorted cooked
   seafood, thawed if frozen

1 tbsp capers in brine, drained

1 oz/25 g pitted black olives in
   brine, drained

¼ cup grated lowfat
   mozzarella cheese

¼ cup freshly grated
   Parmesan cheese

1 Place the pizza dough mix in a
   bowl and stir in the dill. Make the
dough according to the instructions
on the package.

2 Line a cookie sheet with baking
   parchment. Press the herbed
pizza dough into a circle about
10 inches/25 cm wide on the prepared
cookie sheet, then leave in a warm
place to rise.

3 To make the sauce, halve and
   seed the bell pepper and arrange
on a broiler rack. Cook under a
preheated broiler for 8–10 minutes,
until softened and charred. Let cool
slightly, then peel off the skin, and
chop the flesh.

4 Place the bell pepper flesh in a
   pan with the canned tomatoes.
Bring to a boil, then reduce the heat,
and simmer for 10 minutes. Stir in the
tomato paste and season to taste with
salt and pepper.

5 Spread the sauce evenly over the
   pizza base and top with the
seafood. Sprinkle over the capers and
olives, top with the grated cheeses,
and bake in a preheated oven, 400°F/
200°C, for 25–30 minutes. Garnish
with sprigs of fresh dill and serve hot.

COOK'S TIP
Look for packets of prepared
mixed seafood in the chiller
cabinets of large supermarkets.
These have more flavor and a
better texture than frozen.

smoked cod cornmeal

serves four

6½ cups water

generous 2⅓ cups instant cornmeal

7 oz/200 g frozen chopped spinach,
    thawed and drained

3 tbsp butter

½ cup grated romano cheese

generous ¾ cup milk

1 lb/450 g smoked cod
    fillet, skinned

4 eggs, beaten

salt and pepper

1 Bring the water to a boil in a large pan. Add the cornmeal and cook, stirring constantly, for 20–25 minutes.

2 Stir the spinach, butter, and half of the romano cheese into the cornmeal, then season to taste with salt and pepper.

3 Divide the cornmeal mixture among 4 individual ovenproof dishes, spreading it evenly across the bases and up the sides of the dishes.

4 Bring the milk to a boil in a skillet. Add the fish and simmer gently, turning once, for 8–10 minutes, until tender. Remove the fish with a slotted spoon.

5 Remove the pan from the heat. Pour the eggs into the milk in the pan and mix well together.

VARIATION

Try using 12 oz/350 g of
cooked chicken breast with
2 tablespoons chopped
tarragon instead of the
smoked cod, if you like.

6 Using a fork, flake the fish into smaller pieces and place it in the center of the ovenproof dishes.

7 Pour the milk and egg mixture over the fish.

8 Sprinkle the remaining cheese over the top and bake in a preheated oven , 375°F/ 190°C, for 25–30 minutes, or until set and golden. Serve hot.

fillets of red snapper & pasta

serves four

2 lb 4 oz/1 kg red snapper fillets

1¼ cups dry white wine

4 shallots, chopped finely

1 garlic clove, crushed

3 tbsp finely chopped mixed
    fresh herbs

finely grated rind and juice
    of 1 lemon

pinch of freshly grated nutmeg

3 anchovy fillets, chopped coarsely

2 tbsp heavy cream

1 tsp cornstarch

1 lb/450 g dried vermicelli

1 tbsp olive oil

salt and pepper

TO GARNISH

1 fresh mint sprig

lemon slices

strips of lemon rind

1 Place the red snapper fillets in a large casserole. Pour over the wine and add the shallots, garlic, herbs, lemon rind and juice, nutmeg, and anchovies. Season to taste with salt and pepper. Cover and bake in a preheated oven, 350°F/180°C, for 35 minutes.

2 Lift the snapper out of the casserole with a slotted spoon and transfer to a warmed dish, reserving the cooking liquid. Set the fish aside and keep warm.

3 Pour the cooking liquid into a pan and bring to a boil. Simmer for 25 minutes, until reduced by half. Mix the cream and cornstarch to a paste and stir into the sauce to thicken.

4 Meanwhile, bring a pan of lightly salted water to a boil. Add the vermicelli and oil, bring back to a boil, and cook for 8–10 minutes, until tender but still firm to the bite. Drain and transfer to a warmed serving dish.

5 Arrange the red snapper fillets on top of the vermicelli and pour over the sauce. Garnish with a sprig of fresh mint, slices of lemon, and strips of lemon rind, and serve immediately.

italian chicken parcels

serves six

1 tbsp olive oil, for brushing

6 skinless, boneless chicken
   breast portions

9 oz/250 g mozzarella cheese

3½ cups sliced zucchini

6 large tomatoes, sliced

1 small bunch of fresh basil
   or oregano

pepper

rice or pasta, to serve

COOK'S TIP

To aid cooking, place the
vegetables and chicken on the
shiny side of the foil so that
when the parcel is wrapped up,
the dull surface of the foil faces
outward. The heat will be
absorbed into the parcel, and not
reflected away.

VARIATION

This recipe also works well with
monkfish fillet. Use 6 x 5–6 oz/
140–175 g fillets. Remove all the
gray membrane first.

1 Cut out 6 squares of foil, about 10-inches/25-cm wide. Brush the squares lightly with oil and set aside.

2 Slash each chicken breast portion 3–4 times. Slice the mozzarella cheese and tuck the slices between the slashes.

3 Divide the zucchini and tomatoes among the foil squares and season with pepper. Tear or coarsely chop the herbs and sprinkle them over the vegetables in each parcel.

4 Place the chicken on top of each pile of vegetables, then wrap the foil to enclose the chicken and vegetables, sealing at the edges.

5 Place on a cookie sheet and bake in a preheated oven, 400°F/200°C, for about 30 minutes.

6 Unwrap each foil parcel and serve with rice or pasta.

crispy stuffed chicken

serves four

4 skinless, boneless chicken breast
portions, 5½ oz/150 g each

4 fresh tarragon sprigs

½ small orange bell pepper, seeded
and sliced

½ small green bell pepper, seeded
and sliced

¼ cup fresh whole-wheat
bread crumbs

1 tbsp sesame seeds

4 tbsp lemon juice

salt and pepper

fresh tarragon, to garnish

BELL PEPPER SAUCE

small red bell pepper, halved
and seeded

7 oz/200 g canned
chopped tomatoes

1 small fresh red chile, seeded
and chopped

¼ tsp celery salt

salt and pepper

1 Slit the chicken portion with a small, sharp knife to create a pocket in each. Season inside each pocket with salt and pepper to taste.

2 Place a sprig of tarragon and a few slices of orange and green bell pepper in each pocket. Place the chicken portions in a single layer on a nonstick cookie sheet and sprinkle the bread crumbs and sesame seeds over them.

3 Spoon 1 tablespoon of lemon juice over each chicken portion and bake in a preheated oven, 400°F/200°C, for 35–40 minutes, until the chicken is tender and cooked through.

4 Meanwhile, arrange the red bell pepper halves, skin side up, on a broiler rack, and cook under a preheated hot broiler for 5–6 minutes, until the skin starts to char and blister. Let the broiled pepper cool for 10 minutes, then peel off the skin.

5 Place the red bell pepper in a food processor, add the tomatoes, chile, and celery salt and process for a few seconds. Season to taste. Alternatively, finely chop the red bell pepper and press through a strainer with the tomatoes and chile.

6 When the chicken is cooked, heat the sauce, spoon a little onto each of 4 warmed plates, and arrange a chicken portion in the center of each. Garnish with tarragon and serve.

chicken & spinach lasagna

serves four

12 oz/350 g frozen chopped
  spinach, thawed and drained
½ tsp ground nutmeg
1 lb/450 g lean, cooked chicken
  meat, skinned and diced
4 sheets pre-cooked lasagna verde
1½ tbsp cornstarch
1¾ cups skim milk
scant ¾ cup freshly grated
  Parmesan cheese
salt and pepper
TOMATO SAUCE
14 oz/400 g canned
  chopped tomatoes
1 onion, chopped finely
1 garlic clove, crushed
⅔ cup white wine
3 tbsp tomato paste
1 tsp dried oregano
salt and pepper

1 To make the tomato sauce, place the tomatoes in a pan and stir in the onion, garlic, wine, tomato paste, and oregano. Bring to a boil and simmer gently for 20 minutes, stirring occasionally, until thick. Season well with salt and pepper.

2 Drain the spinach again and spread it out on paper towels to make sure that as much water as possible is removed. Layer the spinach in the base of an ovenproof dish. Sprinkle with nutmeg and season.

3 Arrange the diced chicken over the spinach and spoon over the tomato sauce. Arrange the sheets of lasagna over the tomato sauce.

4 Blend the cornstarch with a little of the milk to make a smooth paste. Pour the remaining milk into a pan and stir in the cornstarch paste. Heat gently for 2–3 minutes, stirring constantly, until the sauce thickens. Season to taste with salt and pepper.

5 Pour the sauce over the lasagna and transfer the dish to a cookie sheet. Sprinkle the Parmesan cheese over the sauce and bake in a preheated oven, 400°F/200°C, for 25 minutes, until golden brown. Serve hot.

baked chicken pasta

serves four

2 fennel bulbs

2 red onions, sliced very thinly

1 tbsp lemon juice

4½ oz/125 g white mushrooms

1 tbsp olive oil

8 oz/225 g dried penne pasta

⅓ cup raisins

8 oz/225 g lean, boneless cooked
    chicken, skinned and shredded

13 oz/375 g lowfat soft cheese with
    garlic and herbs

4½ oz/125 g lowfat mozzarella
    cheese, sliced thinly

scant ½ cup freshly grated
    Parmesan cheese

salt and pepper

1 Trim the fennel bulbs, reserving
the green fronds for the garnish,
and slice the bulbs thinly.

2 Generously coat the onions in the
lemon juice. Cut the mushrooms
into fourths.

3 Heat the oil in a large skillet and
cook the fennel, onion, and
mushrooms for 4–5 minutes, stirring,
until just softened. Season well,
transfer the mixture to a large bowl,
and set aside.

4 Bring a pan of lightly salted
water to a boil. Add the pasta,
bring back to a boil, and cook for
8–10 minutes, until tender, but still
firm to the bite. Drain and mix with
the vegetables.

5 Stir the raisins and cooked
chicken into the pasta mixture.
Beat the soft cheese to soften it
further, then mix it into the pasta and
chicken—the heat from the pasta
should make the cheese melt slightly.

6 Transfer the mixture to an
ovenproof dish and place on
a cookie sheet. Arrange slices of
mozzarella cheese over the top and
sprinkle with the Parmesan cheese.

7 Bake in a preheated oven,
400°F/200°C, for 20–25 minutes,
until golden brown.

8 Garnish with chopped fennel
fronds and serve hot.

chicken & ham lasagna

serves four

1 tbsp butter, for greasing

14 sheets pre-cooked lasagna

3½ cups Béchamel Sauce
   (see page 210)

¾ cup freshly grated
   Parmesan cheese

CHICKEN AND MUSHROOM SAUCE

2 tbsp olive oil

2 garlic cloves, crushed

1 large onion, chopped finely

8 oz/225 g exotic
   mushrooms, sliced

2½ cups ground chicken

3 oz/85 g chicken livers,
   chopped finely

¾ cup diced prosciutto

⅔ cup Marsala wine

10 oz/280 g canned
   chopped tomatoes

1 tbsp chopped fresh basil leaves

2 tbsp tomato paste

salt and pepper

1 To make the chicken and mushroom sauce, heat the olive oil in a large pan. Add the garlic, onion, and mushrooms, and cook, stirring frequently, for 6 minutes.

2 Add the ground chicken, chicken livers, and prosciutto, and cook over low heat, stirring frequently, for about 12 minutes, or until the meat has browned.

3 Stir the Marsala, tomatoes, basil, and tomato paste into the mixture and cook for 4 minutes. Season with salt and pepper, cover, and simmer for 30 minutes, stirring occasionally. Uncover the pan, stir, and simmer for 15 minutes more, uncovered.

4 Lightly grease an ovenproof dish with the butter. Arrange sheets of lasagna over the base of the dish, spoon over a layer of chicken and mushroom sauce, then spoon over a layer of béchamel sauce. Place another layer of lasagna on top and repeat the process twice, finishing with a layer of béchamel sauce. Sprinkle the grated Parmesan cheese over the top, then bake in a preheated oven, 375°F/190°C, for 35 minutes, until golden brown and bubbling. Serve immediately.

chicken lasagna

serves four

9 sheets fresh or dried lasagna

1 tbsp butter, for greasing

1 tbsp olive oil

1 red onion, chopped finely

1 garlic clove, crushed

1⅓ cups sliced mushrooms

12 oz/350 g skinless, boneless
    chicken breast portions, diced

⅔ cup red wine, diluted with a
    generous ⅓ cup water

generous 1 cup bottled
    strained tomatoes

1 tsp sugar

¾ cup freshly grated
    Parmesan cheese

salt

BÉCHAMEL SAUCE

5 tbsp butter

generous ⅓ cup all-purpose flour

2½ cups milk

1 egg, beaten

salt and pepper

1 Bring a large pan of lightly salted water to a boil. Add the lasagna and cook according to the instructions on the package. Lightly grease a deep ovenproof dish.

2 Place the oil in a pan over low heat. Add the onion and garlic and cook for 3–4 minutes. Add the mushrooms and chicken and cook for 4 minutes, or until the meat browns.

3 Add the diluted wine, bring the mixture to a boil, then reduce the heat, and simmer for 5 minutes. Stir in the tomatoes and sugar and cook for 3–5 minutes, until the meat is tender and cooked through. The sauce should have thickened, but still be quite runny.

4 To make the Béchamel Sauce, melt the butter in a pan, stir in the flour, and cook for 2 minutes, stirring constantly. Remove the pan from the heat and gradually add the milk, mixing to form a smooth sauce. Return the pan to the heat and bring to a boil, stirring until thickened. Let cool slightly, then beat in the egg and season to taste with salt and pepper. Stir half the Parmesan cheese into the béchamel sauce.

5 Place 3 sheets of lasagna in the base of the prepared dish and spread with half of the chicken mixture. Repeat the layers. Top with the last 3 sheets of lasagna, pour over the béchamel sauce, and sprinkle with the remaining Parmesan cheese. Bake in a preheated oven, 375°F/190°C, for 30 minutes, until golden and the pasta is cooked. Serve immediately.

mustard-baked chicken

serves four

4 large or 8 small chicken pieces

4 tbsp butter, melted

4 tbsp mild mustard (see Cook's Tip)

2 tbsp lemon juice

1 tbsp brown sugar

1 tsp paprika

3 tbsp poppy seeds

14 oz/400 g dried pasta shells

1 tbsp olive oil

salt and pepper

COOK'S TIP

Dijon is the type of mustard most often used in cooking, as it has a clean and mildly spicy flavor, compared to American mustard, which is mild and sweet. German mustard has a sweet-sour taste, although Bavarian mustard is slightly sweeter.

VARIATION

This recipe would also work well with a variety of feathered game, such as guinea fowl and young pheasant.

1 Arrange the chicken pieces in a single layer in the base of a large ovenproof dish.

2 Combine the butter, mustard, lemon juice, sugar, and paprika in a bowl and season with salt and pepper to taste. Brush the mixture over the upper surfaces of the chicken pieces and bake in a preheated oven, 400°F/200°C, for 15 minutes.

3 Remove the dish from the oven and carefully turn over the chicken. Coat the upper surfaces of the chicken pieces with the remaining mustard mixture, sprinkle over the poppy seeds, and return to the oven for 15 minutes more.

4 Meanwhile, bring a large pan of lightly salted water to a boil. Add the pasta shells and olive oil, bring back to a boil, and cook for about 8–10 minutes, or until tender but still firm to the bite.

5 Drain the pasta thoroughly and arrange on 4 warmed serving plates. Top the pasta with the chicken pieces, pour over the mustard sauce, and serve immediately.

roast duckling with apple

serves four

4 duckling pieces, about
    12 oz/350 g each

4 tbsp dark soy sauce

2 tbsp light brown sugar

2 red-skinned apples

2 green-skinned apples

juice of 1 lemon

2 tbsp honey

a few bay leaves

salt and pepper

a selection of fresh vegetables,
    to serve

APRICOT SAUCE

14 oz/400 g canned apricots,
    in natural juice

4 tbsp sweet sherry

1 Wash the duckling and trim off any excess fat. Place on a wire rack over a roasting pan and prick all over with a fork.

2 Brush the duck with the soy sauce. Sprinkle over the brown sugar and season with pepper. Cook in a preheated oven, 375°F/190°C, basting occasionally, for about 50–60 minutes, until the meat is cooked through—the juices should run clear when a skewer is inserted into the thickest part of the meat.

3 Meanwhile, core the apples and cut each of them into 6 wedges. Mix with the lemon juice and honey in a bowl. Place the fruit and liquid in a small roasting pan. Add a few bay leaves and season. Cook alongside the duckling, basting occasionally, for 20–25 minutes, until tender. Discard the bay leaves.

4 To make the sauce, place the apricots and their juices in a blender or food processor with the sherry, then process into a paste. Alternatively, mash the apricots with a fork, then mix in the juice and sherry.

5 Just before serving, heat the apricot sauce in a small pan. Remove the skin from the duckling and pat the flesh with paper towels to absorb any fat. Serve the duckling with the apple wedges, apricot sauce, and fresh vegetables.

pesto-baked partridge

serves four

8 partridge pieces, 115 g/4 oz each

4 tbsp butter, melted

4 tbsp Dijon mustard

2 tbsp lime juice

1 tbsp brown sugar

6 tbsp Pesto Sauce (see page 11)

1 lb/450 g dried rigatoni pasta

1 tbsp olive oil

1 cup freshly grated
    Parmesan cheese

salt and pepper

VARIATION

You could also prepare young
pheasant in the same way.

---

1 Arrange the partridge pieces,
smooth side down, in a single
layer in a large, ovenproof dish.

2 Combine the butter, Dijon
mustard, lime juice, and brown
sugar in a bowl. Season to taste with
salt and pepper. Brush the mixture
over the partridge pieces, reserving
the remaining mixture, and bake in a
preheated oven, 400°F/200°C, for
15 minutes.

3 Remove the dish from the oven
and coat the partridge pieces
with 3 tablespoons of the pesto sauce.
Return the dish to the oven and bake
for 12 minutes more.

4 Remove the dish from the oven
and carefully turn over the
partridge pieces. Coat the top of the
partridge with the remaining mustard
mixture and return to the oven for
another 10 minutes.

5 Meanwhile, bring a large pan of
lightly salted water to a boil. Add
the rigatoni and olive oil, bring back to
a boil, and cook for 8–10 minutes,
until tender but still firm to the bite.
Drain and transfer to a serving dish.

6 Add the remaining pesto sauce
and the Parmesan cheese to the
pasta and toss thoroughly to blend.
Transfer the partridge to serving plates
and serve with the pasta, pouring over
the cooking juices.

honey-glazed duck

serves four

2 large, boneless duck breasts,
about 8 oz/225 g each
MARINADE
1 tsp dark soy sauce
2 tbsp honey
1 tsp garlic vinegar
2 garlic cloves, crushed
1 tsp ground star anise
2 tsp cornstarch
2 tsp water
TO GARNISH
celery leaves
cucumber wedges
fresh chives

COOK'S TIP

If the duck begins to burn
slightly while it is cooking, cover
with foil. Check that the duck
breasts are cooked through by
inserting the point of a sharp
knife into the thickest part of the
meat—the juices should run
clear when the duck is cooked.

1 To make the marinade, combine
the soy sauce, honey, garlic
vinegar, garlic, and star anise in a
bowl. Blend the cornstarch with the
water to form a smooth paste and stir
it into the mixture.

2 Place the duck in a shallow dish.
Brush the marinade over the
duck, turning the meat to coat. Cover
and marinate in the refrigerator for at
least 2 hours, or overnight.

3 Drain the duck, reserving the
marinade. Place in a shallow
ovenproof dish and bake in a
preheated oven, 425°F/220°C, for
20–25 minutes, basting frequently
with the marinade.

4 Remove the duck from the oven
and transfer to a preheated
medium broiler. Broil for 3–4 minutes
to caramelize the top.

5 Remove the duck from the broiler
rack and cut into fairly thin slices.
Arrange the slices on a warmed
serving dish, garnish with celery
leaves, cucumber wedges, and fresh
chives, and serve immediately.

red roast pork in soy sauce

serves four

1 lb/450 g lean pork tenderloin

MARINADE

6 tbsp dark soy sauce

2 tbsp dry sherry

1 tsp Chinese five-spice powder

2 garlic cloves, crushed

2 tsp finely chopped fresh gingerroot

1 large red bell pepper

1 large yellow bell pepper

1 large orange bell pepper

4 tbsp superfine sugar

2 tbsp red wine vinegar

TO GARNISH

shredded scallions

snipped fresh chives

1 Trim away any excess fat and the silver skin from the pork and place in a shallow dish.

2 To make the marinade, mix the soy sauce, sherry, five-spice powder, garlic, and ginger together in a bowl. Spoon over the pork, turning it to coat, cover, and marinate in the refrigerator for at least 1 hour, or until required.

3 Drain the pork, reserving the marinade. Place the pork on a roasting rack over a roasting pan. Cook in a preheated oven, 375°F/190°C, basting occasionally with the marinade, for 1 hour, or until cooked through.

4 Meanwhile, halve and seed the bell peppers. Cut each bell pepper half into 3 equal portions. Arrange them on a cookie sheet and bake alongside the pork for the last 30 minutes of cooking time.

5 Place the sugar and vinegar in a pan and heat gently until the sugar dissolves. Bring to a boil and simmer for 3–4 minutes, until syrupy.

6 When the pork is cooked, remove it from the oven and brush with the sugar syrup. Let stand for about 5 minutes, then slice, and arrange on a warmed serving plate. Garnish with scallions and freshly snipped chives and serve.

braised fennel & linguine

serves four

6 fennel bulbs

⅔ cup Vegetable Bouillon
(see page 11)

2 tbsp butter

6 strips lean smoked
bacon, diced

6 shallots, cut into fourths

¼ cup all-purpose flour

scant ½ cup heavy cream

1 tbsp Madeira

1 lb/450 g dried linguine pasta

1 tbsp olive oil

salt and pepper

1 Trim the fennel bulbs, then peel off and reserve the outer layer of each. Cut the bulbs into quarters and put them in a large pan with the bouillon and the reserved outer layers.

2 Bring to a boil, lower the heat, and simmer for 5 minutes.

3 Using a slotted spoon, transfer the fennel to a large dish, discarding the outer layers of the bulbs. Bring the bouillon to a boil and reduce by half. Set aside.

4 Melt the butter in a skillet over low heat. Add the bacon and shallots and cook, stirring occasionally, for 4 minutes. Add the flour, reduced bouillon, cream, and Madeira and cook, stirring constantly, for 3 minutes, or until the sauce is smooth. Season to taste with salt and pepper and pour over the fennel.

5 Bring a pan of lightly salted water to a boil. Add the pasta and oil, bring back to a boil, and cook for 8–10 minutes, or until tender but still firm to the bite. Drain, and transfer to an ovenproof dish.

6 Add the fennel and the sauce and braise in a preheated oven, 350°F/180°C, for 20 minutes, until the fennel is tender. Serve immediately.

stuffed cannelloni

serves four

8 dried cannelloni tubes

1 tbsp olive oil

⅓ cup freshly grated
   Parmesan cheese

fresh flatleaf parsley sprigs,
   to garnish

FILLING

2 tbsp butter

10½ oz/300 g frozen chopped
   spinach, thawed and drained

½ cup ricotta cheese

⅓ cup freshly grated
   Parmesan cheese

¼ cup chopped ham

pinch of freshly grated nutmeg

2 tbsp heavy cream

2 eggs, lightly beaten

salt and pepper

SAUCE

2 tbsp butter

scant ¼ cup all-purpose flour

1¼ cups milk

2 bay leaves

pinch of freshly grated nutmeg

salt and pepper

1 To make the filling, melt the butter in a pan, add the spinach, and cook for 2–3 minutes. Remove from the heat, transfer to an ovenproof bowl, and stir in the ricotta, Parmesan cheese, and ham. Season to taste with nutmeg, salt, and pepper. Beat in the cream and eggs to make a thick paste.

2 Bring a pan of lightly salted water to a boil. Add the cannelloni and the oil, return to a boil, and cook for 10–12 minutes, or until tender but still firm to the bite. Drain and let cool.

3 To make the sauce, melt the butter in a pan. Stir in the flour and cook, stirring, for 1 minute. Gradually stir in the milk. Add the bay leaves and simmer, stirring, for 5 minutes. Add the nutmeg and salt and pepper to taste. Remove from the heat and discard the bay leaves.

4 Spoon the filling into a pastry bag and fill the cooked cannelloni.

5 Spoon a little sauce into the base of an ovenproof dish. Arrange the cannelloni in the dish in a single layer and pour over the remaining sauce. Sprinkle over the Parmesan cheese and bake in a preheated oven, 375°F/ 190°C, for 40–45 minutes. Garnish with sprigs of fresh flatleaf parsley and serve immediately.

italian calzone

serves four

1 quantity Basic Pizza Dough
(see page 10)

1 egg, beaten

FILLING

1 tbsp tomato paste

1 oz/25 g Italian salami, chopped

1 oz/25 g mortadella, chopped

1 tomato, peeled and chopped

2 tbsp ricotta cheese

2 scallions, trimmed and chopped

¼ tsp dried oregano

salt and pepper

fresh flatleaf parsley, to garnish

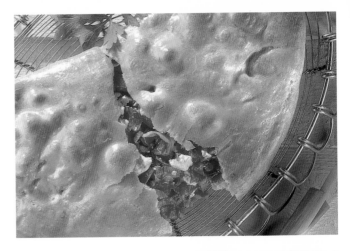

1 Knead the Basic Pizza Dough and roll out on a lightly floured counter into a 9-inch/23-cm circle.

2 Brush the edge of the dough with a little beaten egg. Reserve the remaining egg.

3 Spread the tomato paste over the half of the circle nearest to you.

4 Sprinkle the salami, mortadella, and chopped tomato on top.

5 Dot with the ricotta cheese and then evenly sprinkle over the scallions and oregano. Season to taste.

6 Fold over the other half of the dough to form a semicircle shape. Press the edges together well to prevent the filling from leaking out.

7 Place the calzone on a cookie sheet and brush with beaten egg to glaze. Make a small hole in the top with a knife to allow steam to escape during cooking.

8 Bake in a preheated oven, 400°F/ 200°C, for 20 minutes, or until golden. Transfer to a warmed serving plate, garnish with flatleaf parsley, and serve immediately.

eggplant pasta cake

serves four

1 tbsp butter, for greasing

1 eggplant

10½ oz/300 g dried tricolor
    pasta shapes

½ cup lowfat soft cheese with garlic
    and herbs

1½ cups bottled strained tomatoes

scant ¾ cup freshly grated
    Parmesan cheese

1½ tsp dried oregano

2 tbsp dry white bread crumbs

salt and pepper

fresh oregano sprigs, to garnish

1 Grease an 8-inch/20-cm round springform cake pan and line it with baking parchment.

2 Trim the eggplant. Cut lengthwise into slices about ¼ inch/5 mm thick. Place in a bowl and sprinkle with salt, then let stand for 30 minutes, to remove any bitter juices. Rinse well under cold running water and drain.

3 Bring a pan of water to a boil and blanch the eggplant slices for 1 minute. Drain and pat dry with paper towels. Set aside.

4 Bring a separate large pan of lightly salted water to a boil. Add the pasta shapes, bring back to a boil, and cook for 8–10 minutes, until tender but still firm to the bite. Drain well and return to the pan. Add the lowfat soft cheese and let it melt over the pasta.

5 Stir in the tomatoes, Parmesan cheese, and oregano, and season to taste with salt and pepper. Set aside.

6 Arrange the eggplant slices over the base and sides of the cake pan, overlapping them and making sure there are no gaps.

7 Pile the pasta mixture into the pan, packing it down well, and sprinkle with the bread crumbs. Bake in

a preheated oven, 375°F/190°C, for 20 minutes. Remove from the oven and let stand for 15 minutes.

8 Loosen the cake around the edge of the pan with a spatula, and turn it out, eggplant side uppermost. Garnish with fresh oregano and serve.

pasticcio

serves six

8 oz/225 g dried fusilli, or other
short pasta shapes

1 tbsp olive oil, plus extra
for brushing

4 tbsp heavy cream

salt

fresh rosemary sprigs, to garnish

BEEF SAUCE

2 tbsp olive oil

1 onion, thinly sliced

1 red bell pepper, seeded
and chopped

2 garlic cloves, chopped

1 lb 6 oz/625 g lean ground beef

14 oz/400 g canned
chopped tomatoes

½ cup dry white wine

2 tbsp chopped fresh parsley

1¾ oz/50 g canned anchovies,
drained and chopped

salt and pepper

TOPPING

1¼ cups plain yogurt

3 eggs

pinch of freshly grated nutmeg

½ cup freshly grated
Parmesan cheese

salt and pepper

1 To make the sauce, heat the oil in a large skillet, add the onion and red bell pepper, and cook for 3 minutes. Stir in the garlic and cook for 1 minute. Stir in the beef and cook, stirring frequently, until browned.

2 Add the tomatoes and wine, stir, and bring to a boil. Simmer, uncovered, for 20 minutes, or until the sauce is fairly thick. Stir in the parsley and anchovies and season to taste.

3 Bring a large pan of lightly salted water to a boil. Add the pasta and olive oil, return to a boil, and cook for 8–10 minutes, until tender but still firm to the bite. Drain, then transfer to a bowl. Stir in the cream and set aside.

4 To make the topping, beat together the yogurt, eggs, and nutmeg until well blended, and season with salt and pepper, to taste.

5 Brush a large, shallow ovenproof dish with oil. Spoon in half of the pasta mixture and cover with half of the beef sauce. Repeat the layers, then spread the topping evenly over the final layer. Sprinkle the grated Parmesan cheese on top.

6 Bake in a preheated oven, 375°F/ 190°C, for 25 minutes, or until the topping is golden brown and bubbling. Garnish with sprigs of fresh rosemary and serve.

hot pot chops

serves four

4 lean, boneless lamb leg steaks,
   about 4½ oz/125 g each
1 small onion, sliced thinly
1 carrot, sliced thinly
1 potato, sliced thinly
1 tsp olive oil
1 tsp dried rosemary
salt and pepper
fresh rosemary, to garnish
freshly steamed green vegetables,
   to serve

1 Trim any excess fat from the lamb steaks using a sharp knife.

2 Season both sides of the steaks with salt and pepper to taste and arrange them on a cookie sheet.

3 Alternate layers of sliced onion, carrot, and potato on top of each lamb steak, finishing with a layer of potato on top.

4 Brush the top layer of potato lightly with oil, season with salt and pepper to taste, then sprinkle with a little dried rosemary.

5 Bake the hot pot chops in a preheated oven, 350°F./180°C, for 25–30 minutes, until the lamb is tender and cooked through.

6 Drain the lamb steaks on paper towels and transfer to a warmed serving plate.

7 Garnish with fresh rosemary and serve accompanied by freshly steamed green vegetables.

fruity lamb casserole

serves four

1 lb/450 g lean lamb, trimmed and
cut into 1-inch/2.5-cm cubes

1 tsp ground cinnamon

1 tsp ground coriander

1 tsp ground cumin

2 tsp olive oil

1 red onion, chopped finely

1 garlic clove, crushed

14 oz/400 g canned
chopped tomatoes

2 tbsp tomato paste

4½ oz/125 g no-soak dried apricots

1 tsp superfine sugar

1¼ cups Vegetable Bouillon
(see page 11)

salt and pepper

1 small bunch of fresh cilantro,
to garnish

rice or couscous, to serve

1 Place the lamb in a mixing bowl and add the cinnamon, coriander, cumin, and oil. Mix thoroughly to coat the lamb in the spices.

2 Place a nonstick skillet over a high heat for a few seconds until hot, then add the spiced lamb. Reduce the heat and cook for 4–5 minutes, stirring, until the meat has browned all over. Remove the lamb using a slotted spoon and transfer to a large casserole.

3 Add the onion, garlic, tomatoes, and tomato paste to the skillet and cook, stirring occasionally, for 5 minutes. Season to taste with salt and pepper. Stir in the dried apricots and sugar, add the bouillon, and bring to a boil.

4 Spoon the sauce over the lamb and mix well. Cover and cook in a preheated oven, 350°F/180°C, for 1 hour, removing the lid for the last 10 minutes.

5 Chop the cilantro and use it to garnish the lamb. Serve immediately, straight from the casserole, with rice or couscous.

fresh spaghetti & meatballs

serves four

2½ cups fresh whole-wheat
bread crumbs

⅔ cup milk

1 large onion, chopped

4 cups ground steak

1 tsp paprika

4 tbsp olive oil

1 tbsp butter

1 lb/450 g fresh spaghetti

salt and pepper

fresh tarragon sprigs, to garnish

TOMATO SAUCE

1 tbsp butter

¼ cup whole-wheat flour

generous ¾ cup beef bouillon

14 oz/400 g canned
chopped tomatoes

2 tbsp tomato paste

1 tsp sugar

1 tbsp finely chopped fresh tarragon

salt and pepper

1 Place the bread crumbs in a bowl, add the milk, and soak for about 30 minutes.

2 To make the tomato sauce, melt half of the butter in a pan. Add the flour and cook, stirring constantly, for 2 minutes. Gradually stir in the beef bouillon and cook, stirring, for 5 minutes more. Add the tomatoes, tomato paste, sugar, and tarragon. Season and simmer for 25 minutes.

3 Mix the onion, steak, and paprika into the bread crumbs and season to taste with salt and pepper. Shape the mixture into 14 meatballs.

4 Heat the oil and butter in a skillet over low heat, add the meatballs, and cook, turning, until browned all over. Place the meatballs in a deep casserole, pour over the tomato sauce, cover, and bake in a preheated oven, 350°F/180°C, for 25 minutes.

5 Bring a large pan of lightly salted water to a boil. Add the fresh spaghetti, bring back to a boil, and cook for about 2–3 minutes, or until tender but still firm to the bite.

6 Meanwhile, remove the meatballs from the oven and let cool for 3 minutes. Drain the spaghetti and transfer to a serving dish, then pour the meatballs and their sauce over the top. Garnish with tarragon and serve.

meatballs in red wine sauce

serves four

generous 2½ cups fresh white
   bread crumbs

⅔ cup milk

12 shallots, chopped

4 cups ground steak

1 tsp paprika

5 tbsp olive oil

1 tbsp butter

1 lb/450 g dried egg tagliatelle

salt and pepper

fresh basil sprigs, to garnish

MUSHROOM AND WINE SAUCE

1 tbsp butter

4 tbsp olive oil

3 cups sliced oyster mushrooms

¼ cup whole-wheat flour

generous ¾ cup beef bouillon

⅔ cup red wine

4 tomatoes, peeled and chopped

1 tbsp tomato paste

1 tsp brown sugar

1 tbsp finely chopped fresh basil

salt and pepper

1 Place the bread crumbs in a bowl, add the milk, and let soak for 30 minutes.

2 To make the sauce, heat half of the butter and the oil in a large pan. Add the mushrooms and cook for 4 minutes. Stir in the flour and cook for 2 minutes. Add the bouillon and wine and simmer for 15 minutes. Add the tomatoes, tomato paste, sugar, basil, and seasoning. Simmer for 30 minutes.

3 Mix the shallots, steak, and paprika with the bread crumbs and season to taste with salt and pepper. Shape the mixture into 14 meatballs.

4 Heat 4 tablespoons of the oil and the butter in a large skillet over medium heat. Add the meatballs and cook, turning frequently, until browned all over. Transfer the meatballs to a deep casserole and pour over the wine and mushroom sauce. Cover, and bake in a preheated oven, 350°F/180°C, for 30 minutes.

5 Bring a pan of lightly salted water to a boil. Add the pasta and the remaining oil, bring back to a boil, and cook for 8–10 minutes, or until tender but still firm to the bite. Drain and transfer to a serving dish.

6 Remove the casserole from the oven and let cool for 3 minutes. Pour the meatballs and sauce over the pasta, garnish with sprigs of basil, and serve.

lasagna verde

serves six

Ragù Sauce (see page 10)
1 tbsp olive oil
8 oz/225 g lasagna verde
1 tbsp butter, for greasing
Béchamel Sauce (see page 210)
⅔ cup freshly grated
    Parmesan cheese
salt and pepper
salad greens, tomato salad, or black
    olives, to serve

1 First, make the ragù sauce as
described on page 6, but cook for
10–12 minutes longer than the time
given, uncovered, to let the excess
liquid evaporate. The sauce needs to
be reduced to a thick paste.

2 Bring a large pan of lightly salted,
water to a boil and add the olive
oil. Drop the lasagna sheets into the
boiling water, a few at a time, bringing
back to a boil before adding further
sheets. If you are using fresh lasagna
sheets, cook them for about 8 minutes;
if you are using dried lasagna sheets or
partly pre-cooked lasagna sheets, cook
them according to the instructions on
the package.

3 Remove the lasagna sheets from
the pan with a slotted spoon.
Spread them out in a single layer on
clean, damp dish towels.

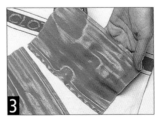

4 Grease a rectangular ovenproof
dish measuring 10–11 inches/
25–28 cm long. Spoon a little of the
meat sauce into the base of the
prepared dish, cover with a layer of
lasagna, then spoon over a little of the
béchamel sauce, and sprinkle with
some of the Parmesan cheese. Repeat
the layers, covering the final layer of
lasagna sheets with the remaining
béchamel sauce.

5 Sprinkle over the remaining
cheese and bake in a preheated
oven, 375°F/190°C, for 40 minutes, or
until the sauce is golden brown and
bubbling. Serve with salad greens, a
tomato salad, or a bowl of black olives.

beef & pasta casserole

serves four

2 lb/900 g steak, cubed

⅔ cup beef bouillon

1 lb/450 g dried macaroni

1¼ cups heavy cream

½ tsp garam masala

salt

KORMA PASTE

½ cup blanched almonds

6 garlic cloves

3 tsp coarsely chopped
    fresh gingerroot

6 tbsp beef bouillon

1 tsp ground cardamom

4 cloves, crushed

1 tsp cinnamon

2 large onions, chopped

1 tsp coriander seeds

2 tsp ground cumin seeds

pinch of cayenne pepper

6 tbsp sunflower oil

TO GARNISH

fresh cilantro

sliced almonds

1 To make the korma paste, grind the blanched almonds finely using a pestle and mortar. Put the ground almonds and the rest of the korma paste ingredients into a food processor and process to a very smooth paste.

2 Put the steak in a shallow dish and spoon over the korma paste, turning the steak to coat thoroughly. Set the meat aside in the refrigerator to marinate for 6 hours.

3 Transfer the steak and korma paste to a large pan and simmer over low heat, adding a little beef bouillon if required, for 35 minutes.

4 Meanwhile, bring a large pan of lightly salted water to a boil. Add the macaroni, bring back to a boil, and cook for 10 minutes, until tender but still firm to the bite. Drain the pasta thoroughly and transfer to a deep casserole. Add the steak, cream, and garam masala.

5 Bake in a preheated oven, 400°F/200°C, for 30 minutes, until the steak is tender. Remove from the oven and let stand for 10 minutes. Garnish the casserole with cilantro and sliced almonds and serve hot.

neopolitan veal cutlets

serves four

¾ cup butter

4 veal cutlets, about 9 oz/250 g
each, trimmed

1 large onion, sliced

2 apples, peeled, cored, and sliced

6 oz/175 g white mushrooms

1 tbsp chopped fresh tarragon

8 black peppercorns

1 tbsp sesame seeds

2 large beefsteak tomatoes,
cut in half

leaves of 1 fresh basil sprig

14 oz/400 g dried marille pasta

scant ½ cup extra virgin olive oil

¾ cup mascarpone cheese

salt and pepper

fresh basil leaves, to garnish

1 Melt ¼ cup of the butter in a skillet. Add the veal and cook over low heat for 5 minutes on each side. Transfer to a dish and keep warm.

2 Add the onion and apple slices to the skillet and cook, stirring occasionally, for 5–8 minutes, until lightly browned. Transfer to an ovenproof dish, place the veal on top, and keep warm.

3 Melt all but 1 tablespoon of the remaining butter in the skillet. Add the mushrooms, tarragon, and peppercorns. Cook over low heat for 3 minutes. Stir in the sesame seeds and transfer to a bowl with the pan juices. Set aside. Add the tomatoes and basil to the pan with the remaining butter, cook for 2–3 minutes. Set aside.

4 Bring a large pan of lightly salted water to a boil. Add the pasta and 1 tablespoon of the oil, bring back to a boil, and cook for 8–10 minutes, or until tender but still firm to the bite.

Drain well and transfer to an ovenproof dish. Dot with the mascarpone and sprinkle over the remaining olive oil.

5 Place the onions, apples, and veal on top of the pasta. Spoon the mushroom mixture onto the cutlets with the pan juices, place the tomatoes and basil leaves around the edge, and bake in a preheated oven, 300°F/ 150°C, for 5 minutes.

6 Remove from the oven and transfer to serving plates. Season, garnish with basil, and serve.

Vegetarian & Vegan

Anyone who ever thought that vegetarian meals were dull will be proved wrong by the rich variety of dishes in this chapter. You'll recognize influences from Middle Eastern and Italian cooking, such as the Stuffed Vegetables, Roasted Bell Pepper Bread, and Sun-dried Tomato Loaf, but there are also traditional recipes such as Pineapple Upside-Down Cake and Fruit Crumble. They all make exciting treats at any time of year and for virtually any occasion. Don't be afraid to substitute some of your own personal favorite ingredients wherever appropriate.

spicy black-eyed peas

serves four

2 cups black-eyed peas, soaked
    overnight in cold water

1 tbsp vegetable oil

2 onions, chopped

1 tbsp honey

2 tbsp molasses

4 tbsp dark soy sauce

1 tsp dry mustard powder

4 tbsp tomato paste

scant 2 cups Vegetable Bouillon
    (see page 11)

1 bay leaf

1 each fresh rosemary, thyme,
    and sage sprig

1 small orange

1 tbsp cornstarch

2 red bell peppers, seeded
    and diced

pepper

2 tbsp chopped fresh flatleaf
    parsley, to garnish

crusty bread, to serve

1 Rinse the black-eyed peas and place in a pan. Cover with water, bring to a boil, and boil rapidly for 10 minutes. Drain the peas and place in a casserole.

2 Meanwhile, heat the oil in a large skillet, add the onions, and cook over low heat, stirring occasionally, for 5 minutes. Stir in the honey, molasses, soy sauce, mustard, and tomato paste. Pour in the bouillon, bring to a boil, and pour over the peas.

3 Tie the bay leaf and herbs together with a clean piece of string and add to the pea mixture in the casserole. Finely pare 3 pieces of orange rind using a swivel vegetable peeler and stir into the pea mixture, with plenty of pepper. Cover and cook in a preheated oven, 300°F/150°C, for 1 hour.

4 Extract the juice from the orange and blend with the cornstarch to form a paste. Remove the casserole from the oven and stir the cornstarch paste into the peas with the red bell peppers. Cover, return to the oven, and cook for 1 hour, until the sauce is rich and thick and the peas are tender. Discard the herbs and orange rind.

5 Garnish the casserole with chopped flatleaf parsley and serve with crusty bread.

pasta & bean casserole

serves six

generous 1 cup dried navy beans,
    soaked overnight and drained

6 tbsp olive oil

2 large onions, sliced

2 garlic cloves, chopped

2 bay leaves

1 tsp dried oregano

1 tsp dried thyme

5 tbsp red wine

2 tbsp tomato paste

3½ cups Vegetable Bouillon
    (see page 11)

8 oz/225 g dried penne, or other
    short pasta shapes

2 celery stalks, sliced

1 fennel bulb, sliced

scant 2 cups sliced mushrooms

8 oz/225 g tomatoes, sliced

1 tsp dark molasses sugar

scant 1 cup dry white bread crumbs

salt and pepper

TO SERVE

salad greens

crusty bread

1 Place the beans in a pan, cover with water, and bring to a boil. Boil rapidly for 20 minutes, then drain.

2 Place the beans in a large flameproof casserole, stir in 5 tablespoons of the olive oil, the onions, garlic, bay leaves, herbs, wine, and tomato paste, and pour in the vegetable bouillon.

3 Bring to a boil, then cover the casserole, and bake in a preheated oven, 350°F/180°C, for 2 hours.

4 Towards the end of the cooking time, bring a large pan of salted water to the boil, add the pasta and the remaining olive oil and cook for 3 minutes. Drain and set aside.

5 Remove the casserole from the oven and add the pasta, celery, fennel, mushrooms, and tomatoes, and season to taste with salt and pepper.

6 Stir in the sugar and sprinkle over the bread crumbs. Cover the casserole, return to the oven, and continue cooking for 1 hour. Serve hot with salad greens and crusty bread.

mushroom cannelloni

serves four

12 oz/350 g crimini mushrooms

1 onion, chopped finely

1 garlic clove, crushed

1 tbsp chopped fresh thyme

½ tsp ground nutmeg

4 tbsp dry white wine

scant 1 cup fresh white
   bread crumbs

12 dried quick-cook cannelloni

salt and pepper

Parmesan shavings, to garnish

TOMATO SAUCE

1 large red bell pepper

¾ cup dry white wine

scant 2 cups bottled
   strained tomatoes

2 tbsp tomato paste

2 bay leaves

1 tsp superfine sugar

1 Finely chop the mushrooms and place in a pan with the onion and garlic. Stir in the thyme, nutmeg, and wine. Bring to a boil, cover, and simmer for 10 minutes.

2 Add the bread crumbs, stir to bind the mixture together, and season to taste. Remove from the heat and let cool for 10 minutes.

3 To make the tomato sauce, cut the bell pepper in half, seed it, and place on the broiler rack. Cook under a preheated hot broiler for 8–10 minutes, until charred. Let cool.

4 When the bell pepper has cooled, peel off the charred skin. Chop the flesh and place in a food processor with the wine. Process into a paste, then pour into a pan.

5 Add the remaining sauce ingredients to the paste and stir. Bring to a boil and simmer for 10 minutes. Discard the bay leaves.

6 Cover the base of an ovenproof dish with a thin layer of tomato sauce. Fill the cannelloni with the mushroom mixture and place in the dish. Spoon over the remaining sauce, cover with foil, and bake in a preheated oven, 400°F/200°C, for 35–40 minutes. Garnish with Parmesan shavings and serve.

stuffed vegetables

serves four

4 large beefsteak tomatoes

4 zucchini

2 orange bell peppers

salt and pepper

FILLING

1¼ cups cracked wheat

¼ cucumber

1 red onion

2 tbsp lemon juice

2 tbsp chopped fresh cilantro

2 tbsp chopped fresh mint

1 tbsp olive oil

2 tsp cumin seeds

salt and pepper

TO SERVE

warm pita bread

hummus

COOK'S TIP

It is a good idea to blanch vegetables (except for tomatoes) before stuffing. Blanch bell peppers, zucchini, and eggplant for 5 minutes.

1 Slice the tops off the tomatoes and reserve, then scoop out the tomato pulp. Chop the pulp and place in a bowl. Season the tomato shells with salt and pepper, then invert them on absorbent paper towels, and set aside to drain.

2 Trim the zucchini and cut a V-shaped groove lengthwise down each one. Finely chop the cut-out wedges and add to the tomato pulp. Season the zucchini shells to taste and set aside. Halve the bell peppers, cutting carefully through the stalks. Cut out the seeds and discard, leaving the stalks intact. Season the bell pepper shells and set aside.

3 To make the filling, soak the cracked wheat according to the instructions on the package. Finely chop the cucumber and add to the reserved tomato pulp and zucchini mixture. Finely chop the red onion and add to the vegetable mixture with the lemon juice, herbs, olive oil, cumin, and seasoning, and mix together well.

4 When the wheat has soaked, mix with the vegetables, and stuff into the tomato, zucchini, and bell pepper shells. Place the tops on the tomatoes, transfer to a roasting pan, and bake in a preheated oven, 400°F/200°C, for about 20–25 minutes, until cooked through. Drain and serve with pita bread and hummus.

lentil & red bell pepper tart

serves six

DOUGH

1¾ cups plain whole-wheat flour,
   plus extra for dusting

⅓ cup vegan margarine, diced

4 tbsp water

FILLING

¾ cup red lentils, rinsed

1¼ cups Vegetable Bouillon
   (see page 11)

1 tbsp vegan margarine

1 onion, chopped

2 red bell peppers, seeded
   and diced

1 tsp yeast extract

1 tbsp tomato paste

3 tbsp chopped fresh parsley

pepper

1 To make the dough, strain the flour into a mixing bowl and add any bran remaining in the strainer. Rub in the vegan margarine with your fingertips until the mixture resembles fine bread crumbs. Stir in the water and bring together to form a dough. Wrap in plastic wrap and chill in the refrigerator for 30 minutes.

2 Meanwhile, to make the filling, put the lentils in a pan with the stick, bring to a boil, then simmer for 10 minutes, until the lentils are tender. Remove from the heat and mash the lentils into a paste.

3 Melt the margarine in a small skillet over low heat, add the onion and red bell peppers and cook for about 3 minutes, stirring occasionally, until just soft.

4 Add the lentil paste, yeast extract, tomato paste, and parsley. Season with pepper. Mix until well blended.

5 Roll out the dough on a lightly floured counter and use it to line a 9½-inch/24-cm loose-based tart pan. Prick the base of the tart shell with a fork and spoon the lentil mixture into the shell.

6 Bake in a preheated oven, 400°F/200°C, for 30 minutes, until the filling is set. Serve immediately.

brazil nut & mushroom pie

serves four

DOUGH

1¾ cups plain whole-
  wheat flour

⅓ cup vegan margarine, diced

4 tbsp water

soy milk, to glaze

FILLING

2 tbsp vegan margarine

1 onion, chopped

1 garlic clove, chopped finely

scant 2 cups sliced
  white mushrooms

1 tbsp all-purpose flour

⅔ cup Vegetable Stock
  (see page 11)

1 tbsp tomato paste

generous 1 cup chopped Brazil nuts

1⅓ cup fresh whole-wheat
  bread crumbs

2 tbsp chopped fresh parsley

½ tsp pepper

1 To make the dough, strain the flour into a mixing bowl and add any bran remaining in the strainer. Rub in the vegan margarine with your fingertips until the mixture resembles fine bread crumbs. Stir in the water and bring together to form a dough. Wrap in plastic wrap and chill in the refrigerator for 30 minutes.

2 Meanwhile, to make the filling, melt half of the margarine in a skillet over low heat. Add the onion, garlic, and mushrooms and cook, stirring occasionally, for 5 minutes, until softened. Add the flour and cook for 1 minute, stirring constantly. Gradually add the bouillon, stirring, until the sauce is smooth and starting to thicken. Stir in the tomato paste, Brazil nuts, bread crumbs, parsley, and pepper. Remove the pan from the heat and let cool slightly.

3 Roll out two-thirds of the dough on a lightly floured counter and use it to line an 8-inch/20-cm loose-based tart pan or pie dish. Spread the filling in the pie shell. Brush the edges of the dough with soy milk. Roll out the remaining dough to fit the top of the pie. Press the edges to seal, then make a slit in the top of the pie to let steam escape during cooking, and brush with soy milk.

4 Bake in a preheated oven, 400°F/ 200°C, for 30–40 minutes, until golden brown. Serve immediately.

245

roasted bell pepper bread

serves four

1 tbsp vegan margarine,
   for greasing
1 red bell pepper, cut in half
   and seeded
1 yellow bell pepper, cut in half
   and seeded
2 fresh rosemary sprigs
1 tbsp olive oil
¼ oz/10 g active dry yeast
1 tsp granulated sugar
1¼ cups lukewarm water
1 lb/450 g strong white bread flour
1 tsp salt

1 Grease a 9-inch/23-cm deep circular cake pan with margarine.

2 Place the bell pepper halves and rosemary sprigs in a shallow roasting pan. Pour over the oil and roast in a preheated oven, 400°F/200°C, for 20 minutes, or until slightly charred. Leave the peppers to cool slightly, then remove the skin, and cut the flesh into slices.

3 Place the yeast and sugar in a bowl and mix with ½ cup of the water. Let stand in a warm place for about 15 minutes, or until frothy.

4 Strain the flour and salt together into a large bowl. Stir in the yeast mixture and the remaining water and bring together with your fingers to form a smooth dough.

5 Knead the dough for 5 minutes, until smooth. Cover with oiled plastic wrap and let rise for about 30 minutes, or until doubled in size.

6 Cut the dough into 3 equal portions. Roll the portions into circles slightly larger than the cake pan.

7 Place 1 circle in the base of the pan so that it reaches up the sides by about ¾ inch/2 cm. Top with half of the bell pepper mixture. Strip the leaves from the rosemary sprigs and sprinkle half of them over the top.

8 Place the second circle of dough on top, followed by the remaining bell pepper mixture and rosemary leaves. Place the last circle of dough on top, pushing the edges of the dough down the sides of the pan.

9 Cover with oiled plastic wrap and let rise for 30–40 minutes. Bake for 45 minutes in the preheated oven, until golden. When the loaf is cooked it should sound hollow when tapped. Turn out onto a wire rack to cool slightly, then cut into slices to serve.

garlic & sage bread

serves six

1 tbsp vegan margarine,
 for greasing

2¼ cups brown bread flour

1 envelope active dry yeast

3 tbsp chopped fresh sage

2 tsp sea salt

3 garlic cloves, chopped finely

1 tsp honey

⅔ cup lukewarm water

1 Grease a cookie sheet with vegan margarine. Strain the flour into a large mixing bowl and add any bran remaining in the strainer.

2 Stir in the dry yeast, sage, and half of the sea salt. Reserve 1 teaspoon of the chopped garlic for sprinkling and stir the rest into the bowl. Add the honey and water and bring together to form a dough.

3 Turn the dough out onto a lightly floured counter and knead it for about 5 minutes. Alternatively, use an electric mixer with a dough hook.

4 Place the dough in a greased bowl, cover, and let rise in a warm place until doubled in size.

5 Knead the dough again for a few minutes to punch it down, then make it into a donut shape (see Cook's Tip), and place on the cookie sheet.

6 Cover and let rise for a further 30 minutes, or until springy to the touch. Sprinkle with the rest of the sea salt and garlic.

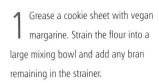

7 Bake the herb bread in a preheated oven, 400°F/200°C, for 25–30 minutes. Transfer to a wire rack to cool before slicing and serving.

COOK'S TIP
Roll the dough into a long sausage and then curve it into a donut shape. You can omit the sea salt for sprinkling, if you like.

sun-dried tomato loaf

serves four

¼ oz/10 g active dry yeast

1 tsp granulated sugar

1¼ cups lukewarm water

1 lb/450 g strong white bread flour,
plus extra for dusting

1 tsp salt

2 tsp dried basil

2 tbsp sun-dried tomato paste or
ordinary tomato paste

1 tbsp vegan margarine,
for greasing

12 sun-dried tomatoes in oil,
drained and cut into strips

1 Place the yeast and sugar in a small bowl and mix with ½ cup of the water. Let stand in a warm place for about 15 minutes, or until frothy.

2 Strain the flour and salt into a large mixing bowl. Make a well in the center and add the dried basil, yeast mixture, tomato paste, and half of the remaining water. Draw the flour into the liquid with a wooden spoon and bring together with your fingers to form a dough, adding the rest of the water gradually.

3 Turn the dough out onto a floured counter and knead for 5 minutes. Cover with oiled plastic wrap and let stand in a warm place for 30 minutes, or until doubled in size.

4 Lightly grease a 2-lb/900-g loaf pan with the vegan margarine.

5 Turn the dough out and knead in the sun-dried tomatoes. Knead for 2–3 minutes more.

6 Place the dough in the prepared pan. Let rise for 30–40 minutes, or until it has doubled in size again. Bake in a preheated oven, 375°F/190°C, for 30–35 minutes, or until golden. When the loaf is cooked, it should sound hollow when tapped on the base. Cool slightly on a wire rack and serve.

eggless sponge cake

serves eight

1 tbsp vegan margarine,
 for greasing

1¾ cups whole-wheat flour

4 tsp baking powder

¾ cup superfine sugar

6 tbsp sunflower oil

1 cup water

1 tsp vanilla extract

4 tbsp strawberry or raspberry
 reduced-sugar spread

superfine sugar,
 for dusting

COOK'S TIP

Standard margarine—packets
that are not labelled vegan—
may contain some animal
products, such as whey, butter
fat, or skim milk.

1 Grease 2 circular layer pans,
 8-inches/20-cm wide, and line
them with baking parchment.

2 Strain the flour and baking
 powder into a large bowl and
add any bran remaining in the strainer.
Stir in the sugar.

3 Pour in the oil, water, and vanilla
 extract. Stir with a wooden spoon
for about 1 minute, until the mixture is
smooth, then divide among the
prepared pans.

4 Bake in a preheated oven, 350°F/
 180°C, for 25–30 minutes, until
firm to the touch.

5 Let the sponge cakes cool in the
 pans, then turn out, and transfer
to a wire rack to cool completely.
Remove the baking parchment.

VARIATION

To make a chocolate-flavored
sponge cake, replace
2 tablespoons of the whole-
wheat flour with unsweetened
cocoa. To make a citrus-flavored
sponge cake, add the grated rind
of ½ lemon or orange to the flour
in step 2. To make a coffee-
flavored sponge cake, replace
2 teaspoons of the flour with
instant coffee powder.

6 Place one sponge cake on a
 serving plate. Cover with the
reduced-sugar fruit spread, spreading it
out to the edges, and place the other
sponge cake lightly on top.

7 Dust the eggless sponge cake
 with a little superfine sugar
before serving.

baked cheesecake

serves six

4 tbsp vegan margarine, melted,
    plus extra for greasing
2¼ cups graham cracker crumbs
⅓ cup chopped pitted dates
4 tbsp lemon juice
grated rind of 1 lemon
3 tbsp water
12 oz/350 g firm bean curd
⅔ cup apple juice
1 banana, mashed
1 tsp vanilla extract
1 mango, peeled, pitted,
    and chopped

1 Lightly grease a 7-inch/18-cm circular loose-based cake pan with a little margarine.

2 Mix together the graham cracker crumbs and melted margarine in a bowl. Press the mixture into the base of the prepared pan.

3 Put the dates, lemon juice, lemon rind, and water into a pan and bring to a boil. Simmer for 5 minutes, until the dates are soft, then mash the mixture coarsely with a fork.

4 Place the mixture in a food processor with the bean curd, apple juice, mashed banana, and vanilla extract and process until the mixture forms a thick, smooth paste.

5 Pour the bean curd paste onto the prepared cracker-crumb base and level the surface with a spatula.

6 Bake in a preheated oven, 350°F/180°C, for 30–40 minutes, until lightly golden. Let cool in the pan, then chill thoroughly in the refrigerator before serving.

7 Place the chopped mango in a food processor and process until smooth. Serve the fruit purée as a sauce with the cheesecake.

pineapple upside-down cake

serves eight

¼ cup vegan margarine, diced, plus
   extra for greasing
15 oz/425 g canned unsweetened
   pineapple pieces in fruit
   juice, drained, with the
   juice reserved
4 tsp cornstarch
¼ cup brown sugar
½ cup water
grated rind of 1 lemon
SPONGE
4 tbsp sunflower oil
⅓ cup brown sugar
⅔ cup water
1¼ cups all-purpose flour
2 tsp baking powder
1 tsp ground cinnamon

1 Grease a deep 7-inch/18-cm circular cake pan with margarine. Mix the juice from the pineapple with the cornstarch to make a smooth paste. Put the paste in a pan with the sugar, margarine, and water, and stir over low heat until the sugar has dissolved. Bring to a boil and simmer for 2–3 minutes, until thickened. Let the pineapple syrup cool slightly.

2 To make the sponge, heat the oil, sugar, and water in a pan over low heat until the sugar has dissolved, but do not let it boil. Remove from the heat and let cool. Sift the flour, baking powder, and ground cinnamon into a mixing bowl. Pour in the cooled oil and sugar mixture and beat well to form a batter.

3 Place the pineapple pieces and lemon rind in the prepared pan. Pour over 4 tablespoons of pineapple syrup. Spoon the batter on top.

4 Bake in a preheated oven, 350°F/ 180°C, for 35–40 minutes, until set and a fine metal skewer inserted into the center comes out clean. Place a plate over the top and carefully invert, let stand for 5 minutes, then remove the pan. Serve immediately with the remaining syrup.

apricot slices

makes twelve

DOUGH

⅓ cup vegan margarine, diced, plus
    extra for greasing

1¾ cups whole-wheat flour

½ cup finely ground
    mixed nuts

4 tbsp water

soy milk, to glaze

FILLING

1 cup dried apricots

grated rind of 1 orange

1¼ cups apple juice

1 tsp ground cinnamon

⅓ cup raisins

COOK'S TIP

These slices will keep in an
airtight container for 3–4 days.

---

1 Lightly grease a 9-inch/23-cm square cake pan. To make the dough, place the flour and nuts in a mixing bowl and rub in the margarine with your fingertips until the mixture resembles bread crumbs. Stir in the water and bring together to form a dough. Wrap in plastic wrap and chill in the refrigerator for 30 minutes.

2 To make the filling, place the apricots, orange rind, and apple juice in a pan and bring to a boil. Simmer gently for 30 minutes, until the apricots are mushy. Cool slightly, then place in a food processor and process into a purée. Alternatively, press the mixture through a fine strainer with the back of a spoon. Add the cinnamon and raisins and stir.

3 Remove the dough from the refrigerator. Divide in half, roll out one half, and use it to line the base of the prepared pan. Spread the apricot purée over the top, leaving a border around the edges, and brush the edges with water. Roll out the rest of the dough to fit over the top. Place over the purée and press the edges to seal.

4 Prick the top of the dough with a fork and brush with soy milk. Bake in a preheated oven, 400°F/ 200°C, for 20–25 minutes, until golden. Let cool slightly before cutting into 12 bars. Serve the apricot slices warm or cold.

date & apricot tart

serves eight

1¾ cups all-purpose whole-wheat
    flour, plus extra for dusting

½ cup ground mixed nuts

⅓ cup vegan margarine, diced

4 tbsp water

1 cup chopped dried apricots

1⅓ cups chopped pitted dates

scant 2 cups apple juice

1 tsp ground cinnamon

grated rind of 1 lemon

soy custard, to serve (optional)

1 Place the flour and ground nuts in a mixing bowl and rub in the margarine with your fingertips until the mixture resembles bread crumbs. Stir in the water and bring together to form a dough. Wrap in plastic wrap and chill in the refrigerator for 30 minutes.

2 Meanwhile, place the apricots and dates in a pan with the apple juice, cinnamon, and lemon rind. Bring to a boil, cover, and simmer over low heat for about 15 minutes, until the fruit has softened. Mash the fruit into a purée and set aside.

3 Remove the dough from the refrigerator. Reserve a small ball of dough for making lattice strips. Roll out the rest of the dough into a circle on a lightly floured counter and use it to line a 9-inch/23-cm loose-based tart pan.

4 Spread the fruit purée evenly over the base of the tart shell. Roll out the reserved dough and cut into strips ½ inch/1 cm wide. Cut the strips to fit the tart and twist them across the top of the fruit to form a decorative lattice pattern. Moisten the edges of the dough strips with a little water and press the ends firmly against the rim of the tart to seal.

5 Bake in a preheated oven, 400°F/ 200°C, for 25–30 minutes, until golden brown. Cut into the tart into slices and serve immediately with soy custard, if you like.

fruit crumble

serves six

1 tbsp vegan margarine,
    for greasing

6 pears, peeled

1 tbsp chopped preserved ginger

1 tbsp dark brown sugar

2 tbsp orange juice

CRUMBLE TOPPING

1½ cups all-purpose flour

6 tbsp vegan margarine, diced

¼ cup sliced almonds

⅓ cup rolled oats

1¾ oz/50 g dark brown sugar

soy custard, to serve (optional)

VARIATION
Stir 1 teaspoon ground allspice into the crumble mixture in step 3 for added flavor, if you like.

1 Lightly grease a 4-cup/1-litre ovenproof dish with the vegan margarine.

2 Core the pears, cut them into fourths, and slice them. Place the pear slices in a bowl with the ginger, sugar, and orange juice and stir to blend. Spoon the mixture evenly across the base of the prepared dish.

3 To make the crumble topping, strain the flour into a large mixing bowl. Add the margarine and rub it in with your fingertips until the mixture resembles fine bread crumbs. Add the sliced almonds, then the rolled oats and sugar. Mix together until thoroughly blended.

4 Sprinkle the crumble topping evenly over the pear and ginger mixture in the dish, pressing it down gently with the back of a spoon.

5 Bake in a preheated oven, 375°F/ 190°C, for 30 minutes, until the topping is golden and the fruit tender. Serve the crumble immediately with soy custard, if you like.

257

Chocolate

Introduction

Chocolate! The mere mention of anything associated with this mouthwatering confection can cause a dreamy look to come into the eyes of the chocoholic.

The cocoa tree, Theobroma cacao, originated in South America, and from the early 7th century it was cultivated by the Maya, who established a flourishing trade and even used the cocoa bean as currency. In 1502, Christopher Columbus took the cocoa bean to Spain, but it wasn't until later that Cortés introduced xocotlatl, a recipe brought from the Mexican court of Montezuma for a drink made from crushed roasted cocoa beans and cold water. Vanilla, spices, honey, and sugar were added to improve the flavor of this thick and bitter brew, and over time it came to be served hot.

In the 17th century, the popularity of cocoa spread to the rest of Europe. France was the first country to fall to its charms, then Holland, where Amsterdam became the most important cocoa port beyond Spain. From there cocoa went to Germany, then north to Scandinavia, and also south to Italy. Cocoa arrived in England in the mid-17th century, and in London chocolate houses quickly began to rival the newly established coffee houses.

In the early 19th century, Dutch chemist Coenraad Van Houten invented a press to extract the fat from the beans, and developed a method of neutralizing the acids. In this way, he was able to produce almost pure cocoa butter, and a hard "cake," which could be milled to a powder for use as a flavoring. As a result, it became possible to eat chocolate as well as to drink it.

In Britain, Fry's chocolate appeared in 1847, and in Switzerland the famous chocolate companies were established. In 1875 chocolate was combined with condensed milk to produce the first milk chocolate. At around this time, Lindt found a way of making the smooth, melting chocolate still associated with his company today. About 20 years later, Hershey introduced his famous chocolate bar in the United States.

Cocoa trees are now grown in many parts of the world. The cocoa beans are left in the sun, then shelled, and the kernels processed to produce cocoa solids. Finally, the cocoa butter is extracted and further processed to become chocolate, in all its many guises.

Basic Recipes

Preparing Chocolate

To melt chocolate on a stove:

1 Break the chocolate into small, equal-size pieces and put it into a heatproof bowl.

2 Place the bowl over a pan of hot, simmering water, making sure the base of the bowl does not come into contact with the water.

3 Once the chocolate starts to melt, stir gently until smooth, then remove from the heat.

Note: Do not melt chocolate over direct heat (unless melting with other ingredients—in this case, keep the heat very low).

To melt chocolate in a microwave oven:

1 Break the chocolate into small pieces and place in a microwave-proof bowl.

2 Put the bowl in the microwave oven and melt. As a guide, melt 4½ oz/125 g semisweet chocolate on High for 2 minutes, and white or milk chocolate on Medium for 2–3 minutes.

Note: As microwave oven temperatures and settings vary, you should consult the manufacturer's instructions first.

3 Stir the chocolate, let stand for a few minutes, then stir again. If necessary, return it to the microwave for another 30 seconds.

Chocolate Decorations

Decorations add a special touch to a cake or pudding. They can be interleaved with non-stick baking parchment and stored in airtight containers. Semisweet chocolate will keep for 4 weeks, and milk or white chocolate for 2 weeks.

Caraque

1 Spread the melted chocolate over a clean acrylic cutting board and let it set.

2 When the chocolate has set, hold the board firmly, position a large, smooth-bladed knife on the chocolate, and pull the blade toward you at an angle of 45°, scraping along the chocolate to form the caraque. You should end up with irregularly shaped long curls.

3 Using the knife blade, lift the caraque off the board.

Quick Curls

1 For quick curls, choose a thick bar of chocolate, and keep it at room temperature.

2 Using a sharp, swivel-bladed vegetable peeler, scrape lightly along the chocolate to form fine curls, or more firmly to form thicker curls.

Note: Before grating chocolate, make sure the chocolate is firm. In warm weather, chill the chocolate in the refrigerator before using.

Leaves

1 Use freshly picked leaves with well-defined veins that are clean, dry, and pliable. Holding a leaf by its stem, paint a smooth layer of melted chocolate onto the underside with a small paint brush or pastry brush.

2 Repeat with the remaining leaves, then place them, chocolate-side up, on a baking sheet lined with waxed paper.

3 Let chill for at least 1 hour until set. When set, peel each leaf away from its chocolate coating.

Cakes, Gâteaux & Loaves

It is hard to resist the pleasure of a sumptuous

piece of chocolate cake and no chocolate book

would be complete without a selection of

cakes, gâteaux, and loaves—there are plenty to choose from in this chapter.

The more experimental among you can vary the fillings of decoration

according to what takes your fancy. Alternatively, follow our easy step-by-step

instructions and look at our glossy pictures to guide you to perfect results.

The gâteaux in this book are a feast for the eyes, and so are the delicious

cakes, many of which can be made with surprising ease. The loaves are the

perfect indulgence to enjoy with coffee and can be made with very little effort.

So next time you feel like a mouthwatering slice of something, these recipes

are sure to be a success.

chocolate almond cake

serves eight

6 oz/175 g semisweet chocolate

¾ cup butter

½ cup superfine sugar

4 eggs, separated

¼ tsp cream of tartar

⅓ cup self-rising flour

1¼ cups ground almonds

1 tsp almond extract

TOPPING

4½ oz/125 g light chocolate

2 tbsp butter

4 tbsp heavy cream

TO DECORATE

2 tbsp toasted slivered almonds

1 oz/25 g semisweet chocolate, melted

1 Lightly grease and line the bottom of a 9-inch/23-cm round springform pan. Break the chocolate into small pieces and place in a small pan with the butter. Heat gently, stirring until melted and well combined.

2 Place ½ cup of the superfine sugar in a bowl with the egg yolks and whisk until pale and creamy. Add the melted chocolate and butter mixture, beating until well combined.

3 Sift the cream of tartar and flour together and fold into the chocolate mixture with the ground almonds and almond extract.

4 Whisk the egg whites in a bowl until standing in soft peaks. Add the remaining superfine sugar and whisk for about 2 minutes by hand, or 45–60 seconds if using an electric mixer, until thick and glossy. Fold the

egg whites into the chocolate mixture and spoon into the prepared pan. Bake in a preheated oven, 375°F/190°C, for 40 minutes, until just springy to the touch. Let cool.

5 Heat the topping ingredients in a bowl over a pan of hot water. Remove from the heat and beat for 2 minutes. Let chill for 30 minutes. Transfer the cake to a plate and spread with the topping. Sprinkle with the slivered almonds and drizzle with melted chocolate. Let the topping set for 2 hours before serving.

chocolate tray bake

serves fifteen

3 cups self-rising flour, sifted

3 tbsp unsweetened cocoa, sifted

1 cup superfine sugar

1 cup soft margarine

4 eggs, beaten

4 tbsp milk

⅓ cup light chocolate chips

⅓ cup semisweet chocolate chips

⅓ cup white chocolate chips

confectioners' sugar, for dusting

VARIATION

For an attractive finish, cut thin strips of paper and lay in a criss-cross pattern on top of the cake. Dust with confectioners' sugar, then remove the paper strips.

1 Grease a 13 x 9 x 2-inch/ 33 x 23 x 5-cm cake pan with a little butter or margarine.

2 Place all of the ingredients except for the chocolate chips and confectioners' sugar in a large mixing bowl and beat together until smooth.

3 Beat in the light, semisweet, and white chocolate chips.

4 Spoon the mixture into the prepared cake pan and smooth the top. Bake in a preheated oven, 350°F/180°C, for 30–40 minutes, until risen and springy to the touch. Let cool in the pan.

5 Once cool, dust with confectioners' sugar. Cut into squares to serve.

chocolate & pineapple cake

serves nine

⅔ cup lowfat spread

½ cup superfine sugar

¾ cup self-rising flour, sifted

3 tbsp unsweetened cocoa, sifted

1½ tsp baking powder

2 eggs

8 oz/225 g canned unsweetened
   pineapple pieces in fruit juice

½ cup lowfat thick plain yogurt

about 1 tbsp confectioners' sugar

grated chocolate, to decorate

COOK'S TIP

Store the cake, undecorated,
in an airtight container for
up to 3 days. Once decorated,
refrigerate and use within
2 days.

1 Lightly grease an 8-inch/20-cm square cake pan.

2 Place the lowfat spread, superfine sugar, flour, unsweetened cocoa, baking powder, and eggs in a large mixing bowl. Beat with a wooden spoon or electric mixer until smooth.

3 Pour the cake mixture into the prepared pan and smooth the surface. Bake in a preheated oven, 325°F/190°C, for 20–25 minutes or until springy to the touch. Let the chocolate and pineapple cake cool slightly in the pan before transferring to a wire rack to cool completely.

4 Drain the pineapple, chop the pineapple pieces, and drain again. Set aside a little pineapple for decoration, then stir the rest of the pineapple into the yogurt and sweeten to taste with confectioners' sugar.

5 Using a spatula, spread the pineapple and yogurt mixture smoothly and evenly over the top of the cake and decorate with the reserved pineapple pieces. Sprinkle with the grated chocolate.

family chocolate cake

serves eight

½ cup soft margarine

½ cup superfine sugar

2 eggs

1 tbsp light corn syrup

1 cup self-rising flour, sifted

2 tbsp unsweetened cocoa, sifted

FILLING AND TOPPING

4 tbsp confectioners' sugar, sifted

2 tbsp butter

3½ oz/100 g white or light cooking
    chocolate

a little light or white chocolate,
    melted (optional)

1 Lightly grease two 7-inch/18-cm
shallow cake pans.

2 Place all of the ingredients for the
cake in a large mixing bowl and
beat with a wooden spoon or electric
mixer to form a smooth mixture.

3 Divide the mixture between
the prepared pans and smooth
the tops. Bake in a preheated oven,
375°F/190°C, for 20 minutes or until
springy to the touch. Cool for a few

minutes in the pans before transferring
to a wire rack to cool completely.

4 To make the filling, beat the
confectioners' sugar and butter
together in a bowl until light and fluffy.
Melt the white or light cooking
chocolate and beat half into the icing
mixture. Use the filling to sandwich the
2 cakes together.

5 Spread the remaining melted
cooking chocolate over the top
of the cake. Pipe circles of contrasting
melted light or white chocolate and
feather into the cooking chocolate with
a toothpick, if desired. Let the cake
set before serving.

chocolate & orange cake

serves eight

¾ cup superfine sugar

¾ cup butter or block margarine

3 eggs, beaten

1½ cups self-rising flour, sifted

2 tbsp unsweetened cocoa, sifted

2 tbsp milk

3 tbsp orange juice

grated rind of ½ orange

FROSTING

1½ cups confectioners' sugar

2 tbsp orange juice

a little melted chocolate

VARIATION

Add 2 tablespoons of rum or brandy to the chocolate mixture instead of the milk. The cake also works well when flavored with grated lemon rind and juice instead of the orange.

---

1 Lightly grease an 8-inch/20-cm deep round cake pan.

2 Beat the sugar and butter or margarine together in a bowl until light and fluffy. Gradually add the eggs, beating well after each addition. Carefully fold in the flour.

3 Divide the mixture in half. Add the unsweetened cocoa and milk to one half, stirring until well combined. Flavor the other half with the orange juice and grated orange rind.

4 Place spoonfuls of each mixture into the prepared pan and swirl together with a skewer, to create a marbled effect. Bake in a preheated oven, 375°F/190°C, for 25 minutes or until the cake is springy to the touch.

5 Let the cake cool in the pan for a few minutes before transferring to a wire rack to cool completely.

6 To make the frosting, sift the confectioner's sugar into a mixing bowl and mix in enough of the orange juice to form a smooth frosting. Spread the frosting over the top of the cake and leave to set. Pipe fine lines of melted chocolate in a decorated pattern over the top.

mocha layer cake

serves eight

1¾ cups self-rising flour

¼ tsp baking powder

4 tbsp unsweetened cocoa

½ cup superfine sugar

2 eggs

2 tbsp light corn syrup

⅔ cup corn oil

⅔ cup milk

FILLING

1 tsp instant coffee powder

1 tbsp boiling water

1¼ cups heavy cream

2 tbsp confectioners' sugar

TO DECORATE

1¾ oz/50 g flock chocolate

chocolate caraque (see page 263)

confectioners' sugar, for dusting

1 Lightly grease three 7-inch/18-cm cake pans with butter.

2 Sift the flour, baking powder, and cocoa into a large mixing bowl. Stir in the sugar. Make a well in the center and stir in the eggs, syrup, oil, and milk. Beat with a wooden spoon, gradually mixing in the dry ingredients to make a smooth batter. Divide the cake mixture between the prepared pans.

3 Bake in a preheated oven, 350°F/180°C, for 35–45 minutes or until springy to the touch. Let cool in the pans for 5 minutes, then turn out onto a wire rack to cool completely.

4 Dissolve the instant coffee in the boiling water and place in a bowl with the cream and confectioners' sugar. Whip until the cream is just holding its shape. Use half of the cream to sandwich the 3 cakes together. Spread the remaining cream over the top and sides of the cake. Lightly press the flock chocolate into the cream around the edge of the cake.

5 Transfer to a serving plate. Lay the caraque over the top of the cake. Cut a few thin strips of baking parchment and place on top of the caraque. Dust lightly with confectioners' sugar, then carefully remove the paper. Serve.

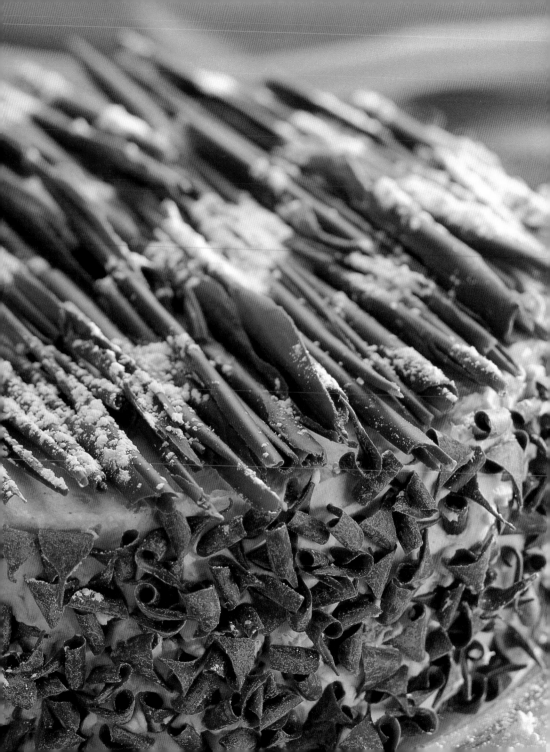

devil's food cake

serves six

3½ oz/100 g semisweet chocolate

2¼ cups self-rising flour

1 tsp baking soda

1 cup butter

2⅔ cups dark brown sugar

1 tsp vanilla extract

3 eggs

½ cup buttermilk

scant 1 cup boiling water

FROSTING

1¼ cups superfine sugar

2 egg whites

1 tbsp lemon juice

3 tbsp orange juice

candied orange peel, to decorate

COOK'S TIP

If you prefer, use vanilla butter frosting to decorate the cake. Cream ¾ cup of butter until soft, then add 3 cups sifted confectioner's sugar and mix together. Stir in vanilla extract to taste. Alternatively, use whipped cream and store in the refrigerator.

1 Lightly grease two 8-inch/20-cm shallow round cake pans and line the bottoms with baking parchment. Melt the chocolate in a pan. Sift the flour and baking soda together.

2 Beat the butter and sugar in a bowl until pale and fluffy. Beat in the vanilla extract and the eggs one at a time, beating well after each addition. Add a little flour if the mixture starts to curdle.

3 Fold the melted semisweet chocolate into the mixture until well blended. Gradually fold in the remaining flour, then gently stir in the buttermilk and boiling water.

4 Divide the mixture between the pans and smooth the tops. Bake in a preheated oven, 375°F/190°C, for 30 minutes, until springy to the touch. Let the cake cool in the pan for 5 minutes, then transfer to a wire rack to cool completely.

5 Place the frosting ingredients in a large bowl set over a pan of gently simmering water. Whisk, preferably with an electric mixer, until thickened and forming soft peaks. Remove from the heat and whisk until the mixture is cool.

6 Sandwich the 2 cakes together with a little of the frosting, then, using a spatula, spread the remainder over the sides and top of the cake, swirling it as you do so. Decorate the top of the cake with the candied orange peel.

chocolate tea bread

serves four

¾ cup butter, softened

⅔ cup light brown sugar

4 eggs, beaten lightly

8 oz/225 g semisweet chocolate
    chips

½ cup raisins

½ cup chopped walnuts

finely grated rind of 1 orange

2 cups self-rising flour

1 Lightly grease a 2-lb/900-g loaf pan and line the bottom with baking parchment.

2 Cream the butter and light brown sugar together in a bowl until they are light and fluffy.

3 Gradually add the eggs, beating well after each addition. If the mixture starts to curdle, beat in 1–2 tablespoons of the flour.

4 Stir in the chocolate chips, raisins, walnuts, and orange rind. Sift the self-rising flour and carefully fold it into the mixture.

5 Spoon the mixture into the prepared loaf pan and then make a slight dip in the center of the top with the back of a spoon.

6 Bake in a preheated oven, 325°F/160°C, for 1 hour or until a fine skewer inserted into the center of the loaf comes out clean.

7 Let the loaf cool in the pan for 5 minutes before carefully turning out on to a wire rack. Let the loaf cool completely.

8 To serve the tea bread, cut it into thin slices.

rich chocolate layer cake

serves ten

7 eggs

scant 1 cup superfine sugar

1¼ cups all-purpose flour

½ cup unsweetened cocoa

4 tbsp butter, melted

FILLING

7 oz/200 g semisweet chocolate

½ cup butter

¼ cup confectioners' sugar

TO DECORATE

¾ cup lightly crushed, toasted
    slivered almonds

quick chocolate curls (see page 263)
    or grated chocolate

1 Grease a deep 9-inch/23-cm square cake pan and line the bottom with baking parchment.

2 Whisk the eggs and superfine sugar in a mixing bowl with an electric mixer for about 10 minutes or until the mixture is very light and foamy and the whisk leaves a trail that lasts a few seconds when lifted.

3 Sift the flour and cocoa together and fold half into the mixture. Drizzle over the melted butter and fold in the rest of the flour and cocoa. Pour into the prepared pan and bake in a preheated oven, 350°F/180°C, for 30–35 minutes or until springy to the touch. Let the cake cool slightly, then remove from the pan and cool completely on a wire rack. Wash and dry the pan and return the cake to it.

4 While the cake is cooling, make the filling. Melt the semisweet chocolate and butter together, then remove from the heat. Stir in the confectioners' sugar, let cool, then beat the filling until it is thick enough to spread.

5 Halve the cooled cake lengthwise and cut each half into 3 layers. Sandwich the layers together with three-quarters of the chocolate filling. Spread the remainder over the cake and mark a wavy pattern on the top. Press the almonds onto the sides. Decorate the cake with chocolate curls or grated chocolate.

chocolate passion cake

serves six

5 eggs

⅔ cup superfine sugar

1¼ cups all-purpose flour

⅓ cup unsweetened cocoa

2 carrots, peeled, grated finely,
    and squeezed until dry

⅓ cup chopped walnuts

2 tbsp corn oil

12 oz/350 g medium-fat soft cheese

1½ cups confectioners' sugar

6 oz/175 g light or semisweet
    chocolate, melted

1 Lightly grease and line the bottom of a 8-inch/20-cm deep round cake pan with baking parchment.

2 Place the eggs and sugar in a large mixing bowl set over a pan of gently simmering water and whisk until the mixture is thick enough to leave a trail.

3 Remove the bowl from the heat. Sift the flour and cocoa into the bowl and carefully fold in. Fold in the grated carrots, walnuts, and oil.

4 Pour into the prepared pan and bake in a preheated oven, 375°F/190°C, for 45 minutes. Turn out onto a wire rack to cool.

5 Beat the soft cheese and confectioners' sugar together until combined. Beat in the melted chocolate. Split the cake in half and sandwich together again with half of the chocolate mixture. Cover the top of the cake with the remainder of the chocolate mixture, swirling it with a knife. Let chill, or serve immediately.

chocolate yogurt cake

serves eight

⅔ cup vegetable oil

⅔ cup whole-milk plain yogurt

1¼ cups brown sugar

3 eggs, beaten

¾ cup whole-wheat self-rising flour

1 cup self-rising flour, sifted

2 tbsp unsweetened cocoa

1 tsp baking soda

1¾ oz/50 g semisweet chocolate,
  melted

FILLING AND TOPPING

⅔ cup whole-milk plain yogurt

⅔ cup heavy cream

8 oz/225 g fresh soft fruit, such as
  strawberries or raspberries

1 Grease a 9-inch/23-cm round deep cake pan and line the bottom with baking parchment.

2 Place the oil, yogurt, sugar, and beaten eggs in a large mixing bowl and beat together until well combined. Sift the flours, cocoa, and baking soda together and beat into the bowl until well combined. Beat in the melted semisweet chocolate.

3 Pour the mixture into the prepared pan and bake in a preheated oven, 350°F/180°C, for 45–50 minutes or until a fine skewer inserted into the center comes out clean. Let the cake cool in the pan for 5 minutes, then turn out onto a wire rack to cool completely. When cold, split the cake into 3 layers.

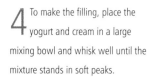

4 To make the filling, place the yogurt and cream in a large mixing bowl and whisk well until the mixture stands in soft peaks.

5 Place one layer of cake onto a serving plate and spread with some of the cream. Top with a little of the fruit (slicing larger fruit such as strawberries). Repeat with the next layer. Top with the final layer of cake and spread with the rest of the cream. Arrange more fruit on top and cut the cake into wedges to serve.

raspberry vacherin

serves ten

3 egg whites

¾ cup superfine sugar

1 tsp cornstarch

1 oz/25 g semisweet chocolate, grated

FILLING

6 oz/175 g semisweet chocolate

2 cups heavy cream, whipped

12 oz/350 g fresh raspberries

a little melted chocolate, to decorate

COOK'S TIP

When whisking egg whites, make sure your bowl is spotlessly clean and free from any grease as the egg whites will not whisk well or hold their shape.

1 Draw 3 rectangles, 4 x 10 inches/ 10 x 25 cm, on sheets of baking parchment, and place on 2 cookie sheets.

2 Whisk the egg whites in a mixing bowl until standing in soft peaks, then gradually whisk in half of the sugar and continue whisking until the mixture is very stiff and glossy.

3 Carefully fold in the rest of the superfine sugar, the cornstarch, and the grated chocolate with a metal spoon or spatula.

4 Spoon the meringue mixture into a pastry bag fitted with a ½-inch/1-cm plain tip and pipe lines across the rectangles.

5 Bake the meringues in a preheated oven, 275°F/140°C, for 1½ hours, changing the positions of

the cookie sheets halfway through. Without opening the oven door, turn off the oven and let the meringues cool inside the oven, then carefully peel away the baking parchment.

6 To make the filling, melt the chocolate and spread it over 2 of the meringues. Let harden.

7 Place 1 chocolate-coated meringue on a plate and top with about one-third of the cream and raspberries. Gently place the second chocolate-coated meringue on top and spread with half of the remaining cream and raspberries.

8 Place the last meringue on the top and decorate with the remaining cream and raspberries. Drizzle a little melted chocolate over the top and serve.

sachertorte

serves ten

6 oz/175 g semisweet chocolate

⅔ cup unsalted butter

⅔ cup superfine sugar

6 eggs, separated

1¼ cups all-purpose flour

FROSTING AND FILLING

6 oz/175 g semisweet chocolate

5 tbsp strong black coffee

1 cup frosting confectioners' sugar

6 tbsp good-quality apricot jelly

1¾ oz/50 g semisweet chocolate, melted, to decorate

COOK'S TIP

The finished cake is delicious served with whipped cream and fresh raspberries or a raspberry coulis.

1 Grease a 9-inch/23-cm springform cake pan and line the bottom with baking parchment. Melt the chocolate. Beat the butter and ⅓ cup of the sugar until pale and fluffy. Add the egg yolks and beat well. Add the chocolate in a thin stream, beating well. Sift the flour and fold it into the mixture. Whisk the egg whites until standing in soft peaks. Add the remaining sugar and whisk for 2 minutes by hand, or 45–60 seconds if using an electric mixer, until glossy. Fold half into the chocolate mixture, then fold in the remainder.

2 Spoon into the prepared pan and smooth the top. Bake in a preheated oven, 300°F/150°C, for 1–1¼ hours until a skewer inserted into the center comes out clean. Cool in the pan for 5 minutes, then transfer to a wire rack and let cool completely.

3 To make the frosting, melt the chocolate and beat in the coffee until smooth. Strain the confectioners' sugar into a bowl. Whisk in the melted chocolate mixture to give a thick frosting. Halve the cake. Warm the apricot jelly, spread over one half of the cake and sandwich together. Invert the cake onto a wire rack. Spoon the frosting over the cake and, using a spatula, spread as smoothly and evenly as possible, to coat the top and sides. Let the frosting set for 5 minutes, allowing any excess to drip through the rack. Transfer to a serving plate and let set for at least 2 hours.

4 To decorate, spoon the melted chocolate into a small pastry bag and pipe the word "Sacher" or "Sachertorte" on the top of the cake. Let it harden before serving the cake.

chocolate marshmallow cake

serves six

6 tbsp unsalted butter

generous 1 cup superfine sugar

½ tsp vanilla extract

2 eggs, beaten lightly

3 oz/85 g semisweet chocolate,
    broken into pieces

⅔ cup buttermilk

1¼ cups self-rising flour

½ tsp baking soda

pinch of salt

2 oz/55 g light chocolate, grated,
    to decorate

FROSTING

6 oz/175 g white marshmallows

1 tbsp milk

2 egg whites

2 tbsp superfine sugar

1 Grease a 3¾-cup ovenproof bowl
with butter. Cream the butter,
sugar, and vanilla together in a bowl
until pale and fluffy, then gradually
beat in the eggs.

2 Melt the semisweet chocolate in a
heatproof bowl over a pan of
simmering water. When the chocolate
has melted, stir in the buttermilk
gradually, until well combined. Remove
the pan from the heat and cool slightly.

3 Sift the flour, baking soda,
and salt into a separate bowl.

4 Add the chocolate mixture and
the flour mixture alternately to the
creamed mixture, a little at a time.
Spoon the mixture into the ovenproof
bowl and smooth the surface.

5 Bake in a preheated oven,
325°F/160°C, for 50 minutes until
a skewer inserted into the center of the
cake comes out clean. Turn out onto a
wire rack to cool.

6 Meanwhile, make the frosting.
Put the marshmallows and milk
in a small pan and heat very gently
until the marshmallows have melted.
Remove the pan from the heat and
set aside to cool.

7 Whisk the egg whites until soft
peaks form, then add the sugar
and continue whisking, until stiff
peaks form. Fold the egg white into
the cooled marshmallow mixture and
set aside for 10 minutes.

8 When the cake is cool, cover
the top and sides with the
marshmallow frosting. Top with
grated light chocolate.

chocolate slab cake

serves ten

1 cup butter

3½ oz/100 g semisweet chocolate, chopped

⅔ cup water

2½ cups all-purpose flour

2 tsp baking powder

1⅔ cups soft brown sugar

⅔ cup sour cream

2 eggs, beaten

FROSTING

7 oz/200 g semisweet chocolate

6 tbsp water

3 tbsp light cream

1 tbsp butter, chilled

1 Grease a 13 x 8-inch/33 x 20-cm square cake pan and line the bottom with baking parchment. In a pan, melt the butter and chocolate with the water over low heat, stirring frequently.

2 Sift the flour and baking powder into a mixing bowl and stir in the sugar. Pour the hot chocolate liquid into the bowl.

3 Beat well until all of the ingredients are evenly mixed. Stir in the sour cream, followed by the beaten eggs and mix well.

COOK'S TIP
Frost the cake while it is still on the wire rack, and place a large cookie sheet underneath to catch any drips. Spoon any drips back onto the cake.

4 Pour the mixture into the prepared pan and bake in a preheated oven, 375°F/190°C, for 40–45 minutes.

5 Let the cake cool in the pan before turning it out onto a wire rack to cool completely.

6 To make the frosting, melt the chocolate with the water in a pan over very low heat, stir in the cream and remove from the heat. Stir in the chilled butter, then pour the frosting over the cooled cake, using a spatula to spread it evenly over the top of the cake.

mousse cake

serves twelve

¾ cup butter

¾ cup superfine sugar

4 eggs, beaten lightly

1 tbsp unsweetened cocoa

1¾ cups self-rising flour

1¾ oz/50 g semisweet, orange-
flavored chocolate, melted

ORANGE MOUSSE

2 eggs, separated

4 tbsp superfine sugar

generous ¾ cup freshly squeezed
orange juice

2 tsp powdered gelatin

3 tbsp water

1¼ cups heavy cream

peeled orange slices, to decorate

1 Grease an 8-inch/20-cm springform cake pan and line the bottom with baking parchment. Beat the butter and sugar together in a bowl until light and fluffy. Gradually add the eggs, beating well after each addition. Sift the cocoa and flour together and fold into the cake mixture. Fold in the melted chocolate.

2 Pour into the prepared pan and smooth the top. Bake in a preheated oven, 350°F/180°C, for 40 minutes or until springy to the touch. Let the cake cool for 5 minutes in the pan, then turn out and cool completely.

3 Meanwhile, make the orange mousse. Beat the egg yolks and sugar until light, then whisk in the orange juice. Sprinkle the gelatin over the water in a small bowl and let it go spongy, then place over a pan of hot water and stir until the gelatin has dissolved. Stir into the mousse.

4 Whip the cream until holding its shape, set aside a little for decoration, and fold the rest into the mousse. Whisk the egg whites until standing in soft peaks, then fold in. Let stand in a cool place until starting to set, stirring occasionally.

5 Cut the cold cake into 2 layers. Place half of the cake in the pan. Pour in the mousse and press the second cake layer on top. Chill until set. Transfer to a plate, pipe cream rosettes on the top, and arrange orange slices in the center.

chocolate roulade

serves six

5½ oz/150 g semisweet chocolate

2 tbsp water

6 eggs

¾ cup superfine sugar

¼ cup all-purpose flour

1 tbsp unsweetened cocoa

FILLING

1¼ cups heavy cream

2¾ oz/75 g sliced strawberries

TO DECORATE

confectioners' sugar, for dusting

chocolate leaves (see page 263)

fresh strawberries, to serve

1 Line a 15 x 10-inch/38 x 25-cm jelly roll pan. Melt the chocolate in the water, stirring. Let cool slightly.

2 Place the eggs and sugar in a bowl and whisk for 10 minutes or until the mixture is pale and foamy and the whisk leaves a trail when lifted. Whisk in the chocolate in a thin stream. Sift the flour and cocoa together and fold into the mixture. Pour into the pan and smooth the top.

3 Bake in a preheated oven, 400°F/200°C, for 12 minutes. Dust a sheet of baking parchment with a little confectioners' sugar. Turn out the roulade and remove the lining paper. Roll up the roulade with the fresh parchment inside. Place on a wire rack, cover with a damp dish towel, and let cool.

4 Whisk the cream. Unroll the roulade and sprinkle over the fruit. Spread three-quarters of the cream over the roulade and re-roll. Dust with confectioners' sugar.

5 Place the roulade on a plate. Pipe the rest of the cream down the center. Make the chocolate leaves and use to decorate the roulade. Serve with strawberries.

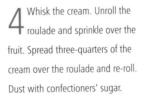

chocolate & coconut roulade

serves eight

3 eggs

⅓ cup superfine sugar

⅓ cup self-rising flour

1 tbsp block creamed coconut,
   softened with 1 tbsp boiling
   water

¼ cup shredded coconut

6 tbsp good-quality raspberry jelly

CHOCOLATE COATING

7 oz/200 g semisweet chocolate

5 tbsp butter

2 tbsp light corn syrup

RASPBERRY COULIS

8 oz/225 g fresh or frozen
   raspberries, thawed if frozen

2 tbsp water

4 tbsp confectioners' sugar

1 Grease and line a 9 x 12-inch/
23 x 30-cm jelly roll pan. Whisk
the eggs and superfine sugar in a large
mixing bowl with an electric mixer for
about 10 minutes or until the mixture
is very light and foamy and the whisk
leaves a trail that lasts a few seconds
when lifted.

2 Sift the flour and fold in with a
metal spoon or spatula. Fold in
the creamed coconut and shredded
coconut. Pour into the prepared pan
and bake in a preheated oven,
400°F/200°C, for 10–12 minutes
or until springy to the touch.

3 Sprinkle a sheet of baking
parchment with a little superfine
sugar and place on top of a damp dish
towel. Turn the cake out onto the
paper and carefully peel away the
lining parchment. Spread the raspberry
jelly over the sponge and roll up from
one of the short ends, using the dish
towel to help you. Place the roulade
seam-side down on a wire rack and let
cool completely.

4 Meanwhile, make the coating.
Melt the chocolate and butter,
stirring. Stir in the syrup and let the
mixture cool for 5 minutes. Spread it
over the roulade and let stand until set.

5 to make the coulis, blend the fruit
to a purée in a food processor
with the water and sugar, and strain to
remove the seeds. Cut the roulade into
slices and serve with the coulis and a
few fresh raspberries.

chocolate brownie roulade

serves eight

5 ½ oz/150 g semisweet chocolate,
 broken into pieces

3 tbsp water

¾ cup superfine sugar

5 eggs, separated

2 tbsp raisins, chopped

2 tbsp chopped pecans

pinch of salt

1¼ cups heavy cream, whipped
 lightly

confectioners' sugar, for dusting

1 Grease a 12 x 8-inch/30 x 20-cm
 jelly roll pan, line with baking
parchment, and grease the parchment.

2 Melt the chocolate with the water
 in a small pan over low heat until
the chocolate has just melted. Let the
chocolate cool.

3 Whisk the sugar and egg yolks In
 a bowl for 2–3 minutes with
an electric mixer until thick and pale.

4 Fold in the cooled chocolate,
 raisins, and pecans.

5 Whisk the egg whites In a
 separate bowl with the salt. Fold
one-quarter of the egg whites into the
chocolate mixture, then fold in the rest
of the whites, working lightly and
quickly so as not to lose any air.

6 Transfer the mixture to the
 prepared pan and bake in a
preheated oven, 350°F/180°C, for
25 minutes, until risen and just firm
to the touch. Let the cake cool before
covering with a sheet of non-stick
baking parchment and a damp clean
dish towel. Set aside until cold.

7 Turn the roulade out onto another
 piece of baking parchment dusted
with confectioners' sugar and remove
the lining paper.

8 Spread the cream over the
 roulade. Starting from a short
end, roll the roulade away from you
using the parchment to guide you. Trim
the ends of the roulade to make a neat
finish and transfer to a serving plate.
Chill in the refrigerator until ready to
serve. Dust with a little confectioners'
sugar before serving.

almond & hazelnut gâteau

serves eight

4 eggs

½ cup superfine sugar

½ cup ground almonds

½ cup ground hazelnuts

⅓ cup all-purpose flour

½ cup slivered almonds

FILLING

3½ oz/100 g semisweet chocolate

1 tbsp butter

1¼ cups heavy cream

confectioners' sugar, for dusting

1 Grease 2 round 7-inch/18-cm layer cake pans and line the bottoms with baking parchment.

2 Whisk the eggs and superfine sugar in a large mixing bowl with an electric mixer for about 10 minutes or until the mixture is very light and foamy and the whisk leaves a trail that lasts a few seconds when lifted.

3 Fold in the ground nuts, sift the flour and fold in with a metal spoon or spatula. Pour the mixture into the prepared pans.

4 Sprinkle the slivered almonds over the top of one of the cakes. Bake both of the cakes in a preheated oven, 375°F/190°C, for 15–20 minutes or until springy to the touch.

5 Let the cakes cool slightly in the pans. Carefully remove the cakes from the pans and transfer them to a wire rack to cool completely.

6 Meanwhile, make the filling. Melt the chocolate, remove from the heat, and stir in the butter. Let the mixture cool slightly. Whip the cream until just holding its shape, then fold in the melted chocolate until mixed.

7 Place the cake without the extra almonds on a serving plate and spread the filling over it. Let the filling set slightly, then place the almond-topped cake on top and let chill for about 1 hour. Dust the cake with confectioners' sugar and serve.

layered meringue gâteau

serves eight

6 egg whites

¾ cup superfine sugar

1½ cups confectioners' sugar

2 tbsp cornstarch

FILLING

1 cup heavy cream

5 oz/140 g semisweet chocolate

4 tsp dark rum

TO DECORATE

⅔ cup heavy cream

4 tsp superfine sugar

1–2 tsp unsweetened cocoa

1 Prepare 5 sheets of baking parchment by drawing a 7-inch/18-cm circle on each. Use them to line cookie sheets.

2 Whisk the egg whites until they form soft peaks. Mix together both sugars and cornstarch and strain it into the egg whites, a little at a time, whisking until firm peaks form.

3 Spoon the meringue mixture into a pastry bag fitted with a round tip. Starting from the center, carefully pipe 5 spirals, measuring 7 inches/ 18 cm, on each of the prepared pieces of baking parchment.

4 Bake in a preheated oven, at the lowest possible temperature with the oven door kept slightly ajar, for 6 hours or overnight.

5 After baking, carefully peel the meringue spirals from the parchment and cool on wire racks.

6 To make the filling, pour the cream into a pan and place over low heat. Break the chocolate into small pieces and add to the pan. Stir until melted. Remove from the heat and beat the mixture with a hand-held whisk. Beat in the rum, then cover with plastic wrap and chill overnight or for as long as the meringues are baking.

7 To assemble the gâteau, beat the filling with an electric mixer until thick and smooth. Place 3 of the meringue layers on a counter and spread the filling over them. Stack the 3 meringue layers, one on top of the other, and place an uncovered meringue layer on top. Crush the fifth meringue layer into crumbs.

8 To make the decoration, whip the cream with the sugar until thick. Carefully spread the cream mixture over the top of the gâteau. Sprinkle the meringue crumbs on top of the cream and dust the center of the gâteau with unsweetened cocoa. Serve within 1–2 hours.

chocolate & walnut cake

serves eight

4 eggs

½ cup superfine sugar

1 cup all-purpose flour

1 tbsp unsweetened cocoa

2 tbsp butter, melted

2¾ oz/75 g semisweet chocolate,
   melted

1¼ cups finely chopped walnuts

FROSTING

2¾ oz/75 g semisweet chocolate

½ cup butter

1¼ cups confectioners' sugar

2 tbsp milk

walnut halves, to decorate

1 Grease a deep 7-inch/18-cm round cake pan and line the bottom. Place the eggs and superfine sugar in a mixing bowl and beat with an electric mixer for 10 minutes or until the mixture is light and foamy and the whisk leaves a trail that lasts a few seconds when lifted.

2 Sift the flour together and cocoa and fold in with a metal spoon or spatula. Fold in the melted butter and chocolate, and the chopped walnuts. Pour into the prepared pan and bake in

a preheated oven, 325°F/160°C, for 30–35 minutes or until the cake is springy to the touch.

3 Let the cake cool in the pan for 5 minutes, then transfer to a wire rack to cool completely.

4 Meanwhile, make the frosting. Melt the semisweet chocolate and let it cool slightly. Beat the butter, confectioners' sugar, and milk together in a bowl until pale and fluffy. Whisk in the melted chocolate.

5 Cut the cold cake into 2 layers. Sandwich the 2 layers with some of the frosting and place on a serving plate. Spread the remaining frosting over the top of the cake with a spatula, swirling it slightly as you do so. Decorate the finished cake with the walnut halves and serve.

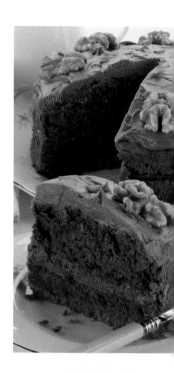

dobos torte

serves eight

3 eggs

½ cup superfine sugar

1 tsp vanilla extract

¾ cup all-purpose flour

FILLING

6 oz/175 g semisweet chocolate

¾ cup butter

2 tbsp milk

3 cups confectioners' sugar

CARAMEL

½ cup granulated sugar

4 tbsp water

1 Draw four 7-inch/18-cm circles on sheets of baking parchment. Place 2 of them upside down on 2 cookie sheets.

2 Beat the eggs and superfine sugar in a large mixing bowl with an electric mixer for 10 minutes or until light and foamy. Fold in the vanilla extract. Sift the flour and fold in.

3 Spoon one-quarter of the mixture onto one of the cookie sheets and spread out to the size of the circle. Repeat with the other circle. Bake in a preheated oven, 400°F/200°C, for 5–8 minutes. Cool on wire racks. Repeat with the remaining mixture.

4 To make the filling, melt the chocolate and cool slightly. Beat the butter, milk, and confectioners' sugar together until pale and fluffy. Whisk in the melted chocolate.

5 Place the sugar and water for the caramel in a heavy-based pan. Heat gently, stirring, to dissolve the sugar. Boil gently until pale golden in color. Remove from the heat. Pour over one cake layer as a topping. Let harden slightly, then carefully mark into 8 portions with an oiled knife.

6 Remove the cakes from the parchment. Trim the edges. Sandwich the layers together with some of the filling, finishing with the caramel-topped cake. Spread the sides with the filling, and pipe rosettes around the top.

apricot & chocolate ring

1 Grease a 10-inch/25-cm round cake pan and line the bottom with baking parchment.

2 Rub the butter into the flour until the mixture resembles fine bread crumbs. Stir in the superfine sugar, eggs, and milk to form a soft dough.

3 Roll out the dough on a lightly floured counter to form a 14-inch/35-cm square.

4 Brush the melted butter over the surface of the dough. Mix together the apricots and chocolate chips and, using a spoon or knife, spread them over the dough to within 1 inch/2.5 cm of the top and bottom.

5 Roll up the dough tightly, like a jelly roll, and cut it into 1-inch/2.5-cm slices. Stand the slices in a ring around the edge of the prepared pan at a slight tilt. Brush the surface with a little milk to glaze.

6 Bake in a preheated oven, 350°F/180°C, for 30 minutes or until cooked and golden. Let cool in the pan for about 15 minutes, then transfer to a wire rack to cool.

7 Drizzle the melted chocolate over the ring to decorate.

semisweet & white chocolate torte

serves six

4 eggs

½ cup superfine sugar

¾ cup all-purpose flour

DARK CHOCOLATE CREAM

⅔ cup heavy cream

5½ oz/150 g semisweet chocolate,
    broken into small pieces

WHITE CHOCOLATE FROSTING

2¾ oz/75 g white chocolate

1 tbsp butter

1 tbsp milk

4 tbsp confectioners' sugar

chocolate caraque (see page 263)

1   Grease an 8-inch/20-cm round
    springform cake pan and line the
bottom. Beat the eggs and superfine
sugar in a large mixing bowl with an
electric mixer for about 10 minutes
or until the mixture is very light and
foamy and the whisk leaves a trail
that lasts a few seconds when lifted.

2   Sift the flour and fold in with
    a metal spoon or spatula. Pour
into the prepared pan and bake in a
preheated oven, 350°F/180°C, for
35–40 minutes or until springy to the
touch. Let the cake cool slightly, then

transfer to a wire rack and let
cool completely.

3   While the cake is cooling, make
    the chocolate cream. Place the
cream in a pan and bring to a boil,
stirring. Add the chocolate and stir until
melted and well combined. Remove
from the heat, transfer to a bowl, and
let cool. Beat the chocolate cream with
a wooden spoon until thick.

4   Cut the cold cake into 2 layers
    horizontally. Sandwich the layers
back together with the chocolate cream
and place on a wire rack.

5   To make the frosting, melt the
    chocolate and butter together and

stir until blended. Whisk in the milk
and confectioners' sugar, and continue
whisking until cool. Pour over the cake
and spread with a spatula to coat the
top and sides. Decorate with chocolate
caraque and let the frosting set.

bistvitny torte

serves ten

CHOCOLATE TRIANGLES

1 oz/25 g semisweet chocolate,
   melted

1 oz/25 g white chocolate, melted

CAKE

¾ cup soft margarine

¾ cup superfine sugar

½ tsp vanilla extract

3 eggs, beaten lightly

2 cups self-rising flour

1¾ oz/50 g semisweet chocolate

SYRUP

½ cup granulated sugar

6 tbsp water

3 tbsp brandy or sherry

⅔ cup heavy cream

1 Grease a 9-inch/23-cm ring pan. To make the triangles, place a sheet of baking parchment onto a cookie sheet and place alternate spoonfuls of the semisweet and white chocolate onto the paper. Spread together to form a thick marbled layer, and let set. Cut into squares, then into triangles.

2 To make the cake, beat the margarine and sugar until light and fluffy. Beat in the vanilla extract. Gradually add the eggs, beating well. Fold in the flour. Divide the mixture in half. Melt the semisweet chocolate and stir into one half.

3 Place spoonfuls of each mixture into the prepared pan and swirl them together with a toothpick to create a marbled effect.

4 Bake in a preheated oven, 375°F/190°C, for 30 minutes or until the cake is springy to the touch. Let the cake cool in the pan for a few minutes, then transfer it to a wire rack and let cool completely.

5 To make the syrup, place the sugar in a small pan with the water and heat until the sugar has dissolved. Boil for 1–2 minutes. (Do not leave the pan unattended while the syrup is boiling.) Remove from the heat and stir in the brandy or sherry. Let the syrup cool slightly, then spoon it slowly all over the cake, letting it soak into the sponge. Whip the cream and pipe swirls of it on top of the cake. Decorate with the marbled chocolate triangles and serve.

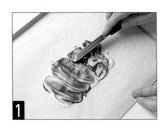

chocolate & almond torte

serves ten

8 oz/225 g semisweet chocolate,
   broken into pieces

3 tbsp water

1 cup brown sugar

¾ cup butter, softened

¼ cup ground almonds

3 tbsp self-rising flour

5 eggs, separated

⅔ cup finely chopped blanched
   almonds

confectioners' sugar, for dusting

heavy cream, to serve

COOK'S TIP

For a nuttier flavor, toast
the chopped almonds in a
dry skillet over medium
heat for about 2 minutes
until lightly golden.

1 Grease a 9-inch/23-cm loose-bottomed cake pan and line the bottom with baking parchment.

2 Melt the chocolate with the water in a pan set over very low heat, stirring until smooth. Add the sugar and stir until dissolved, taking the pan off the heat to prevent it overheating.

3 Add the butter in small amounts until it has melted into the chocolate. Remove from the heat and lightly stir in the ground almonds and flour. Add the egg yolks one at a time, beating well after each addition.

4 Whisk the egg whites in a large mixing bowl, until they stand in soft peaks, then fold them into the chocolate mixture with a metal spoon. Stir in the chopped almonds. Pour the mixture into the prepared cake pan and smooth the surface.

5 Bake in a preheated oven, 350°F/180°C, for 40–45 minutes, until well risen and firm (the cake will crack on the surface during cooking).

6 Let cool in the pan for 30–40 minutes, then turn out onto a wire rack to cool completely. Dust with confectioners' sugar and serve in slices with cream.

date & chocolate cake

serves eight

4 oz/115 g semisweet chocolate,
   broken into pieces

1 tbsp grenadine

1 tbsp light corn syrup

½ cup unsalted butter, 2 tsp extra
   for greasing

4 tbsp superfine sugar

2 large eggs

⅔ cup self-rising flour

1 tbsp extra for dusting

2 tbsp ground rice

1 tbsp confectioners' sugar,
   to decorate

FILLING

⅔ cup chopped dried dates

1 tbsp lemon juice

1 tbsp orange juice

1 tbsp raw brown sugar

¼ cup chopped blanched almonds

2 tbsp apricot jelly

1 Grease and flour two 7-inch/
18-cm layer cake pans. Put the
chocolate, grenadine, and syrup in
the top of a double boiler or in a
heatproof bowl set over a pan of barely
simmering water. Stir over low heat
until the chocolate has melted and the
mixture is smooth. Remove from the
heat and let the mixture cool.

2 Cream the butter and superfine
sugar together until pale and
fluffy, then gradually beat in the eggs,
then the cooled chocolate mixture.

3 Sift the flour into another bowl
and stir in the ground rice.
Carefully fold the flour mixture into
the creamed mixture.

4 Divide the mixture between the
prepared cake pans and smooth
the surface with a spatula. Bake in a
preheated oven, 350°F/180°C, for
20–25 minutes, until golden and firm
to the touch. Turn the cakes out onto a
wire rack to cool.

5 To make the filling, put all the
ingredients into a pan and stir
over low heat for 4–5 minutes, until
fully incorporated. Remove from the
heat, let cool, and then use the filling
to sandwich the cakes together. Dust
the top of the cake with confectioners'
sugar to decorate.

white truffle cake

serves twelve

2 eggs

4 tbsp superfine sugar

⅓ cup all-purpose flour

1¾ oz/50 g white chocolate, melted

TRUFFLE TOPPING

1¼ cups heavy cream

12 oz/350 g white chocolate,
   broken into pieces

9 oz/250 g mascarpone cheese

TO DECORATE

semisweet, light, or white chocolate
   caraque (see page 263)

unsweetened cocoa, for dusting

1 Grease an 8-inch/20-cm round
   springform cake pan and line.

2 Whisk the eggs and superfine
   sugar in a mixing bowl for
10 minutes or until the mixture is very
light and foamy and the whisk leaves
a trail that lasts a few seconds when
lifted. Sift the flour and fold in with a
metal spoon. Fold in the melted white
chocolate. Pour into the pan and bake
in a preheated oven, 350°F/180°C,
for 25 minutes or until springy to the
touch. Let cool slightly, then transfer
to a wire rack until completely cold.
Return the cold cake to the pan.

3 To make the topping, place the
   cream in a pan and bring to a
boil, stirring to prevent it sticking to the
bottom of the pan. Cool slightly, then

add the white chocolate pieces and stir
until melted and combined. Remove
from the heat and stir until almost cool,
then stir in the mascarpone cheese.
Pour the mixture on top of the cake
and let chill for 2 hours.

4 Remove the cake from the pan
   and transfer to a plate. Make the
caraque (see page 7) and then use it to
decorate the top of the cake.

chocolate & vanilla loaf

serves ten

¾ cup superfine sugar

¾ cup soft margarine

½ tsp vanilla extract

3 eggs

2 cups self-rising flour, sifted

1¾ oz/50 g semisweet chocolate

confectioners' sugar, for dusting

COOK'S TIP

Freeze the loaf undecorated
for up to 2 months. Thaw at
room temperature.

1 Lightly grease a 1-lb/450-g loaf pan and set aside.

2 Beat the sugar and soft margarine together in a bowl until the mixture is light and fluffy.

3 Beat in the vanilla extract. Gradually add the eggs, beating well after each addition. Carefully fold the flour into the mixture.

4 Divide the mixture in half. Gently melt the semisweet chocolate and stir it carefully into one half of the mixture until well combined.

5 Place the vanilla mixture in the pan and smooth the top. Spread the chocolate layer over the vanilla layer.

6 Bake in a preheated oven, 375°F/190°C, for 30 minutes or until springy to the touch.

7 Let the loaf cool in the pan for a few minutes before transferring to a wire rack to cool completely.

8 Serve the loaf dusted with confectioners' sugar.

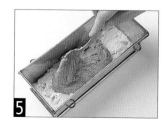

no-bake refrigerator cake

serves eight

1 cup unsalted butter, diced

8 oz/225 g semisweet chocolate,
  broken into pieces

⅓ cup chopped candied cherries

½ cup chopped walnuts

12 rectangular semisweet chocolate
  cookies

1 Line a 1-lb/450-g loaf pan with waxed paper or baking parchment. Set aside.

2 Put the butter and chocolate into the top of a double boiler or in a heatproof bowl set over a pan of barely simmering water. Stir constantly over low heat until they have melted and the mixture is smooth. Remove from the heat and cool slightly.

3 Mix the cherries and walnuts together in a bowl. Spoon one-third of the chocolate mixture into the prepared pan, cover with a layer of cookies, and top with half the cherries and walnuts. Make further layers, ending with the chocolate mixture. Cover with plastic wrap and let chill in the refrigerator for at least 12 hours. When thoroughly chilled, turn the cake out onto a serving dish.

chocolate ganache cake

serves ten

¾ cup butter

¾ cup superfine sugar

4 eggs, beaten lightly

1¾ cups self-rising flour

1 tbsp unsweetened cocoa

1¾ oz/50 g semisweet chocolate,
   melted

GANACHE

2 cups heavy cream

13 oz/375 g semisweet chocolate,
   broken into pieces

7 oz/200 g chocolate-flavored cake
   covering, to finish

1 Lightly grease an 8-inch/20-cm springform cake pan and line the bottom. Beat the butter and sugar until light and fluffy. Gradually add the eggs, beating well. Sift the flour and cocoa together. Fold into the cake mixture. Fold in the melted chocolate.

2 Pour into the prepared pan and smooth the top. Bake in a preheated oven, 350°F/180°C, for 40 minutes or until springy to the touch. Let cool for 5 minutes in the pan, then turn out onto a wire rack. Cut the cold cake into 2 layers.

3 To make the ganache, place the cream in a pan and bring to a boil, stirring. Add the chocolate and stir until melted and combined. Pour into a bowl and whisk for about 5 minutes or until the ganache is fluffy and cool.

4 Set aside one-third of the ganache. Use the remaining ganache to sandwich the cake together and spread smoothly and evenly over the top and sides of the cake.

5 Melt the cake covering and spread it over a large sheet of baking parchment. Let cool until just set. Cut into strips a little wider than the height of the cake. Place the strips around the edge of the cake, overlapping them slightly.

6 Using a pastry bag fitted with a fine tip pipe the reserved ganache in tear drops or shells to cover the top of the cake. Let the finished cake chill for 1 hour in the refrigerator before serving.

chocolate truffle cake

serves twelve

⅓ cup butter

⅓ cup superfine sugar

2 eggs, beaten lightly

⅔ cup self-rising flour

½ tsp baking powder

¼ cup unsweetened cocoa

½ cup ground almonds

TRUFFLE TOPPING

12 oz/350 g semisweet chocolate

½ cup butter

1¼ cups heavy cream

1¼ cups plain cake crumbs

3 tbsp dark rum

TO DECORATE

Cape gooseberries

1¾ oz/50 g semisweet chocolate,
   melted

1 Lightly grease an 8-inch/20-cm round springform cake pan and line the bottom. Beat the butter and sugar together until light and fluffy. Gradually add the eggs to the creamed butter and sugar, beating well after each addition.

2 Sift the flour, baking powder, and cocoa together and fold into the mixture along with the ground almonds. Pour into the prepared pan and bake in a preheated oven, 350°F/180°C, for 20–25 minutes or until springy to the touch. Let the cake cool slightly in the pan, then transfer to a wire rack to cool completely. Wash and dry the pan and return the cooled cake to the pan.

3 To make the topping, heat the chocolate, butter, and cream in a heavy-based pan over low heat and stir until smooth. Cool, then let chill for 30 minutes. Beat well with a wooden spoon and chill for another 30 minutes. Beat the mixture again, then add the cake crumbs and rum, beating until well combined. Spoon the topping over the sponge cake and let chill for 3 hours.

4 Meanwhile, dip the Cape gooseberries in the melted chocolate until partially covered. Set aside on baking parchment to set. Transfer the cake to a serving plate, decorate with the chocolate-dipped Cape gooseberries and serve.

bûche de noël

serves ten

CAKE

4 eggs

½ cup superfine sugar

⅔ cup self-rising flour

2 tbsp unsweetened cocoa

FROSTING

5½ oz/150 g semisweet chocolate

2 egg yolks

⅔ cup milk

½ cup butter

4 tbsp confectioners' sugar

2 tbsp rum, optional

TO DECORATE

a little white glacé or royal frosting

confectioners' sugar, for dusting

holly leaves

1 Grease and line a 12 x 9-inch/ 30 x 23-cm jelly roll pan.

2 Beat the eggs and superfine sugar in a bowl with an electric mixer for 10 minutes or until the mixture is very light and foamy and the whisk leaves a trail. Sift the flour and cocoa and fold in. Pour into the prepared pan and bake in a preheated oven, 400°F/200°C, for 12 minutes or until springy to the touch. Turn out onto baking parchment sprinkled with a little superfine sugar. Peel off the lining parchment and trim the edges. Cut a small slit halfway into the cake, ½ inch/ 1 cm from one of the short ends. Starting at that end, roll up tightly, enclosing the parchment. Place on a wire rack to cool.

3 To make the frosting, break the chocolate into pieces and melt in a heatproof bowl set over a pan of hot water. Beat in the egg yolks, whisk in the milk and cook stirring until the mixture thickens enough to coat the back of a wooden spoon. Cover with dampened waxed paper and cool. Beat the butter and sugar until pale. Beat in the custard and rum (if using).

4 Unroll the sponge, spread with one-third of the frosting, and roll up. Place on a serving plate. Spread the remaining frosting over the cake and mark with a fork to give the effect of bark. Let the frosting set. Pipe white frosting to form the rings of the log. Sprinkle with sugar and decorate.

chocolate bread dessert

serves four

6 thick slices white bread, crusts
 removed

scant 2 cups milk

6 fl oz/175 ml canned evaporated
 milk

2 tbsp unsweetened cocoa

2 eggs

2 tbsp brown sugar

1 tsp vanilla extract

confectioners' sugar, for dusting

HOT FUDGE SAUCE

2 oz/55 g semisweet chocolate,
 broken into pieces

1 tbsp unsweetened cocoa

2 tbsp light corn syrup

¼ cup butter or margarine

2 tbsp brown sugar

⅔ cup milk

1 tbsp cornstarch

1 Grease a shallow ovenproof dish. Cut the bread into squares and layer them in the dish.

2 Put the milk, evaporated milk, and unsweetened cocoa in a pan and heat gently, stirring occasionally, until the mixture is lukewarm.

3 Whisk the eggs, sugar, and vanilla extract together. Add the warm milk mixture and beat well.

4 Pour into the prepared dish, making sure that all the bread is completely covered. Cover the dish with plastic wrap and let chill in the refrigerator for 1–2 hours.

5 Bake the dessert in a preheated oven 350°F/180°C, for 35–40 minutes, until set. Let stand for 5 minutes.

6 To make the sauce, put all the ingredients into a pan, heat gently, stirring constantly until smooth.

7 Dust the dessert with confectioners' sugar and serve immediately with the hot fudge sauce.

chocolate layer log

serves eight

½ cup soft margarine

½ cup superfine sugar

2 eggs

¾ cup self-rising flour

¼ cup unsweetened cocoa

2 tbsp milk

WHITE CHOCOLATE BUTTER CREAM

2¾ oz/75 g white chocolate

2 tbsp milk

⅔ cup butter

¾ cup confectioners' sugar

2 tbsp orange-flavored liqueur

quick chocolate curls (see page 263),
   to decorate

1 Grease and line the sides of two 14-oz/400-g food cans.

2 Beat the margarine and sugar together in a bowl until light and fluffy. Gradually add the eggs, beating well after each addition. Sift the flour and cocoa together and fold into the cake mixture. Fold in the milk.

3 Divide the mixture between the prepared cans. Stand the cans on a cookie sheet and bake in a preheated oven, 350°F/180°C, for

40 minutes or until springy to the touch. Let cool for about 5 minutes in the cans, then turn out and cool completely on a wire rack.

4 Meanwhile, make the butter cream. Put the chocolate and milk in a pan and heat gently until the chocolate has melted, stirring until well combined. Let cool slightly. Beat the butter and confectioners' sugar together until light and fluffy. Beat in the orange liqueur. Gradually beat in the chocolate mixture.

5 Cut both cakes into ½-inch/1-cm thick slices, then reassemble them by sandwiching the slices together with some of the butter cream.

6 Place the cake on a serving plate and spread the remaining butter cream over the top and sides. Decorate with chocolate curls then serve, cut diagonally into slices.

chocolate & apricot squares

serves twelve

½ cup butter

6 oz/175 g white chocolate, chopped

4 eggs

½ cup superfine sugar

1¾ cups all-purpose flour, sifted

1 tsp baking powder

pinch of salt

3½ oz/100 g no-soak dried apricots, chopped

1 Lightly grease a 9-inch/20-cm square cake pan and line the bottom with baking parchment.

2 Melt the butter and chocolate in a heatproof bowl set over a pan of simmering water. Stir frequently with a wooden spoon until the mixture is smooth and glossy. Let the chocolate mixture cool slightly.

3 Beat the eggs and superfine sugar into the butter and chocolate mixture until well combined.

4 Fold in the flour, baking powder, salt, and chopped dried apricots, and mix together well.

5 Pour the mixture into the pan and bake in a preheated oven, 350°F/180°C, for 25–30 minutes.

6 The center of the cake may not be completely firm when you take it out of the oven, but it will set as it cools. Let it cool in the pan.

7 When the cake is completely cold turn it out of the pan and carefully slice into squares or bars to serve.

Hot Desserts

Chocolate is comforting at any time but no more so than when served in a steaming hot dessert. It is hard to think of anything more 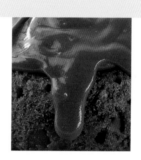 warming, comforting, and homely than tucking into a steamed hot Chocolate Fudge Dessert or a Hot Chocolate Soufflé, and children will love the chocolate Bread & Butter Dessert. In fact, there are several old favorite recipes that have been given the chocolate treatment, bringing them right up to date and putting them firmly on every chocolate lover's map.

When you are feeling in need of something a little more sophisticated, try the new-style Chocolate Apple Crêpe Stacks, or Chocolate Pear & Almond Tart, or Chocolate Zabaglione for an elegant creamy, warm dessert set to get your taste buds in a whirl!

mini chocolate gingers

serves four

generous ⅓ cup soft margarine

¾ cup self-rising flour, sifted

½ cup superfine sugar

2 eggs

¼ cup unsweetened cocoa, sifted

1 oz/25 g semisweet chocolate

1¾ oz/50 g preserved ginger

CHOCOLATE CUSTARD

2 egg yolks

1 tbsp superfine sugar

1 tbsp cornstarch

1¼ cups milk

3½ oz/100 g semisweet chocolate, broken into pieces

confectioners' sugar, for dusting

1 Lightly grease 4 small individual ovenproof bowls. Place the margarine, flour, sugar, eggs, and cocoa in a mixing bowl and beat until well combined and smooth. Chop the chocolate and preserved ginger and stir into the mixture, ensuring they are well combined.

2 Spoon the cake mixture into the prepared bowls and smooth the top. The mixture should three-quarters fill the bowls. Cover the bowls with discs of baking parchment and cover with a pleated sheet of foil. Steam the mini chocolate ginger for 45 minutes until the sponges are cooked and springy to the touch.

3 Meanwhile, make the custard. Beat the egg yolks, sugar, and cornstarch together to form a smooth paste. Heat the milk until boiling and pour over the egg mixture. Return to the pan and cook over very low heat, stirring until thick. Remove from the heat and beat in the chocolate. Stir until the chocolate melts.

4 Lift the mini chocolate gingers from the steamer, run a knife around the edge of the bowls, and carefully turn out onto serving plates. Dust each chocolate ginger with sugar and drizzle chocolate custard over the top. Serve the remaining chocolate custard separately.

chocolate queen of desserts

serves four

1¾ oz/50 g semisweet chocolate

2 cups chocolate-flavored milk

1⅔ cups fresh white bread crumbs

½ cup superfine sugar

2 eggs, separated

4 tbsp black cherry jelly

VARIATION

If you prefer, add ½ cup shredded coconut to the bread crumbs and omit the jelly.

1 Break the chocolate into small pieces and place in a pan with the chocolate-flavored milk. Heat gently, stirring until the chocolate melts. Bring almost to a boil, then remove the pan from the heat.

2 Place the bread crumbs in a large mixing bowl with 5 teaspoons of the sugar. Pour over the chocolate milk and mix well to incorporate. Beat in the egg yolks.

3 Spoon into a 5-cup pie dish and bake in a preheated oven, 350°F/180°C, for 25–30 minutes or until set and firm to the touch.

4 Whisk the egg whites in a large clean bowl until standing in soft peaks. Gradually whisk in the remaining superfine sugar and whisk until you have a glossy, thick meringue.

5 Spread the jelly over the chocolate mixture and pile the meringue on top. Return to the oven for about 15 minutes or until the meringue is crisp and golden.

322

chocolate eve's dessert

serves four

2 eating apples, peeled, cored, and
   sliced thickly

8 oz/225 g fresh or frozen
   raspberries

4 tbsp seedless raspberry jelly

2 tbsp port, optional

SPONGE TOPPING

4 tbsp soft margarine

4 tbsp superfine sugar

⅔ cup self-rising flour, sifted

1¾ oz/50 g white chocolate, grated

1 egg

2 tbsp milk

BITTER CHOCOLATE SAUCE

3 oz/85 g semisweet chocolate

⅔ cup light cream

VARIATION

Use semisweet chocolate in the
sponge and top with apricot
halves, covered with peach
schnapps and apricot jelly.

---

1 Place the apple slices and
raspberries in a shallow 5-cup
ovenproof dish and set aside while you
warm the jelly and port (if using).

2 Place the raspberry jelly and
port in a small pan and heat
gently until the jelly melts and
combines with the port. Pour the
mixture over the fruit.

3 Place all of the ingredients for the
sponge topping in a large mixing
bowl and beat thoroughly with an
electric mixer until the mixture is
completely smooth.

4 Spoon the sponge mixture over
the fruit and smooth the top. Bake
in a preheated oven, 350°F/180°C, for
40–45 minutes or until the sponge is
springy to the touch.

5 To make the sauce, break the
chocolate into small pieces and
place in a heavy-based pan with the
cream. Heat gently, beating until a
smooth sauce is formed. Serve the
sauce warm with the dessert.

bread & butter dessert

serves four

8 oz/225 g brioche

1 tbsp butter

⅓ cup semisweet chocolate chips

1 egg, plus 2 egg yolks

4 tbsp superfine sugar

15 fl oz/425 ml canned light
evaporated milk

1 Cut the brioche into thin slices using a sharp knife. Lightly butter one side of each brioche slice.

2 Place a layer of brioche, buttered-side down, in the bottom of a shallow ovenproof dish. Sprinkle a few chocolate chips over the top.

3 Continue layering the brioche and chocolate chips, finishing with a layer of bread on top.

VARIATION

For a double chocolate dessert, heat the milk with 1 tablespoon of unsweetened cocoa, stirring until dissolved. Continue from step 4.

4 Whisk the egg, egg yolks, and sugar together until well combined. Heat the milk in a small pan until it just starts to simmer. Gradually add to the egg mixture, whisking well.

5 Pour the custard over the bread and let stand for 5 minutes. Press the brioche down into the milk.

6 Place the dessert in a roasting pan and fill with boiling water to come halfway up the side of the dish (this is known as a bain-marie). Bake in a preheated oven, 350°F/180°C, for 30 minutes or until the custard has set. Let the dessert cool for about 5 minutes before serving.

chocolate fruit crumble

serves four

14 oz/400 g canned apricots in
   fruit juice

1 lb/450 g tart cooking apples,
   peeled and sliced thickly

¾ cup all-purpose flour

6 tbsp butter

⅔ cup porridge oats

4 tbsp superfine sugar

⅔ cup semisweet chocolate chips

VARIATION

Other fruits can be used to make
this crumble—fresh pears mixed
with fresh or frozen raspberries
work well. If you do not use
canned fruit, add 4 tablespoons
of orange juice to the fresh fruit.

1 Lightly grease an ovenproof dish
with a little butter.

2 Drain the apricots, reserving
4 tablespoons of the juice. Place
the apples and apricots in the prepared
ovenproof dish with the reserved
apricot juice and toss to mix.

3 Sift the flour into a mixing bowl.
Cut the butter into small cubes
and rub in with your fingertips until the
mixture resembles fine bread crumbs.
Stir in the porridge oats, sugar, and
chocolate chips.

4 Sprinkle the crumble mixture over
the apples and apricots and
smooth the top roughly. Do not press
the crumble into the fruit.

5 Bake in a preheated oven,
350°F/180°C, for 40–45 minutes
or until the topping is golden. Serve
the crumble hot or cold.

chocolate & banana crêpes

serves four

3 large bananas

6 tbsp orange juice

grated rind of 1 orange

2 tbsp orange- or banana-flavored
   liqueur

HOT CHOCOLATE SAUCE

1 tbsp unsweetened cocoa

2 tsp cornstarch

3 tbsp milk

1½ oz/40 g semisweet chocolate

1 tbsp butter

½ cup light corn syrup

¼ tsp vanilla extract

CRÊPES

¾ cup all-purpose flour

1 tbsp unsweetened cocoa

1 egg

1 tsp corn oil

1¼ cups milk

oil, for cooking

1 Peel and slice the bananas and arrange them in a dish with the orange juice and rind and the liqueur. Set the bananas aside.

2 Mix the cocoa and cornstarch in a bowl, then stir in the milk. Break the semisweet chocolate into pieces and place in a pan with the butter and light corn syrup. Heat gently, stirring until well blended. Add the cocoa mixture and bring to a boil over gentle heat, stirring. Simmer for 1 minute, then remove from the heat and stir in the vanilla extract.

3 To make the crêpes, sift the flour and cocoa into a mixing bowl and make a well in the center. Add the egg and oil. Gradually whisk in the milk to form a smooth batter. Heat a little oil in a heavy-based skillet and pour off any excess. Pour in a little batter and tilt the pan to coat the bottom. Cook over medium heat until the underside is browned. Flip over and cook the other side. Slide the crêpe out of the skillet and keep warm. Repeat until all the crêpe batter has been used. Keep the crêpes warm.

4 To serve, re-heat the chocolate sauce for 1–2 minutes. Fill the crêpes with the bananas and fold in half or into triangles. Pour a little chocolate sauce over the crêpes and serve immediately.

326

chocolate fudge dessert

serves six

generous ⅓ cup soft margarine

1¼ cups self-rising flour

½ cup light corn syrup

3 eggs

¼ cup unsweetened cocoa

CHOCOLATE FUDGE SAUCE

3½ oz/100 g semisweet chocolate

½ cup condensed milk

4 tbsp heavy cream

1 Lightly grease a 5-cup heatproof bowl.

2 Place the ingredients for the sponge in a separate mixing bowl and beat until well combined and smooth.

3 Spoon into the prepared bowl and smooth the top. Cover with a disk of waxed paper and tie a pleated sheet of foil over the bowl. Steam for 1½–2 hours, until the sponge is cooked and springy to the touch.

4 To make the sauce, break the chocolate into small pieces and place in a small pan with the condensed milk. Heat gently, stirring until the chocolate melts.

5 Remove the pan from the heat and stir in the cream.

6 To serve the dessert, turn it out onto a serving plate and pour over a little of the chocolate fudge sauce. Serve the remaining sauce separately.

331

chocolate meringue pie

serves six

8 oz/225 g semisweet chocolate
  graham crackers

4 tbsp butter

FILLING

3 egg yolks

4 tbsp superfine sugar

4 tbsp cornstarch

2½ cups milk

3½ oz/100 g semisweet chocolate,
  melted

MERINGUE

2 egg whites

½ cup superfine sugar

¼ tsp vanilla extract

1 Place the graham crackers in a plastic bag and crush with a rolling pin. Pour into a mixing bowl. Melt the butter and stir it into the cracker crumbs until well mixed. Press the mixture firmly into the bottom and up the sides of a 23-cm/9-inch tart pan or dish.

2 To make the filling, beat the egg yolks, superfine sugar, and cornstarch in a large bowl until they form a smooth paste, adding a little of the milk if necessary. Heat the milk until almost boiling, then slowly pour it onto the egg mixture, whisking well.

3 Return the mixture to the pan and cook gently, whisking constantly, until it thickens. Remove from the heat. Whisk in the melted chocolate, then pour it onto the graham cracker pie shell. Smooth out the filling.

4 To make the meringue, whisk the egg whites in a large mixing bowl until standing in soft peaks. Gradually whisk in about two-thirds of the sugar until the mixture is stiff and glossy. Fold the remaining sugar and vanilla extract into the meringue.

5 Spread the meringue over the filling, swirling the surface with the back of a spoon to give it an attractive finish. Bake in the center of a preheated oven, 325°F/160°C, for 30 minutes or until the meringue is golden. Serve the pie hot or just warm.

apple crêpe stacks

serves four

2 cups all-purpose flour

1½ tsp baking powder

4 tbsp superfine sugar

1 egg

1 tbsp butter, melted

1¼ cups milk

1 eating apple

⅓ cup semisweet chocolate chips

Chocolate Sauce (see page 338) or

maple syrup, to serve

COOK'S TIP

To keep the cooked crêpes
warm, pile them on top of each
other with waxed paper in
between to prevent them from
sticking to one another.

1 Sift the flour and baking powder into a mixing bowl. Stir in the superfine sugar. Make a well in the center and add the egg and melted butter. Gradually whisk in the milk to form a smooth batter.

2 Peel, core, and grate the apple and stir it into the batter together with the chocolate chips.

3 Heat a griddle pan or heavy-based skillet over medium heat and grease it lightly. For each crêpe, place about 2 tablespoons of the batter onto the griddle or skillet and spread to make a 3-inch/7.5-cm circle.

4 Cook for a few minutes until you see bubbles appear on the surface of the crêpe. Turn over and cook for another minute. Remove from the pan and keep warm. Repeat with the remaining batter to make about 12 crêpes.

5 To serve, stack 3 or 4 crêpes on an individual serving plate and serve them with the Chocolate Sauce, or maple syrup.

chocolate fondue

serves four

CHOCOLATE FONDUE

8 oz/225 g semisweet chocolate

generous ¾ cup heavy cream

2 tbsp brandy

TO SERVE

selection of fruit

white and pink marshmallows

sweet cookies

1 Break the chocolate into small pieces and place in a small pan with the cream.

2 Heat the mixture gently, stirring constantly, until the chocolate has melted and blended with the cream.

3 Remove the pan from the heat and stir in the brandy.

4 Pour into a fondue pot or a small flameproof dish and keep warm, preferably over a small burner.

5 Serve with a selection of fruit, marshmallows, and cookies for dipping. The fruit and marshmallows can be spiked on fondue forks, wooden skewers, or ordinary forks.

COOK'S TIP

To prepare the fruit for dipping, cut larger fruit into bite-size pieces. Fruit that discolors, such as bananas, apples, and pears, should be dipped in a little lemon juice as soon as it is cut.

chocolate ravioli

serves four

1½ cups all-purpose flour

4 tbsp unsweetened cocoa

2 tbsp confectioners' sugar

2 eggs, beaten lightly, plus 1 extra
   beaten egg for brushing

1 tbsp vegetable oil

FILLING

6 oz/175 g white chocolate, broken
   into pieces

1 cup mascarpone cheese

1 egg

1 tbsp finely chopped preserved
   ginger

fresh mint sprigs, to decorate

heavy cream, to serve

1 Sift the flour, cocoa, and sugar together onto a clean counter. Make a well in the center and pour the 2 beaten eggs and the oil into it. Gradually draw in the flour with your fingertips until it is fully incorporated. Alternatively, sift the flour, cocoa, and sugar into a food processor, add the eggs and oil and process until mixed. Knead the dough until it is smooth and elastic, then cover with plastic wrap and place in the refrigerator for 30 minutes to chill.

2 Meanwhile, to make the filling, put the white chocolate in the top of a double boiler or in a heatproof bowl set over a pan of barely simmering water. When the chocolate has melted, remove it from the heat and let cool slightly, then beat in the mascarpone cheese and the egg. Stir in the preserved ginger.

3 Remove the pasta dough from the refrigerator, cut it in half, and keep one half tightly wrapped in plastic wrap. Roll out the first half of the dough into a rectangle on a lightly floured counter, then cover with a clean, damp dish towel. Roll out the other half into a rectangle. Spoon the chocolate and ginger filling into a pastry bag and pipe small mounds in even rows at intervals of about 1½ inches/4 cm over 1 dough rectangle. Brush the spaces between the mounds with beaten egg, then, using a rolling pin to lift it, position

the second dough rectangle on top of the first. Press firmly between the mounds with your finger to seal and push out any pockets of air. Cut the dough into squares around the mounds using a serrated ravioli or dough cutter or a sharp knife. Transfer the ravioli to a lightly floured dish towel and let rest for 30 minutes.

4 Bring a large pan of water to a boil, then lower the heat to medium and cook the ravioli, in batches, stirring to prevent them from sticking together, for 4–5 minutes, until tender, but still firm to the bite. Remove with a slotted spoon. Serve immediately on individual plates, garnished with mint sprigs, and hand the cream separately.

saucy chocolate dessert

serves four

1¼ cups milk

2¾ oz/75 g semisweet chocolate

½ tsp vanilla extract

½ cup superfine sugar

generous ⅓ cup butter

1¼ cups self-rising flour

2 tbsp unsweetened cocoa

confectioners' sugar, for dusting

CHOCOLATE SAUCE

3 tbsp unsweetened cocoa

⅓ cup brown sugar

1¼ cups boiling water

1 Lightly grease a 3¾-cup ovenproof dish with butter.

2 Place the milk in a small pan. Break the chocolate into small pieces and add to the milk. Heat gently, stirring until the chocolate melts. Let the mixture cool slightly. Stir in the vanilla extract.

3 Beat the superfine sugar and butter together in a bowl until light and fluffy. Sift the flour and cocoa together. Add to the bowl with the chocolate milk and beat until smooth. Pour into the prepared dish.

4 To make the chocolate sauce, mix the cocoa and sugar together in a small bowl. Add a little boiling water to the mixture and stir to a smooth paste, then stir in the remaining boiling water. Carefully pour the chocolate sauce over the surface of the dessert mixture but do not mix in.

5 Place the dish on a cookie sheet and bake in a preheated oven, 350°F/180°C, for 40 minutes or until the dessert is dry on top and springy to the touch. Let the dessert stand for about 5 minutes, then dust lightly with a little confectioners' sugar just before serving.

pecan fudge ring

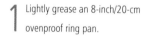

serves six

FUDGE SAUCE

3 tbsp butter

3 tbsp brown sugar

4 tbsp light corn syrup

2 tbsp milk

1 tbsp unsweetened cocoa

1½ oz/40 g semisweet chocolate

⅓ cup finely chopped pecan nuts

CAKE

generous ⅓ cup soft margarine

⅔ cup brown sugar

1 cup self-rising flour

2 eggs

2 tbsp milk

1 tbsp light corn syrup

1 Lightly grease an 8-inch/20-cm ovenproof ring pan.

2 To make the fudge sauce, place the butter, sugar, syrup, milk, and cocoa in a small pan and heat gently, stirring until combined.

3 Break the chocolate into pieces, add to the mixture and stir until melted. Stir in the chopped nuts. Pour into the bottom of the pan and let cool.

4 To make the cake, place all of the ingredients in a large mixing bowl and beat thoroughly until smooth. Carefully spoon the cake mixture over the chocolate fudge sauce in the bottom of the pan.

5 Bake in a preheated oven, 350°F/180°C, for 35 minutes or until the cake is springy to the touch.

6 Let the fudge ring cool in the pan for 5 minutes, then turn out onto a serving plate and serve.

hot chocolate soufflé

serves four

3½ oz/100 g semisweet chocolate

1¼ cups milk

2 tbsp butter

4 large eggs, separated

1 tbsp cornstarch

4 tbsp superfine sugar

½ tsp vanilla extract

⅔ cup semisweet chocolate chips

superfine and confectioners' sugar,
    for dusting

CHOCOLATE CUSTARD

2 tbsp cornstarch

1 tbsp superfine sugar

2 cups milk

1¾ oz/50 g semisweet chocolate

1 Grease a 5-cup soufflé dish and sprinkle with superfine sugar. Break the chocolate into pieces.

2 Heat the milk with the butter in a pan until almost boiling. Mix the egg yolks, cornstarch, and superfine sugar in a bowl and pour on some of the hot milk, whisking. Return it to the pan and cook gently, stirring constantly, until thickened. Add the chocolate and stir until melted. Remove from the heat and stir in the extract.

3 Whisk the egg whites until standing in soft peaks. Fold half of the egg whites into the chocolate mixture. Fold in the rest with the chocolate chips. Pour into the dish and bake in a preheated oven, 350°F/180°C, for 40–45 minutes, until well risen.

4 Meanwhile, make the custard. Put the cornstarch and sugar in a small bowl and mix to a smooth paste with a little of the milk. Heat the remaining milk until almost boiling. Pour a little of the hot milk onto the cornstarch, mix well, then pour back into the pan. Cook gently, stirring until thickened. Break the chocolate into pieces and add to the custard, stirring gently until melted.

5 Dust the soufflé with sugar and serve immediately with the chocolate custard.

fudge dessert

serves four

4 tbsp margarine

½ cup brown sugar

2 eggs, beaten

1¼ cups milk

⅓ cup chopped walnuts

¼ cup all-purpose flour

2 tbsp unsweetened cocoa

confectioners' sugar and
    unsweetened cocoa, for dusting

1 Lightly grease a 4-cup ovenproof dish. Set aside.

2 Cream the margarine and sugar together in a large mixing bowl until fluffy. Beat in the eggs.

3 Gradually stir in the milk and add the walnuts.

4 Sift the flour and cocoa into the mixture and fold in gently with a metal spoon, until well mixed.

5 Spoon the mixture into the dish and cook in a preheated oven, 350°F/180°C, for 35–40 minutes or until the sponge is cooked.

6 Dust with confectioners' sugar and cocoa and serve.

chocolate zabaglione

serves four

4 egg yolks

4 tbsp superfine sugar

1¾ oz/50 g semisweet chocolate

½ cup Marsala wine

unsweetened cocoa, for dusting

COOK'S TIP

Make the dessert just before serving as it will separate if you let it stand. If it starts to curdle, remove it from the heat immediately and place it in a bowl of cold water to stop the cooking. Whisk the chocolate zabaglione furiously until the mixture comes together.

1 Whisk the egg yolks and superfine sugar together in a mixing bowl until you have a very pale mixture, using an electric mixer.

2 Grate the chocolate finely and fold into the egg yolk and superfine sugar mixture.

3 Fold the Marsala wine into the chocolate mixture.

4 Place the mixing bowl over a pan of gently simmering water and set the electric whisk on the lowest speed or change to a hand-held balloon whisk. Cook gently, whisking constantly until the mixture thickens. Take care not to overcook or the mixture will curdle. If this happens, follow the Cook's Tip.

5 Spoon the hot mixture into warmed individual glass dishes or coffee cups (as here) and dust with cocoa. Serve the zabaglione as soon as possible after you make it so that it is still warm, light, and fluffy.

steamed coffee sponge

serves four

2 tbsp margarine

2 tbsp brown sugar

2 eggs

⅓ cup all-purpose flour

¾ tsp baking powder

6 tbsp milk

1 tsp coffee extract

SAUCE

1¼ cups milk

1 tbsp brown sugar

1 tsp unsweetened cocoa

2 tbsp cornstarch

1 Lightly grease a 2½-cup heatproof bowl. Cream the margarine and sugar until fluffy and beat in the eggs.

2 Gradually stir the flour and baking powder and then the milk and coffee extract into the margarine and sugar, to make a smooth batter.

3 Spoon the mixture into the prepared heatproof bowl and cover with a pleated piece of baking parchment and then a pleated piece of foil, securing around the bowl with string. Place in a steamer or large pan and half fill with boiling water. Cover and steam for 1–1¼ hours or until cooked through.

4 To make the sauce, put the milk, soft brown sugar, and cocoa in a pan and heat until the sugar dissolves. Blend the cornstarch with 4 tablespoons of cold water to make a paste and stir into the pan. Bring to a boil, stirring until thickened. Cook over gentle heat for 1 minute.

5 Turn the coffee sponge carefully out onto a serving plate and spoon the chocolate sauce over the top. Serve.

COOK'S TIP

The sponge is covered with pleated paper and foil to allow it to rise. The foil will react with the steam and must therefore not be placed directly against the sponge.

chocolate dessert with rum

serves four

4 tbsp unsalted butter

1¼ cups self-rising flour

2 oz/55 g semisweet chocolate

¼ tsp vanilla extract

scant ⅔ cup superfine sugar

2 eggs, beaten lightly

5 tbsp milk

SAUCE

1¼ cups milk

2 tbsp cornstarch

2 tbsp superfine sugar

2 tbsp dark rum

1 Grease and flour a 5-cup ovenproof bowl. Put the butter, chocolate, and vanilla in the top of a double boiler or a heatproof bowl set over a pan of barely simmering water. Heat gently until melted, then remove from the heat and cool slightly. Stir the sugar into the chocolate mixture, then beat in the eggs. Sift in the flour, stir in the milk, and mix well. Pour the mixture into the prepared ovenproof bowl, cover the top with a pleated piece of foil, and tie with string. Steam for 1 hour, topping off with boiling water if necessary.

2 To make the sauce, pour the milk into a small pan set over medium heat. Stir in the cornstarch, then stir in the sugar until dissolved. Bring to a boil, stirring constantly, then lower the heat and let simmer until thickened and smooth. Remove from the heat and stir in the rum.

3 To serve, remove the sponge from the heat and discard the foil. Run a round-bladed knife around the side of the bowl, place a serving plate on top of the sponge, and, holding them together, carefully invert. Serve the dessert immediately, handing the rum sauce separately.

345

sticky chocolate sponges

serves six

½ cup butter, softened

1 cup brown sugar

3 eggs, beaten

pinch of salt

¼ cup unsweetened cocoa

1 cup self-rising flour

1 oz/25 g semisweet chocolate,
    chopped finely

2¾ oz/75 g white chocolate,
    chopped finely

SAUCE

⅔ cup heavy cream

½ cup brown sugar

2 tbsp butter

1 Lightly grease 6 individual ¾-cup
individual dessert molds.

2 Cream the butter and sugar
together in a bowl until pale and
fluffy. Beat in the eggs a little at a time,
beating well after each addition.

3 Sift the salt, cocoa, and flour into
the creamed mixture, and fold
through the mixture. Stir the chopped
chocolate into the mixture until evenly
combined throughout.

4 Divide the mixture between the
prepared molds. Lightly grease
6 squares of foil and use them to cover
the tops of the molds. Press around the
edges to seal them.

5 Place the molds in a roasting pan
and pour in boiling water to come
halfway up the sides of the molds.

6 Bake in a preheated oven,
350°F/180°C, for 50 minutes or
until a skewer inserted into the center
of the sponges comes out clean.

7 Remove the molds from the
roasting pan and set aside while
you prepare the sauce.

8 To make the sauce, put the
cream, sugar, and butter into a
pan and bring to a boil over gentle
heat. Simmer gently until the sugar
has completely dissolved.

9 To serve, run a knife around the
edge of each sponge, then turn
out onto serving plates. Pour the sauce
over the top of the chocolate sponges
and serve immediately.

tropical fruit kabobs

serves four

DIP

4½ oz/125 g semisweet chocolate,
broken into pieces

2 tbsp light corn syrup

1 tbsp unsweetened cocoa

1 tbsp cornstarch

generous ¾ cup milk

KABOBS

1 mango

1 papaya

2 kiwifruit

½ small pineapple

1 large banana

2 tbsp lemon juice

⅔ cup white rum

1 Put all the ingredients for the chocolate dip into a heavy-based pan. Heat over the barbecue grill or over low heat, stirring constantly, until thickened and smooth. Keep warm at the edge of the barbecue grill.

2 Slice the mango on each side of its large, flat pit. Cut the flesh into chunks, removing the peel. Halve, seed, and peel the papaya and cut it into chunks. Peel the kiwifruit and slice into chunks. Peel and cut the pineapple into chunks. Peel and slice the banana and dip the pieces in the lemon juice, turning them to coat evenly, to prevent it from discoloring.

3 Thread the pieces of fruit alternately onto 4 skewers. Place them in a shallow dish and pour over the rum. Set aside to soak up the flavor of the rum for at least 30 minutes, until ready to cook.

4 Cook the kabobs over the hot coals, turning frequently, for about 2 minutes, until seared. Serve, accompanied by the hot chocolate dip.

stuffed nectarines

serves six

3 oz/85 g bittersweet chocolate,
    chopped finely

1 cup amaretti cookie crumbs

1 tsp finely grated lemon rind

1 large egg, separated

6 tbsp Amaretto liqueur

6 nectarines, halved and pitted

1¼ cups white wine

2 oz/55 g light chocolate, grated

whipped cream or ice cream, to
    serve

1 Mix the chocolate, amaretti crumbs and lemon rind together in a large bowl. Lightly beat the egg white and add it to the mixture with half the Amaretto liqueur. Using a small sharp knife, slightly enlarge the cavities in the nectarines. Add the removed nectarine flesh to the chocolate and crumb mixture and mix together well.

2 Preheat the oven to 375°F/190°C. Place the nectarines, cut-side up, in an ovenproof dish just large enough to hold them in a single layer. Pile the chocolate and crumb mixture into the cavities, dividing it equally among them. Mix the wine and remaining Amaretto and pour it into the dish around the nectarines. Bake in a

preheated oven for 40–45 minutes, until the nectarines are tender. Transfer 2 nectarine halves to each individual serving plate and spoon over a little of the cooking juices. Sprinkle over the grated light chocolate and serve the nectarines immediately with whipped cream or, if you prefer, vanilla or chocolate ice cream.

banana empanadas

serves four

about 8 sheets of phyllo pastry, cut
into half lengthwise

melted butter, for brushing

2 ripe sweet bananas

1–2 tsp sugar

juice of ½ lemon

6–7 oz/175–200 g semisweet
chocolate, broken into pieces

confectioners' sugar and ground
cinnamon, for dusting

COOK'S TIP

You could use ready-made puff
pie dough instead of phyllo for
a more puffed-up effect.

1 Working one at a time, lay a long
rectangular sheet of phyllo pastry
out in front of you and then brush it all
over with butter.

2 Peel and dice the bananas and
place in a bowl. Add the sugar
and lemon juice and stir well to
combine. Stir in the chocolate.

3 Place 2 teaspoons of the banana
and chocolate mixture in one
corner of the phyllo pastry, then fold
over into a triangle shape to enclose
the filling. Continue to fold in a
triangular shape, until the pastry is
completely wrapped around the filling.

4 Dust the parcels with
confectioners' sugar and
cinnamon. Place them on a cookie
sheet and continue the process with
the remaining phyllo pastry and
banana or chocolate filling.

5 Bake in a preheated oven,
375°F/190°C, for 15 minutes or
until the empanadas are golden.
Remove from the oven and serve
immediately—warn people that the
filling is very hot.

chocolate fudge pears

serves four

4 pears

1–2 tbsp lemon juice

1¼ cups water

5 tbsp superfine sugar

2-inch/5-cm piece of cinnamon stick

2 cloves

scant 1 cup heavy cream

½ cup milk

scant 1 cup brown sugar

2 tbsp unsalted butter, diced

2 tbsp maple syrup

7 oz/200 g semisweet chocolate,
  broken into pieces

1 Peel the pears using a swivel vegetable peeler. Carefully cut out the cores from underneath, but leave the stalks intact because they look more attractive. Brush the pears with the lemon juice to prevent discoloration.

2 Pour the water into a large, heavy-based pan and add the superfine sugar. Stir over low heat until the sugar has dissolved. Add the pears, cinnamon, and cloves and bring to a boil. (Add a little more water if the pears are not almost covered.) Lower the heat and simmer for 20 minutes.

3 Meanwhile, pour the cream and milk into another heavy-based pan and add the brown sugar, butter, and maple syrup. Stir over low heat until the sugar has dissolved and the butter has melted. Bring to a boil, then boil, stirring, for 5 minutes, until thick and smooth. Remove from the heat and stir in the chocolate, a little at a time, waiting until each batch has melted before adding the next. Set aside.

4 Transfer the pears to serving plates. Bring the poaching syrup back to a boil and cook until reduced. Discard the cinnamon and cloves, then fold the syrup into the chocolate sauce. Pour over the pears and serve.

chocolate crêpes

serves six

⅔ cup all-purpose flour

1 tbsp unsweetened cocoa

1 tsp superfine sugar

2 eggs, beaten lightly

¾ cup milk

2 tsp dark rum

6 tbsp sweet butter

confectioners' sugar, for dusting

FILLING

5 tbsp heavy cream

8 oz/225 g semisweet chocolate

3 eggs, separated

2 tbsp superfine sugar

BERRY SAUCE

2 tbsp butter

4 tbsp superfine sugar

⅔ cup orange juice

2 cups mixed berries, such as
    raspberries, blackberries, and
    strawberries

3 tbsp white rum

1 To make the batter for the chocolate crêpes, sift the flour, cocoa, and superfine sugar into a bowl. Make a well in the center and add the eggs, beating them in a little at a time. Add the milk and beat until smooth. Stir in the rum.

2 Melt all the butter and stir 2 tablespoonfuls into the batter. Cover with plastic wrap and let stand for 30 minutes.

3 To cook the crêpes, brush the bottom of a 7-inch/18-cm crêpe pan or non-stick skillet with melted butter and set over medium heat. Stir the batter and pour 3 tablespoonfuls into the pan, swirling it to cover. Cook for 2 minutes or until the underside is golden, flip over, cook for 30 seconds, then slide on to a plate. Cook another 11 crêpes and stack interleaved with baking parchment.

4 For the filling, pour the cream into a heavy-based pan, add the chocolate and melt over low heat, stirring. Remove from the heat. Beat the egg yolks with half of the superfine sugar in a bowl until creamy, then beat in the chocolate cream.

5 Whisk the egg whites in a separate bowl until soft peaks form, add the rest of the superfine sugar and beat into stiff peaks. Stir a spoonful of the whites into the chocolate mixture, then fold the mixture into the remaining egg whites.

6 Brush a cookie sheet with melted butter. Spread 1 crêpe with 1 tablespoon of the filling, then fold it in half and in half again to make a triangle. Place on the cookie sheet. Repeat with the remaining crêpes. Brush the tops with the remaining melted butter and bake in a preheated oven 400°F/200°C for 20 minutes.

7 For the berry sauce, melt the butter in a heavy-based skillet over low heat, stir in the sugar, and cook until golden. Stir in the orange juice and cook until syrupy. Add the mixed berries to the pan and warm through, stirring gently. Add the rum, heat gently for 1 minute, then ignite. Shake the pan until the flames have died down. Transfer the flambéed crêpes to serving plates, and dust with confectioner's sugar. Add a little of the sauce and serve immediately.

chocolate cranberry sponge

serves four

4 tbsp unsalted butter

4 tbsp brown sugar, plus 2 tsp extra
    for sprinkling

¾ cup cranberries, thawed if frozen

1 large tart cooking apple

2 eggs, beaten lightly

⅔ cup self-rising flour

3 tbsp unsweetened cocoa

SAUCE

6 oz/175 g semisweet chocolate,
    broken into pieces

1¾ cups canned evaporated milk

1 tsp vanilla extract

½ tsp almond extract

1 Grease a 5-cup ovenproof bowl,
sprinkle with brown sugar to coat
the sides, and tip out any excess. Put
the cranberries in a bowl. Peel, core,
and dice the apple and mix with the
cranberries. Put the fruit into the
prepared ovenproof bowl.

2 Place the butter, brown sugar, and
eggs in a large bowl. Sift in the
flour and cocoa and beat well until
thoroughly mixed. Pour the mixture
into the ovenproof bowl on top of the
fruit, cover the top with a pleated piece
of foil, and tie with string. Steam for
about 1 hour, until risen, topping off
with boiling water if necessary.

3 Meanwhile, to make the sauce,
put the semisweet chocolate and
milk into the top of a double boiler or a
heatproof bowl set over a pan of
barely simmering water. Stir until the
chocolate has melted, then remove
from the heat. Whisk in the vanilla and
almond extracts and continue to beat
until the sauce is thick and smooth.

4 To serve, remove the sponge from
the heat and discard the foil. Run
a round-bladed knife around the side
of the bowl, place a serving plate on
top of the sponge and, holding them
together, carefully invert. Serve the
sponge immediately, handing the
sauce separately.

chocolate castle puddings

serves four

3 tbsp butter

3 tbsp superfine sugar

1 large egg, beaten lightly

⅔ cup self-rising flour

2 oz/55 g semisweet chocolate,
    melted

SAUCE

2 tbsp unsweetened cocoa

2 tbsp cornstarch

⅔ cup light cream

1¼ cups milk

1–2 tbsp brown sugar

1 Grease 4 muffin cups or small heatproof bowls. In a mixing bowl, cream the butter and sugar together until pale and fluffy. Gradually add the egg, beating well after each addition.

2 Sift the flour into a separate bowl, fold it into the butter mixture with a metal spoon, then stir in the melted chocolate. Divide the mixture among the muffin cups, filling them to about two-thirds full to allow for expansion during cooking. Cover each cup with a circle of foil, and tie in place with string.

3 Bring a large pan of water to a boil and set a steamer over it. Place the muffin cups in the steamer and cook for 40 minutes. Check the water level from time to time and top off with boiling water necessary. Do not allow the pan to boil dry.

4 To make the sauce, put the cocoa, cornstarch, cream, and milk in a heavy-based pan. Bring to a boil, then lower the heat and simmer over low heat, whisking constantly, until thick and smooth. Cook for another 2–3 minutes, then stir in brown sugar to taste. Pour the sauce into a pitcher.

5 Lift the muffin cups out of the steamer and remove the foil circles from them. Run a knife blade around the sides of the cups and turn out the chocolate castles onto warmed individual plates. Serve immediately, handing the sauce separately.

italian drowned ice cream

serves four

2 cups freshly made espresso coffee

chocolate-coated coffee beans, to
    decorate

VANILLA ICE CREAM

1 vanilla bean

6 large egg yolks

²/₃ cup superfine sugar, or vanilla-
    flavored sugar (sugar that has
    been stored with a vanilla bean)

2¼ cups milk

1 cup plus 2 tbsp heavy cream

1 To make the vanilla ice cream, slit
the vanilla bean lengthwise and
using a knife scrape out the tiny brown
seeds. Set aside.

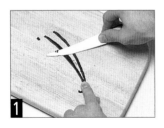

2 Put the yolks and sugar into a
heatproof bowl that will sit over
a pan with plenty of room underneath.
Beat the eggs and sugar together until
thick and creamy.

3 Put the milk, cream, and vanilla
pods in the pan over low heat
and bring to a simmer. Pour the milk
over the egg mixture, whisking. Pour
1 inch/2.5 cm of water in the bottom of
a pan. Place the bowl on top, ensuring
that the base does not touch the water.
Turn the heat to medium–high.

4 Cook the mixture, stirring
constantly, until it is thick enough
to coat the back of the spoon. Remove
the pan from the heat, transfer the
mixture to a bowl, and let cool.

5 Churn the mixture in an
ice-cream maker, following
the manufacturer's instructions.
Alternatively, place it in a freezerproof
container and freeze for 1 hour. Turn
out into a bowl and whisk to break up
the ice crystals, then return to the
freezer. Repeat the process 4 times at
30-minute intervals.

6 Transfer the ice cream to a
freezerproof bowl, smooth the
top, and cover with plastic wrap or
foil. Freeze for up to 3 months.

7 Let soften in the refrigerator for
20 minutes before serving.
Place scoops of ice cream in each
bowl. Pour over coffee and sprinkle
with coffee beans.

french chocolate sauce

makes ⅔ cup

6 tbsp heavy cream

3 oz/85 g semisweet chocolate,
 broken into small pieces

2 tbsp orange-flavored liqueur

1 Bring the cream gently to a boil in a small, heavy-based pan over low heat. Remove the pan from the heat, add the chocolate and stir the sauce until smooth.

2 Stir in the orange-flavored liqueur and serve immediately. Alternatively, if you prefer, keep the sauce warm until required.

Cold Desserts

Cool, creamy, sumptuous, and indulgent are just a few of the words that spring to mind when you think of cold chocolate desserts. The desserts contained in this chapter are a combination of all of these.

Some of the desserts are surprisingly quick and simple to make, while others are more elaborate. One of the best things about these desserts is that they can all be made in advance, sometimes days before you need them, making them perfect for entertaining. A quick decoration when necessary is all that is needed on the day. Even the Baked Chocolate Alaska can be assembled in advance and popped into the oven just before serving.

iced white chocolate terrine

serves eight

2 tbsp granulated sugar

5 tbsp water

10½ oz/300 g white chocolate

3 eggs, separated

1¼ cups heavy cream

COOK'S TIP

To make a coulis, place 8 oz/
225 g soft fruit of your choice,
such as strawberries or mangoes
in a food processor. Add 1–2
tablespoons of confectioners'
sugar and blend. If the fruit
contains seeds, push the mixture
through a strainer. Serve chilled.

1 Line a 1-lb/450-g loaf pan with foil or plastic wrap, pressing out as many creases as you can. Set the prepared loaf pan aside.

2 Place the granulated sugar and water in a heavy-based pan and heat gently, stirring until the sugar has dissolved. Bring to a boil, then boil for 1–2 minutes until syrupy. Remove the pan from the heat.

3 Break the white chocolate into small pieces and stir it into the syrup, continuing to stir until the chocolate has melted and combined with the syrup. Let cool slightly.

4 Beat the egg yolks into the chocolate mixture. Set aside to cool completely.

5 Lightly whip the cream until just holding its shape, and fold it into the chocolate mixture.

6 Whisk the egg whites in a clean bowl until they are standing in soft peaks. Fold the whites into the chocolate mixture. Pour into the prepared loaf pan and freeze overnight.

7 To serve, remove the terrine from the freezer about 10–15 minutes before serving. Turn out of the pan, cut into slices to serve.

banana coconut cheesecake

serves ten

8 oz/225 g chocolate chip cookies

4 tbsp butter

12 oz/350 g medium-fat soft cheese

⅓ cup superfine sugar

1¾ oz/50 g fresh coconut, grated

2 tbsp coconut-flavored liqueur

2 ripe bananas

4½ oz/125 g semisweet chocolate

1 envelope powdered gelatin

3 tbsp water

⅔ cup heavy cream

TO DECORATE

1 banana

lemon juice

a little melted chocolate

COOK'S TIP

To crack the coconut, carefully pierce 2 of the "eyes" and drain off all the liquid. Tap hard around the center of the coconut with a hammer until it cracks and lever it apart. Cut into slices or grate the flesh.

1 Place the cookies in a plastic bag and crush with a rolling pin. Pour into a mixing bowl. Melt the butter and stir into the cookie crumbs until well coated. Firmly press the cookie mixture into the bottom and up the sides of an 8-inch/20-cm springform cake pan.

2 Beat the soft cheese and superfine sugar together until well combined, then beat in the grated coconut and coconut-flavored liqueur. Mash the 2 bananas and beat them in. Melt the semisweet chocolate and beat in until well combined.

3 Sprinkle the gelatin over the water in a heatproof bowl and let it go spongy. Place over a pan of hot water and stir until dissolved. Stir into the chocolate mixture. Whip the cream until just holding its shape and stir into the chocolate mixture. Spoon the filling over the biscuit shell and let chill for 2 hours, until set.

4 To serve, carefully transfer to a serving plate. Slice the banana, toss in the lemon juice, and arrange around the edge of the cheesecake. Drizzle with melted chocolate and let set before serving.

chocolate rum pots

serves six

8 oz/225 g semisweet chocolate

4 eggs, separated

⅓ cup superfine sugar

4 tbsp dark rum

4 tbsp heavy cream

TO DECORATE

a little whipped cream (optional)

marbled chocolate shapes
  (see page 396)

1 Melt the semisweet chocolate and let cool slightly (see page 262).

2 Whisk the egg yolks with the superfine sugar in a bowl until very pale and fluffy.

3 Drizzle the chocolate into the egg yolk and sugar mixture and fold in together with the dark rum and the heavy cream.

4 Whisk the egg whites in a clean bowl until standing in soft peaks. Fold the egg whites into the chocolate mixture in 2 batches. Divide the mixture between 6 individual dishes, and let chill for at least 2 hours before serving.

5 To serve, decorate with a little whipped cream if wished and a marbled chocolate shape.

chocolate hazelnut pots

serves six

2 eggs

2 egg yolks

1 tbsp superfine sugar

1 tsp cornstarch

2½ cups milk

3 oz/85 g semisweet chocolate

4 tbsp chocolate hazelnut spread

TO DECORATE

grated chocolate or quick chocolate
   curls (see page 263)

1 Beat the eggs, egg yolks,
superfine sugar, and cornstarch
together until well combined. Heat the
milk until it is almost boiling.

2 Gradually pour the milk onto the
eggs, whisking as you do so. Melt
the chocolate and hazelnut spread in a
bowl set over a pan of gently simmering
water, then whisk the melted chocolate
mixture into the eggs.

3 Pour into 6 small ovenproof
dishes and cover the dishes
with foil. Place them in a roasting pan.
Fill the pan with boiling water until
halfway up the sides of the dishes.

4 Bake in a preheated oven,
325°F/160°C, for 35–40 minutes,
until the custard is just set. Remove
from the pan and cool, then chill until
required. Serve decorated with grated
chocolate or chocolate curls.

369

chocolate cheese pots

serves four

1¼ cups ricotta cheese, drained

⅔ cup lowfat unsweetened yogurt

2 tbsp confectioners' sugar

4 tsp lowfat drinking chocolate
      powder

4 tsp unsweetened cocoa

1 tsp vanilla extract

2 tbsp dark rum, optional

2 medium egg whites

4 chocolate cake decorations

TO SERVE

pieces of kiwifruit, orange, and
      banana

strawberries and raspberries

1 Mix the ricotta cheese and lowfat yogurt together in a bowl. Sift in the sugar, drinking chocolate, and cocoa and mix well.

2 Add the vanilla extract, and dark rum (if using).

3 Whisk the egg whites in another bowl, until stiff. Using a metal spoon, carefully fold the egg whites into the chocolate mixture.

4 Spoon the yogurt and chocolate mixture into 4 small china dessert pots or ramekins and let chill in the refrigerator for about 30 minutes.

5 Decorate each chocolate cheese pot with a chocolate cake decoration and serve with an assortment of fresh fruit, such as pieces of kiwifruit, orange, and banana, and a few whole strawberries and raspberries or other fruit of your choice.

quick chocolate desserts

1 Pour the water into a pan and add the sugar. Stir over low heat until the sugar has dissolved. Bring to a boil and continue to boil, without stirring, for 3 minutes. Remove the pan from the heat and let cool slightly.

2 Put the chocolate in a food processor and add the hot syrup. Process until the chocolate has melted, then add the egg yolks and process briefly until smooth. Finally, add the cream to the mixture and process until fully incorporated.

3 Pour the mixture into 4 glasses or individual bowls, cover with plastic wrap, and let chill in the refrigerator for 2 hours, until set. Serve with sweet cookies of your choice.

champagne mousse

SPONGE

4 eggs

½ cup superfine sugar

⅔ cup self-rising flour

2 tbsp unsweetened cocoa

2 tbsp butter, melted

MOUSSE

1 envelope powdered gelatin

3 tbsp water

1¼ cups champagne

1¼ cups heavy cream

2 egg whites

⅓ cup superfine sugar

TO DECORATE

2 oz/50 g semisweet chocolate-
flavored cake covering, melted

1 Line a 15 x 10-inch/38 x 25-cm jelly roll pan with greased baking parchment. Place the eggs and sugar in a bowl and beat, using an electric mixer if you have one, until the mixture is very thick and the whisk leaves a trail when lifted. If using a balloon whisk, stand the bowl over a pan of hot water while whisking. Strain the flour and cocoa together and fold into the egg mixture. Fold in the butter. Pour into the pan and bake in a preheated oven, 400°F/200°C, for 8 minutes or until springy to the touch. Let cool for 5 minutes, then turn out onto a wire rack until cold. Meanwhile, line four 4-inch/10-cm baking rings with baking parchment. Line the sides with 1-inch/2.5-cm strips of cake and the bottom with circles.

2 For the mousse, sprinkle the gelatin over the water and let it go spongy. Place the bowl over a pan of hot water and stir until the gelatin has dissolved. Stir in the champagne.

3 Whip the cream until just holding its shape. Fold in the champagne mixture. Stand in a cool place until on the point of setting, stirring. Whisk the egg whites until standing in soft peaks, add the sugar and whisk until glossy. Carefully fold the egg whites into the setting mixture. Spoon into the sponge cases, allowing the mixture to go above the sponge. Let chill for 2 hours. Pipe the cake covering in squiggles on a piece of parchment, let them set, then use the set squiggles to decorate the mousses.

black forest trifle

serves six

6 thin slices chocolate butter cream
    jelly roll

1 lb 12 oz/800 g canned black
    cherries

2 tbsp kirsch

1 tbsp cornstarch

2 tbsp superfine sugar

generous 1¾ cups milk

3 egg yolks

1 egg

2¾ oz/75 g semisweet chocolate

1¼ cups heavy cream, whipped
    lightly

TO DECORATE

chocolate caraque (see page 263)

maraschino cherries (optional)

1 Place the slices of chocolate jelly roll in the bottom of a glass serving bowl.

2 Drain the black cherries, reserving 6 tablespoons of the juice. Place the cherries and the reserved juice on top of the cake. Sprinkle the kirsch over the black cherries. Set aside.

3 Mix the cornstarch and superfine sugar in a bowl. Stir in enough of the milk to mix to a smooth paste. Beat in the egg yolks and the whole egg.

4 Heat the remaining milk in a small pan until almost boiling, then gradually pour it onto the egg mixture, whisking well until it is combined.

5 Place the bowl over a pan of hot water and cook over low heat until the custard thickens, stirring. Add the chocolate and stir until melted.

6 Pour the chocolate custard over the cherries and cool. When cold, spread the cream over the custard, swirling with the back of a spoon. Let chill before decorating.

7 Decorate with chocolate caraque and whole maraschino cherries, (if using) before serving.

chocolate marquise

serves six

7 oz/200 g semisweet chocolate

generous ⅓ cup butter

3 egg yolks

⅓ cup superfine sugar

1 tsp chocolate extract or 1 tbsp
    chocolate-flavored liqueur

1¼ cups heavy cream

TO SERVE

crème fraîche

chocolate-dipped fruits

unsweetened cocoa, for dusting

1 Break the chocolate into pieces. Place the chocolate and butter in a bowl set over a pan of gently simmering water and stir until melted and well combined. Remove the pan from the heat and let the chocolate cool.

2 Place the egg yolks in a mixing bowl with the sugar and whisk until pale and fluffy. Using an electric mixer running on low speed, slowly whisk in the cool chocolate mixture. Stir in the chocolate extract or chocolate-flavored liqueur.

3 Whip the cream until just holding its shape. Fold into the chocolate mixture. Spoon into 6 small custard pots or individual metal molds. Chill the desserts for at least 2 hours.

4 To serve, turn out the desserts onto individual serving dishes. If you have difficulty turning them out, dip the pots or molds into a bowl of warm water for a few seconds to help the marquise to slip out. Serve with chocolate-dipped fruit and crème fraîche and dust with cocoa.

chocolate mint swirl

serves six

1¼ cups heavy cream

⅔ cup mascarpone cheese

2 tbsp confectioners' sugar

1 tbsp crème de menthe

6 oz/175 g semisweet chocolate

semisweet chocolate, to decorate

COOK'S TIP

Pipe the patterns freehand or draw patterns onto baking parchment first, turn the parchment over, and then pipe the chocolate, following the drawn outline.

1 Place the cream in a large mixing bowl and whip it until standing in soft peaks.

2 Fold in the mascarpone cheese and confectioners' sugar, then place about one-third of the mixture in a smaller bowl. Stir the crème de menthe into the smaller bowl. Melt the semisweet chocolate and stir it into the remaining mixture.

3 Place alternate spoonfuls of the 2 mixtures into serving glasses, then swirl the mixture together, using a spoon or knife, to give a decorative two-color effect. Chill until required.

4 To make the piped chocolate decorations, melt a small amount of semisweet chocolate and place in a paper pastry bag.

5 Place a sheet of baking parchment on a board and pipe squiggles, stars, or flower shapes with the melted chocolate. Alternatively, to make curved decorations, pipe decorations onto a long strip of baking parchment, then carefully place the strip over a rolling pin, securing with sticky tape. Let the chocolate set, then carefully remove from the baking parchment.

6 Decorate each dessert with the piped chocolate decorations and serve. The desserts can be decorated and then chilled, if preferred.

377

chocolate banana sundae

serves four

GLOSSY CHOCOLATE SAUCE

2 oz/55 g semisweet chocolate

4 tbsp light corn syrup

1 tbsp butter

1 tbsp brandy or rum, optional

SUNDAE

4 bananas

2/3 cup heavy cream

8–12 scoops good-quality vanilla
  ice cream

3/4 cup slivered or chopped almonds,
  toasted

grated chocolate, for sprinkling

4 fan wafer cookies, to serve

1 To make the chocolate sauce, break the chocolate into small pieces and place in a heatproof bowl with the syrup and butter. Heat over a pan of hot water until melted, stirring until well combined. Remove from the heat and stir in the brandy (if using).

2 Slice the bananas and whip the cream until just holding its shape. Place a scoop of ice cream in the bottom of 4 tall sundae dishes. Top with slices of banana, some chocolate sauce, a spoonful of cream, and a good sprinkling of nuts.

3 Repeat the ice cream, banana, and chocolate sauce layers, finishing with a good dollop of whipped cream, sprinkled with nuts, and a little grated chocolate. Serve the chocolate banana sundaes with fan wafer cookies.

white chocolate ice cream

serves six

ICE CREAM

1 egg, plus 1 extra egg yolk

3 tbsp superfine sugar

5½ oz/150 g white chocolate

1¼ cups milk

⅔ cup heavy cream

COOKIE CUPS

1 egg white

4 tbsp superfine sugar

2 tbsp all-purpose flour, sifted

2 tbsp unsweetened cocoa, sifted

2 tbsp butter, melted

semisweet chocolate, melted, to
   decorate

1 Place baking parchment on 2 cookie sheets. To make the ice cream, beat the egg, egg yolk, and sugar. Break the chocolate into pieces, place in a bowl with 3 tablespoons of milk, and melt over a pan of hot water. Heat the milk until almost boiling and pour onto the eggs, whisking. Place over a pan of simmering water and stir until the mixture thickens. Whisk in the chocolate. Cover with dampened baking parchment and let cool.

2 Whip the cream and fold into the custard. Transfer to a freezer proof container and freeze the mixture for 1–2 hours. Scrape into a bowl and beat until smooth. Re-freeze until firm.

3 Beat the egg white and sugar. Beat in the flour and cocoa, then the butter. Place 1 tablespoon on 1 cookie sheet and spread out into a 5-inch/12.5-cm circle. Bake in a preheated oven, 400°F/200°C, for 4–5 minutes. Remove and mold over an upturned cup. Let set, then cool. Repeat to make 6 cookie cups. Serve the ice cream in the cups, drizzled with melted chocolate.

379

marble cheesecake

serves ten

BASE

8 oz/225 g toasted oat cereal

½ cup toasted hazelnuts, chopped

4 tbsp butter

1 oz/25 g semisweet chocolate

FILLING

12 oz/350 g full-fat soft cheese

½ cup superfine sugar

generous ¾ cup thick yogurt

1¼ cups heavy cream

1 envelope powdered gelatin

3 tbsp water

6 oz/175 g semisweet chocolate, melted

6 oz/175 g white chocolate, melted

1 Place the toasted oat cereal in a plastic bag and crush it coarsely with a rolling pin. Pour the crushed cereal into a mixing bowl and stir in the toasted chopped hazelnuts.

2 Melt the butter and chocolate together over low heat and stir into the cereal mixture, stirring until well coated.

3 Using the bottom of a glass, press the mixture into the bottom and up the sides of an 8-inch/20-cm springform cake pan.

4 Beat the cheese and sugar together with a wooden spoon until smooth. Beat in the yogurt. Whip the cream until just holding its shape and fold into the mixture. Sprinkle the gelatin over the water in a heatproof bowl and let it go spongy. Place over a pan of hot water and stir until dissolved. Stir into the mixture.

5 Divide the mixture in half and beat the semisweet chocolate into one half and the white chocolate into the other half.

6 Place alternate spoonfuls of mixture on top of the cereal base. Swirl the filling together with the tip of a knife to give a marbled effect. Smooth the top with a scraper or a spatula. Chill the cheesecake for at least 2 hours, until set, before serving.

chocolate fruit tartlets

serves six

2¼ cups all-purpose flour

3 tbsp unsweetened cocoa

⅔ cup butter

3 tbsp superfine sugar

2–3 tbsp water

1¾ oz/50 g semisweet chocolate

½ cup chopped mixed nuts, toasted

12 oz/350 g prepared fruit

3 tbsp apricot jelly or red currant jelly

VARIATION

If liked, you can fill the cases with a little sweetened cream before topping with the fruit. For a chocolate-flavored filling, blend 8 oz/225 g chocolate hazelnut spread with 5 tablespoons of thick yogurt or whipped cream.

1 Sift the flour and cocoa into a mixing bowl. Cut the butter into small pieces and rub into the flour with your fingertips until the mixture resembles fine bread crumbs.

2 Stir in the sugar. Add enough of the water to mix to a soft dough—about 1–2 tablespoons. Cover and chill for 15 minutes.

3 Roll out the pie dough on a lightly floured counter and use to line 6 tartlet pans, each 4 inches/10 cm across. Prick the shells with a fork and line with a little crumpled foil. Bake in a preheated oven, 375°F/190°C, for 10 minutes.

4 Remove the foil and bake for another 5–10 minutes, until the pie dough is crisp. Place the pans on a wire rack to cool completely.

5 Melt the chocolate. Spread out the toasted chopped mixed nuts on a plate. Remove the pie shells from the pans. Spread melted chocolate on the rims, then dip in the nuts. Let the chocolate set.

6 Arrange the fruit in the tartlet shells. Melt the apricot or red currant jelly with the remaining tablespoon of water and brush it over the fruit. Chill the tartlets until required.

chocolate cheesecake

serves twelve

¾ cup all-purpose flour

¾ cup ground almonds

1⅓ cups raw brown sugar

⅔ cup margarine

1½ lb/675 g firm bean curd, drained

¼ cup vegetable oil

½ cup orange juice

¾ cup brandy

½ cup unsweetened cocoa, plus
  extra to decorate

2 tsp almond extract

TO DECORATE

confectioners' sugar

Cape gooseberries

1 Put the flour, ground almonds, and 1 tablespoon of the sugar in a bowl and mix well. Rub the margarine into the mixture to form a dough.

2 Lightly grease and line the bottom of a 9-inch/23-cm springform cake pan. Press the dough into the bottom of the pan to cover, pushing the dough up to the edge of the pan.

3 Coarsely chop the bean curd and put it in a food processor with the vegetable oil, orange juice, brandy, cocoa, almond essence, and remaining

sugar, and process until smooth and creamy. Pour the mixture evenly over the dough in the pan and smooth out, using a spatula. Cook in a preheated oven, 325°F/160°C, for 1–1¼ hours or until set.

4 Let cool in the pan for 5 minutes, then remove from the pan and chill. Dust with confectioners' sugar and cocoa. Decorate the chocolate cheesecake with Cape gooseberries and serve.

tiramisù layers

serves six

⅔ cup heavy cream

10½ oz/300 g semisweet chocolate

14 oz/400 g mascarpone cheese

1¾ cup black coffee with

   ¼ cup superfine sugar, cooled

6 tbsp dark rum or brandy

36 ladyfingers, about 14 oz/400 g

unsweetened cocoa, for dusting

VARIATION

Try adding ⅓ cup toasted, chopped hazelnuts to the chocolate cream mixture in Step 1, if you prefer.

1 Whip the cream until it just holds its shape. Melt the chocolate in a bowl set over a pan of simmering water, stirring occasionally. Let the chocolate cool slightly, then stir it into the mascarpone cheese and cream.

2 Mix the coffee and rum together in a bowl. Dip the ladyfingers into the mixture briefly so that they absorb the coffee and rum mixture but do not become soggy.

3 Place 3 ladyfingers on 3 individual serving plates.

4 Spoon a layer of the chocolate, mascarpone, and cream mixture over the ladyfingers.

5 Place 3 more lady fingers on top of the chocolate and mascarpone mixture. Spread another layer of chocolate and mascarpone and place 3 more ladyfingers on top.

6 Let the tiramisù chill in the refrigerator for at least 1 hour. Dust the dessert with unsweetened cocoa just before serving.

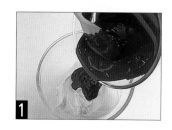

strawberry cheesecake

serves eight

BASE

¼ cup unsalted butter

2⅔ cups crushed graham crackers

½ cup chopped walnuts

FILLING

2 cups mascarpone cheese

2 eggs, beaten

3 tbsp superfine sugar

9 oz/250 g white chocolate, broken
  into pieces

2 cups strawberries, hulled and
  quartered

TOPPING

¾ cup mascarpone cheese

chocolate caraque (see page 263)

16 whole strawberries

1 Melt the butter over low heat and stir in the crushed crackers and the nuts. Spoon the mixture into a 9-inch/23-cm loose-bottomed cake pan and press evenly over the bottom with the back of a spoon. Set aside.

2 Preheat the oven to 300°F/150°C. To make the filling, beat the cheese until smooth, then beat in the eggs and sugar. Put the chocolate into the top of a double boiler or in a heatproof bowl set over a pan of barely simmering water. Stir over low heat until melted and smooth. Remove from the heat and cool slightly, then stir into the cheese mixture. Finally, stir in the strawberries.

3 Spoon the mixture into the cake pan, spread out evenly and smooth the surface. Bake in a preheated oven for 1 hour, until the filling is just firm. Turn off the oven but and let the cheesecake cool inside it until completely cold.

4 Transfer the cheesecake to a serving plate and spread the mascarpone cheese on top. Decorate with chocolate caraque and whole strawberries.

chocolate brandy torte

serves twelve

BASE
9 oz/250 g gingersnaps

2¾ oz/75 g semisweet chocolate

generous ⅓ cup butter

FILLING
8 oz/225 g semisweet chocolate

9 oz/250 g mascarpone cheese

2 eggs, separated

3 tbsp brandy

1¼ cups heavy cream

4 tbsp superfine sugar

TO DECORATE
scant ½ cup heavy cream

chocolate-coated coffee beans

3 Lightly whip the cream until just holding its shape and carefully fold in the chocolate mixture.

4 Whisk the egg whites in a clean bowl until standing in soft peaks. Add the superfine sugar a little at a time and whisk until thick and glossy. Fold into the chocolate mixture, in 2 batches, until just mixed.

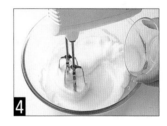

5 Spoon into the gingersnap shell and let chill for at least 2 hours. Transfer to a serving plate. Whip the cream and pipe rosettes onto the cheesecake, then add the chocolate-coated coffee beans.

1 Crush the gingersnaps in a plastic bag with a rolling pin or in a food processor. Melt the chocolate and butter together and pour over the gingersnaps. Mix well, then use to line the bottom and sides of a 9-inch/23-cm loose-bottomed fluted flan pan. Chill while preparing the filling.

2 To make the filling, melt the chocolate in a pan, remove from the heat, and beat in the mascarpone cheese, egg yolks, and brandy.

rich chocolate ice cream

serves six

ICE CREAM

1 egg

3 egg yolks

scant ½ cup superfine sugar

1¼ cups whole milk

9 oz/250 g semisweet chocolate

1¼ cups heavy cream

TRELLIS CUPS

3½ oz/100 g semisweet chocolate

1 Beat the egg, egg yolks, and superfine sugar together in a mixing bowl until well combined. Heat the milk until it is almost boiling.

2 Gradually pour the hot milk onto the eggs, whisking as you do so. Place the bowl over a pan of gently simmering water and cook, stirring constantly, until the custard mixture thickens sufficiently to thinly coat the back of a wooden spoon.

3 Break the semisweet chocolate into small pieces and add to the hot custard. Stir until has melted. Cover with a sheet of dampened baking parchment and let cool.

4 Whip the cream until just holding its shape, then fold into the cooled chocolate custard. Transfer to a freezer proof container and freeze for 1–2 hours until the mixture is frozen 1 inch/2.5 cm from the sides.

5 Scrape the ice cream into a chilled bowl and beat again until smooth. Re-freeze until firm.

6 To make the trellis cups, invert a muffin pan and cover 6 alternate mounds with plastic wrap. Melt the chocolate, place it in a paper pastry bag, and snip off the end.

7 Pipe a circle around the bottom of the mound, then pipe chocolate back and forth over it to form a trellis; carefully pipe a double thickness. Pipe around the bottom again. Chill until set, then lift from the pan and remove the plastic wrap. Serve the chocolate ice cream in the trellis cups.

chocolate freezer cake

serves eight

4 eggs

¾ cup superfine sugar

¾ cup self-rising flour

scant ⅓ cup unsweetened cocoa

2¼ cups chocolate and mint ice
cream

Glossy Chocolate Sauce (see
page 360)

1 Lightly grease a 9-inch/23-cm ring
pan. Place the eggs and sugar in
a large mixing bowl. Using an electric
mixer if you have one, whisk the
mixture until it is very thick and the
whisk leaves a trail. If using a balloon
whisk, stand the bowl over a pan of
hot water while whisking.

2 Sift the flour and cocoa together
and fold into the egg mixture.
Pour into the prepared pan and bake in
a preheated oven, 350°F/180°C, for
30 minutes or until springy to the
touch. Let cool in the pan before
turning out on to a wire rack to cool
completely.

3 Rinse the cake pan and line
with a strip of plastic wrap,
overhanging slightly. Carefully cut off
the top ½ inch/1 cm of the cake in one
slice, and then set aside.

4 Return the cake to the pan. Using
a spoon, scoop out the center of
the cake, leaving a shell about
1-cm/½-inch thick.

5 Remove the ice cream from the
freezer and let stand for a few
minutes, then beat with a wooden
spoon until softened a little. Fill the
center of the cake with the ice cream,
carefully smoothing the top. Replace
the top of the cake.

6 Cover with the overhanging
plastic wrap and freeze the cake
for at least 2 hours.

7 To serve, turn the chocolate
freezer cake out onto a serving
dish and drizzle over some of the
Chocolate Sauce in an attractive
pattern, if wished. Cut the cake into
slices and then serve the remaining
chocolate sauce separately.

chocolate mousse

serves eight

3½ oz/100 g semisweet chocolate,
    melted

1¼ cups unsweetened yogurt

⅔ cup Quark

4 tbsp superfine sugar

1 tbsp orange juice

1 tbsp brandy

1½ tsp gelozone (vegetarian gelatin)

9 tbsp cold water

2 large egg whites

coarsely grated semisweet and
    white chocolate and orange rind,
    to decorate

1 Put the melted chocolate, yogurt, Quark, sugar, orange juice, and brandy in a food processor and process for 30 seconds. Transfer the mixture to a large bowl.

2 Sprinkle the gelozone over the water and stir until dissolved.

3 Put the gelozone and water in a pan and boil for 2 minutes. Cool slightly, then stir into the chocolate.

4 Whisk the egg whites until stiff peaks form and fold into the chocolate mixture using a metal spoon.

5 Line a 1 lb 2-oz/500-g loaf pan with plastic wrap. Spoon the mousse into the pan. Chill in the refrigerator for 2 hours, until set. Turn the mousse out onto a serving plate and decorate with grated chocolate and orange rind.

chocolate charlotte

serves eight

about 22 ladyfingers

4 tbsp orange-flavored liqueur

9 oz/250 g semisweet chocolate

⅔ cup heavy cream

4 eggs

⅔ cup superfine sugar

TO DECORATE

⅔ cup whipping cream

2 tbsp superfine sugar

½ tsp vanilla extract

quick semisweet chocolate curls (see
    page 263)

chocolate decorations, optional

1 Line the bottom of a Charlotte
mold or a deep 7-inch/18-cm
round cake pan.

2 Place the ladyfingers on a tray
and sprinkle with half of the
orange-flavored liqueur. Use to line the
sides of the mold or pan, trimming if
necessary to make a tight fit.

3 Break the chocolate into small
pieces, place in a bowl and melt
over a pan of hot water. Remove from
the heat and stir in the heavy cream.

4 Separate the eggs and place
the whites in a large clean bowl.
Set aside. Beat the egg yolks into the
chocolate and cream mixture.

5 Whisk the egg whites until
standing in stiff peaks, then
gradually add the superfine sugar,
whisking until stiff and glossy. Carefully
fold the egg whites into the chocolate
mixture in 2 batches, taking care not
to knock out all of the air. Pour into
the center of the mold. Trim the
ladyfingers so that they are level with
the chocolate mixture. Chill the
chocolate charlotte in the refrigerator
for at least 5 hours before decorating
and serving.

6 To decorate, whip the cream,
sugar, and vanilla extract until
standing in soft peaks. Turn out the
Charlotte onto a serving plate. Pipe
cream rosettes around the bottom
and decorate with chocolate curls and
other decorations of your choice.

mocha swirl mousse

serves four

1 tbsp coffee and chicory extract

2 tsp unsweetened cocoa, plus extra
    for dusting

1 tsp low-fat drinking chocolate
    powder

⅔ cup lowfat crème fraîche, plus
    4 tsp to serve

2 tsp powdered gelatin

2 tbsp boiling water

2 large egg whites

2 tbsp superfine sugar

4 chocolate-coated coffee beans,
    to serve

1 Place the coffee and chicory extract in one bowl, and 2 teaspoons of cocoa and the drinking chocolate in another bowl. Divide the crème fraîche between the 2 bowls and mix both well.

2 Dissolve the gelatin in the boiling water and set aside. Whisk the egg whites and sugar in a clean bowl, until stiff and divide this evenly between the 2 mixtures.

3 Divide the dissolved gelatin between the 2 mixtures and, using a large metal spoon, gently fold until well mixed.

4 Spoon small amounts of the 2 mousses alternately into 4 serving glasses and swirl together gently. Chill for 1 hour or until set.

5 To serve, top each mousse with a teaspoon of crème fraîche, a chocolate coffee bean, and a light dusting of cocoa. Serve immediately.

layered chocolate mousse

serves four

3 eggs

1 tsp cornstarch

4 tbsp superfine sugar

1¼ cups milk

1 envelope powdered gelatin

3 tbsp water

1¼ cups heavy cream

2¾ oz/75 g semisweet chocolate

2¾ oz/75 g white chocolate

2¾ oz/75 g light chocolate

chocolate caraque, to decorate (see page 263)

1 Line a 1-lb/450-g loaf pan with baking parchment. Separate the eggs, putting each egg white in a separate bowl. Place the egg yolks, cornstarch, and sugar in a large mixing bowl and whisk until well combined. Place the milk in a pan and heat gently, stirring until almost boiling. Pour the milk onto the egg yolks, whisking.

2 Set the bowl over a pan of gently simmering water and cook, stirring until the mixture thickens enough to thinly coat the back of a wooden spoon.

3 Sprinkle the gelatin over the water in a small heatproof bowl and let it go spongy. Place over a pan of hot water and stir until dissolved. Stir into the hot mixture. Let the mixture cool.

4 Whip the cream until just holding its shape. Fold into the egg custard, then divide the mixture into 3. Melt the 3 types of chocolate separately. Fold the semisweet chocolate into one egg custard portion. Whisk one egg white until standing in soft peaks and fold into the semisweet chocolate custard until combined. Pour into the prepared pan and smooth the top. Chill in the refrigerator until just set. The remaining mixtures should stay at room temperature.

5 Fold the white chocolate into another portion of the egg custard. Whisk another egg white and fold in. Pour on top of the semisweet chocolate layer and chill quickly. Repeat with the remaining light chocolate and egg white. Chill for at least 2 hours, until set. Turn out onto a serving dish and decorate with chocolate caraque.

chocolate & vanilla creams

serves four

scant 2 cups heavy cream

⅓ cup superfine sugar

1 vanilla bean

generous ¾ cup crème fraîche

2 tsp powdered gelatin

3 tbsp water

1¾ oz/50 g semisweet chocolate

MARBLED CHOCOLATE SHAPES

a little melted white chocolate

a little melted semisweet chocolate

1 Place the cream and sugar in a pan. Cut the vanilla bean into 2 pieces and add to the cream. Heat gently, stirring until the sugar has dissolved, then bring to a boil. Lower the heat and let simmer for 2–3 minutes.

2 Remove the pan from the heat and take out the vanilla bean. Stir in the crème fraîche.

3 Sprinkle the gelatin over the water in a small heatproof bowl and let it go spongy, then place over a pan of hot water and stir until dissolved. Stir the gelatin into the cream mixture. Pour half of this mixture into another mixing bowl.

4 Melt the semisweet chocolate and stir it into one half of the cream mixture. Pour the chocolate mixture into 4 individual glass serving dishes and chill for 15–20 minutes until just set. While the chocolate mixture is chilling, keep the vanilla mixture at room temperature.

5 Take the serving dishes out of the refrigerator spoon the vanilla mixture on top of the chocolate mixture and chill again until the vanilla is set.

6 Meanwhile, make the shapes for the decoration. Spoon the melted white chocolate into a paper pastry bag and snip off the tip. Spread some melted semisweet chocolate on a piece of baking parchment. While still wet, pipe a fine line of white chocolate in a scribble over the top. Use the tip of a toothpick to marble the white chocolate into the semisweet. When firm but not too hard, carefully cut into shapes with a small shaped cutter or a sharp knife. Chill the marbled chocolate shapes until firm, then use to decorate the desserts.

raspberry chocolate boxes

serves twelve

7 oz/200 g semisweet chocolate,
broken into pieces

1½ tsp cold, strong black coffee

1 egg yolk

1½ tsp coffee liqueur

2 egg whites

7 oz/200g raspberries

SPONGE CAKE

1 egg, plus 1 egg white

¼ cup superfine sugar

scant ½ cup all-purpose flour

1 To make the mocha mousse, melt 2 oz/55 g of the chocolate in a heatproof bowl set over a pan of barely simmering water. Add the coffee and stir over low heat until smooth, then remove from the heat and let cool slightly. Stir in the egg yolk and the coffee liqueur.

2 Whisk the egg whites into stiff peaks. Fold into the chocolate mixture, cover with plastic wrap, and let chill for 2 hours, until set.

3 For the sponge cake, lightly grease an 8-inch/20-cm square cake pan and line the bottom with baking parchment. Put the egg and extra white with the sugar in a heatproof bowl set over a pan of barely simmering water. Whisk over low heat for 5–10 minutes, until pale and thick. Remove from the heat and continue whisking for 10 minutes, until cold and the whisk leaves a ribbon trail when lifted.

4 Preheat the oven to 350°F/180°C. Sift the flour over the egg mixture and gently fold it in. Pour into the prepared pan. Bake in the preheated oven for 20–25 minutes, until firm. Turn out onto a wire rack to cool, then

invert the cake, keeping the baking parchment in place.

5 To make the chocolate boxes, grease a 12 x 9-inch/30 x 23-cm jelly roll pan and line with waxed paper. Place the remaining chocolate in a heatproof bowl set over a pan of barely simmering water. Stir over low heat until melted, but not too runny. Pour it into the pan and spread evenly with a spatula. Set aside in a cool place for about 30 minutes, until set.

6 Turn out the set chocolate, cut it into 36 rectangles, measuring 3 x 1 inches/7.5 x 2.5 cm. Cut 12 of these in half to make 24 rectangles measuring 1½ x 1 inches/4 x 2.5 cm.

7 Trim the sponge cake, then cut into 12 slices, measuring 3 x 1¼ inches/7.5 x 3 cm. Spread a little of the mousse along the sides of each sponge rectangle and press 2 long and 2 short chocolate rectangles on each side to make boxes. Divide the remaining mousse among the boxes and top with the raspberries.

mocha creams

serves four

8 oz/225 g semisweet chocolate

1 tbsp instant coffee powder

1¼ cups boiling water

1 envelope powdered gelatin

3 tbsp cold water

1 tsp vanilla extract

1 tbsp coffee-flavored liqueur,
   optional

1¼ cups heavy cream

4 chocolate-coated coffee beans

8 amaretti cookies

VARIATION

To add a delicious almond
flavor to the dessert, replace
the coffee-flavored liqueur
with Amaretto liqueur.

1 Break the chocolate into small
pieces and place in a pan with
the coffee. Stir in the boiling water
and heat gently, stirring until the
chocolate melts.

2 Sprinkle the gelatin over the
cold water and let it go spongy,
then whisk it into the hot chocolate
mixture to dissolve it.

3 Stir in the vanilla extract and
coffee-flavored liqueur (if using).
Let the chocolate mixture stand in a
cool place until just starting to thicken.
Whisk from time to time.

4 Whisk the cream until it is
standing in soft peaks, then set
aside a little for decorating the desserts
and fold the remainder into the
chocolate mixture. Spoon the mixture
into tall glass serving dishes and let set.

5 Decorate with the reserved cream
and chocolate coffee beans and
serve with the amaretti cookies.

banana cream profiteroles

serves four

DOUGH

⅔ cup water

5 tbsp butter

¾ cup strong all-purpose flour, sifted

2 eggs

CHOCOLATE SAUCE

3½ oz/100 g semisweet chocolate,
  broken into pieces

2 tbsp water

4 tbsp confectioners' sugar

2 tbsp sweet butter

FILLING

1¼ cups heavy cream

1 banana

2 tbsp confectioners' sugar

2 tbsp banana-flavored liqueur

1 Lightly grease a cookie sheet and sprinkle with a little water. To make the choux pastry dough, place the water in a pan. Cut the butter into small pieces and add to the pan. Heat gently until the butter melts, then bring to a rolling boil. Remove the pan from the heat and add the flour in one go, beating well until the mixture leaves the sides of the pan and forms a ball. Let cool slightly, then gradually beat in the eggs to form a smooth, glossy mixture. Spoon the choux pastry dough into a large pastry bag fitted with a ½-inch/1-cm plain tip.

2 Pipe about 18 small balls of the dough onto the cookie sheet, allowing enough room for them to expand during cooking. Bake in a preheated oven, 425°F/220°C, for 15–20 minutes, until crisp and golden. Remove from the oven and, using a sharp knife, make a small slit in each one for steam to escape. Cool the profiteroles on a wire rack.

3 To make the chocolate sauce, place all the ingredients in a heatproof bowl set over a pan of simmering water, and heat until combined to make a smooth, glossy sauce, stirring constantly.

4 To make the filling, whip the cream until standing in soft peaks. Mash the banana with the sugar and liqueur. Fold into the cream. Place in a pastry bag fitted with a ½-inch/1-cm plain tip and pipe into the profiteroles. Serve the profiteroles mounded up on a glass cake stand, with the sauce poured over.

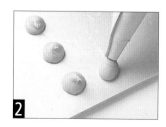

cardamom cream horns

serves six

1 egg white

4 tbsp superfine sugar

2 tbsp all-purpose flour

2 tbsp unsweetened cocoa

2 tbsp butter, melted

1¾ oz/50 g semisweet chocolate

CARDAMOM CREAM

⅔ cup heavy cream

1 tbsp confectioners' sugar

¼ tsp ground cardamom

pinch of ground ginger

1 oz/25 g preserved ginger,
    chopped finely

1 Place a sheet of baking parchment on 2 cookie sheets. Lightly grease 6 cream horn molds. To make the horns, beat the egg white and sugar in a mixing bowl until well combined. Sift the flour and cocoa together, then beat into the egg white and sugar mixture followed by the melted butter.

2 Bake 1 chocolate cone at a time. Place 1 tablespoon of the mixture onto 1 cookie sheet and spread out to form a 5-inch/13-cm circle. Bake in a preheated oven, 400°F/200°C, for 4–5 minutes.

3 Working quickly, remove the cookie with a spatula and wrap around the cream horn mold to form a cone. Let the cone set, then remove from the mold. Repeat with the remaining mixture to make 6 cones.

4 Melt the chocolate and dip the open edges of the horn in the chocolate. Place on a piece of baking parchment and let the chocolate set.

5 To make the cardamom cream, place the cream in a bowl and sift the confectioners' sugar and ground spices over the surface. Whisk the heavy cream until standing in soft peaks. Fold in the chopped preserved ginger and use the mixture to fill the chocolate cones.

chocolate shortcake towers

serves six

1 cup butter

½ cup brown sugar

1¾ oz/50 g semisweet chocolate

scant 2½ cups all-purpose flour

COULIS

12 oz/350 g fresh raspberries

2 tbsp confectioners' sugar

WHITE CHOCOLATE CREAM

1¼ cups heavy cream

3 tbsp milk

3½ oz/100 g white chocolate,
     melted

confectioners' sugar, for dusting

1 Lightly grease a cookie sheet. Beat the butter and sugar together until light and fluffy. Grate the chocolate and beat it into the mixture. Mix in the all-purpose flour to form a stiff dough.

2 Roll out the dough on a lightly floured counter and stamp out 18 circles, 3 inches/7.5 cm across, with a fluted cookie cutter. Place the circles on the cookie sheet and bake in a preheated oven, 400°F/200°C, for 10 minutes, until they are crisp and golden. Let the shortcake circles cool on the sheet.

3 To make the coulis, set aside about 3½ oz/100 g of the raspberries. Blend the remainder in a food processor with the confectioners' sugar, then push through a strainer to remove the seeds. Chill. Set aside 2 teaspoons of the cream. Whip the remainder until just holding its shape. Fold in the milk and the melted chocolate.

4 For each tower, spoon a little coulis onto a serving plate. Drop small dots of the reserved cream into the coulis around the edge of the plate and use a toothpick to drag through the cream to make an attractive pattern.

5 Place a shortcake circle on the plate and spoon on a little of the chocolate cream. Top with 2 or 3 raspberries, top with another short-cake, and repeat. Place a third biscuit on top. Dust with sugar to serve.

403

baked chocolate alaska

serves four

2 eggs

4 tbsp superfine sugar

¼ cup all-purpose flour

2 tbsp unsweetened cocoa

3 egg whites

⅔ cup superfine sugar

4 cups good-quality chocolate ice
cream

1 Grease a 7-inch/18-cm round
cake pan and line the bottom
with baking parchment.

2 Whisk the eggs and the
4 tablespoons of sugar in a
mixing bowl until very thick and pale.
Sift the flour and cocoa together and
carefully fold in.

3 Pour into the prepared pan
and bake in a preheated oven,
425°F/220°C, for 7 minutes or until
springy to the touch. Transfer to a
wire rack to cool completely.

4 Whisk the egg whites in a clean
bowl until they are standing in
soft peaks. Gradually add the superfine
sugar, whisking until you have a thick,
glossy meringue.

5 Place the sponge on a cookie
sheet and pile the ice cream onto
the center in a heaped dome.

COOK'S TIP

This dessert is delicious served
with a black currant coulis. Cook
a few black currants in a little
orange juice until soft, blend to a
purée and push through a
strainer, then sweeten to taste
with a little confectioners' sugar.

6 Pipe or spread the meringue
over the ice cream, making sure
the ice cream is completely enclosed.
(At this point the dessert can be
frozen, if wished.)

7 Return the dessert to the oven, for
5 minutes, until the meringue is
just golden. Serve immediately.

chocolate orange sherbet

serves four

2 tsp vegetable oil, for brushing

8 oz/225 g semisweet chocolate, broken into small pieces

4 cups crushed ice

2¼ cups freshly squeezed orange juice

⅔ cup water

¼ cup superfine sugar

finely grated rind of 1 orange

juice and finely grated rind of 1 lemon

1 tsp powdered gelatin

3 tbsp orange-flavored liqueur

fresh mint sprigs, to decorate

1 Brush a 3¼-cup mold with oil, drain well, then chill in the refrigerator. Put the chocolate in the top of a double boiler or into a heatproof bowl set over a pan of barely simmering water. Stir the chocolate over low heat until melted, then remove from the heat.

2 Remove the mold from the refrigerator and pour in the melted chocolate. Tip and turn the mold to coat the interior. Place the mold on a bed of crushed ice and continue tipping and turning until the chocolate has set. Return the mold to the refrigerator.

3 Set aside 3 tablespoons of the orange juice in a small, heatproof bowl. Pour the remainder into a pan and add the water, sugar, orange rind, and lemon juice and rind. Stir over low heat until the sugar has dissolved, then increase the heat and bring the mixture to a boil. Remove the pan from the heat.

4 Sprinkle the gelatin over the orange juice. Set aside for 2 minutes to soften, then set over a pan of barely simmering water until dissolved. Stir the gelatin and the liqueur into the orange juice mixture. Pour into a freezerproof container and freeze for 30 minutes.

5 Remove the sherbet from the freezer, transfer to a bowl, and beat thoroughly to break up the ice crystals. Return it to the container and freeze for 1 hour. Repeat this process 3 more times.

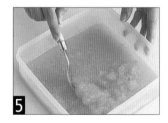

6 Remove the sherbet from the freezer, and beat well. Remove the mold from the refrigerator and spoon the sherbet into it. Freeze overnight. When ready to serve, unmold the sherbet and decorate with mint.

chocolate & almond tart

serves eight

PIE DOUGH

1¼ cups all-purpose flour

2 tbsp superfine sugar

½ cup butter, cut into small pieces

1 tbsp water

FILLING

½ cup light corn syrup

4 tbsp butter

½ cup soft brown sugar

3 eggs, beaten lightly

½ cup whole blanched almonds,
chopped coarsely

3½ oz/100 g white chocolate,
chopped coarsely

cream, to serve (optional)

1 To make the tart shell, place the flour and sugar in a mixing bowl and rub in the butter with your fingertips. Add the water and work the mixture together into a soft dough. Wrap and let chill for 30 minutes.

2 Roll out the dough on a lightly floured counter and use to line a 9½-inch/24-cm loose-bottomed flan pan. Prick the tart shell with a fork and let chill for 30 minutes. Line the shell with foil and baking beans and bake in a preheated oven, 375°F/190°C, for 15 minutes. Remove the foil and baking beans and cook for another 15 minutes.

3 To make the filling, gently melt the syrup, butter, and sugar together in a pan. Remove from the heat and let cool slightly. Stir in the beaten eggs, almonds, and chocolate.

4 Pour the chocolate and nut filling into the prepared tart shell and cook in the oven for 30–35 minutes or until just set. Let cool before removing the tart from the pan. Serve the tart with cream, if wished.

chocolate pear tart

serves eight

DOUGH

scant 1 cup all-purpose flour

pinch of salt

2 tbsp superfine sugar

½ cup diced unsalted butter

1 egg yolk

1 tbsp lemon juice

TOPPING

4 oz/115 g semisweet chocolate,
  grated

4 pears

½ cup light cream

1 egg, plus 1 egg yolk

½ tsp almond extract

3 tbsp superfine sugar

1 To make the dough, sift the flour
and a pinch of salt into a mixing
bowl. Add the sugar and butter and
mix well with a dough blender
or 2 forks until thoroughly
incorporated. Stir in the egg yolk and
the lemon juice to form a dough. Form
the dough into a ball, wrap in plastic
wrap, and let it chill in the refrigerator
for 30 minutes.

2 Roll out the dough on a lightly
floured counter and use it to line
a 10-inch/25-cm loose-bottomed tart
pan. Sprinkle the grated semisweet
chocolate over the bottom of the tart
shell. Peel the pears, cut them in half
lengthwise, and remove the cores.
Thinly slice each pear half and fan out
slightly. Using a spatula, scoop up each
sliced pear half and arrange neatly in
the tart shell.

3 Beat the cream, egg, extra yolk,
and almond extract together, and
spoon the mixture over the pears.
Sprinkle the sugar over the tart.

4 Bake in a preheated oven 400°F/
200°C for 10 minutes, then lower
the temperature to 350°F/180°C and
bake for another 20 minutes, until the
pears are starting to caramelize and the
filling is just set. Remove from the
oven. Decorate and serve.

chocolate pecan pie

serves ten

PIE DOUGH

2½ cups all-purpose flour

½ cup unsweetened cocoa

1 cup confectioners' sugar

scant 1 cup unsalted butter, diced

1 egg yolk

pinch of salt

FILLING

3 oz/85 g semisweet chocolate,
    broken into small pieces

3 cups shelled pecans

6 tbsp unsalted butter

generous 1 cup brown sugar

3 eggs

2 tbsp heavy cream

¼ cup all-purpose flour

1 tbsp confectioners' sugar, for
    dusting

1 To make the pie dough, sift the flour, cocoa, sugar, and salt into a mixing bowl and make a well in the center. Put the butter and egg yolk in the well and gradually mix in the dry ingredients. Knead lightly into a ball. Cover with plastic wrap and chill in the refrigerator for 1 hour.

2 Unwrap the dough and roll it out on a lightly floured counter. Use the dough to line a 10-inch/25-cm non-stick springform pie pan and prick the shell all over with a fork. Line the pie shell with baking parchment and fill with baking beans. Bake the pie shell in the preheated oven 350°F/180°C for 15 minutes. Remove from the oven, discard the beans and paper, and let the pie shell cool.

3 To make the filling, put the chocolate in a heatproof bowl set over a pan of barely simmering water. Stir until melted. Remove from the heat and set aside. Coarsely chop 2 cups of the pecans and set aside. Mix the butter with ⅓ cup of the brown sugar. Beat in the eggs, one at a time, then add the remaining brown sugar and mix well. Stir in the cream, flour, melted chocolate, and chopped pecans.

4 Spoon into the pie shell. Cut the remaining pecans in half and arrange in concentric circles over the pie.

5 Bake in the preheated oven at the same temperature for 30 minutes, then cover the top with foil. Bake for another 25 minutes. Remove from the pan and transfer to a wire rack to cool completely. Dust with confectioners' sugar and serve.

mississippi mud pie

serves eight

2 cups all-purpose flour

¼ cup unsweetened cocoa

⅔ cup butter

2 tbsp superfine sugar

about 2 tbsp cold water

FILLING

¾ cup butter

2⅓ cups brown sugar

4 eggs, beaten lightly

4 tbsp unsweetened cocoa, sifted

5½ oz/150 g semisweet chocolate

1¼ cups light cream

1 tsp chocolate extract

TO DECORATE

1¾ cups heavy cream, whipped

chocolate flakes and quick chocolate

curls (see page 263)

1 To make the pie dough, sift the flour and cocoa into a mixing bowl. Rub in the butter until the mixture resembles fine bread crumbs. Stir in the sugar and enough cold water to mix to a soft dough. Chill for 15 minutes.

2 Roll out the dough on a lightly floured counter and use to line a deep 9-inch/23-cm loose-bottomed flan pan or ceramic flan dish. Line with foil or baking parchment and baking beans. Bake blind in a preheated oven, 375°F/190°C, for 15 minutes. Remove the beans and foil or parchment and cook the pie shell for another 10 minutes, until it is crisp.

3 To make the filling, beat the butter and sugar in a bowl and gradually beat in the eggs with the cocoa. Melt the chocolate and beat it into the mixture with the light cream and the chocolate extract.

4 Pour the mixture into the cooked pie shell and bake at 325°F/160°C, for 45 minutes or until the filling is set.

5 Let the mud pie cool completely, then transfer the pie to a serving plate, if preferred. Cover with the whipped cream and let chill.

6 Decorate the pie with quick chocolate curls and chocolate flakes and then let it chill.

white chocolate molds

4½ oz/125 g white chocolate,
    broken into pieces

scant 1 cup heavy cream

3 tbsp crème fraîche

2 eggs, separated

3 tbsp water

1½ tsp powdered gelatin

1 cup sliced strawberries

scant 1 cup raspberries

1¼ cups black currants

5 tbsp superfine sugar

½ cup raspberry flavored liqueur

12 black currant leaves, if available

1 Put the chocolate into the top of a double boiler or in a heatproof bowl set over a pan of barely simmering water. Stir over low heat until melted and smooth. Remove from the heat and set aside.

2 Meanwhile, pour the cream into a pan and bring to just below boiling point over low heat. Remove from the heat, then stir the cream and crème fraîche into the chocolate and cool slightly. Beat in the egg yolks, one at a time.

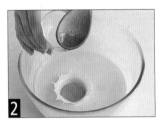

3 Pour the water into a small, heatproof bowl and sprinkle the gelatin on the surface. Let stand for 2–3 minutes to soften, then set over a pan of barely simmering water until completely dissolved. Stir the gelatin into the chocolate mixture and let stand until nearly set.

4 Brush the inside of 6 timbales, dariole molds, or small cups with oil, and line the bottoms with baking parchment. Whisk the egg whites until soft peaks form, then fold them into the chocolate mixture. Divide the mixture evenly among the prepared

molds and smooth the surface. Cover with plastic wrap and chill in the refrigerator for 2 hours, until set.

5 Put the strawberries, raspberries, and black currants in a bowl and sprinkle with the superfine sugar. Pour in the liqueur and stir gently to mix. Cover with plastic wrap and let chill in the refrigerator for 2 hours.

6 To serve, run a round-bladed knife around the sides of the molds and carefully turn out onto individual serving plates. Divide the fruit among the plates and serve immediately, decorated with black currant leaves, if available.

chocolate sherbet

serves six

5 oz/140 g bittersweet chocolate,
chopped coarsely
5 oz/140 g semisweet continental
chocolate, chopped coarsely
scant 2 cups water
1 cup superfine sugar
langues de chat cookies,
to serve

1 Put the bittersweet and
semisweet chocolate into a food
processor and process them briefly
until they are very finely chopped.

2 Pour the water into a heavy-
based pan and add the sugar.
Stir over medium heat to dissolve, then
bring to a boil. Boil for 2 minutes,
without stirring, then remove the pan
from the heat.

3 With the motor of the food
processor running, pour the hot
syrup onto the chocolate. Process for
about 2 minutes, until all the chocolate
has melted and the mixture is smooth.
Scrape down the sides of the food
processor if necessary. Carefully strain
the chocolate mixture into a freezerproof
container and let cool completely.

4 When the mixture is cool, place
it in the freezer for about 1 hour,
until slushy, but starting to become
firm around the edges. Tip the mixture
into the food processor and process
until smooth. Return to the container
and freeze the chocolate sherbet for at
least 2 hours, until firm.

5 Remove the sherbet from the
freezer about 10 minutes
before serving and let stand at room
temperature to let it soften slightly.
Serve the chocolate in scoops and
accompany with langues de chat
cookies.

chocolate & honey ice cream

serves six

2 cups milk

7 oz/200 g semisweet chocolate, broken into pieces

4 eggs, separated

scant ½ cup superfine sugar

2 tbsp honey

pinch of salt

12 fresh strawberries, washed and hulled

1 Pour the milk into a pan, add 5½ oz/150 g of the chocolate, and stir over medium heat for 3–5 minutes, until melted. Remove the pan from the heat and set aside.

2 Beat the egg yolks with all but 1 tablespoon of the sugar in a separate bowl until pale and thickened. Gradually beat in the milk mixture, a little at a time. Return the mixture to a clean pan and cook over low heat, whisking constantly, until smooth and thickened. Remove from the heat and set aside to cool. Cover with plastic wrap and chill in the refrigerator for 30 minutes.

3 Whisk the egg whites with a pinch of salt until soft peaks form. Gradually whisk in the remaining sugar and continue whisking until stiff and glossy. Remove the chocolate mixture from the refrigerator and stir in the honey, then gently fold in the egg whites.

4 Divide the mixture among 6 individual freezerproof molds and place in the freezer for at least 4 hours, until frozen. Meanwhile, put the remaining chocolate into the top of a double boiler or in a heatproof bowl set over a pan of barely simmering water. Stir over low heat until melted and smooth, then dip the strawberries in the melted chocolate so that they are half-coated. Place on a sheet of baking parchment to set. Transfer the ice cream to the refrigerator for 10 minutes before serving. Turn out onto serving plates and decorate with the chocolate-coated strawberries.

marshmallow ice cream

serves four

3 oz/85 g semisweet chocolate,
   broken into pieces
6 oz/175 g white marshmallows
⅔ cup milk
1¼ cups heavy cream

1 Put the semisweet chocolate and marshmallows in a pan and pour in the milk. Warm over very low heat until the chocolate and marshmallows have melted. Remove from the heat and let cool completely.

2 Whisk the cream until thick, then fold it into the cold chocolate mixture with a metal spoon. Pour into a 1-lb/450-g loaf pan and freeze for at least 2 hours, until firm (it will keep for 1 month in the freezer). Serve the ice cream with fresh fruit.

chocolate & hazelnut parfait

serves six

1½ cups blanched hazelnuts

6 oz/175 g semisweet chocolate, broken into small pieces

2½ cups heavy cream

3 eggs, separated

2½ cups confectioners' sugar

1 tbsp unsweetened cocoa, for dusting

6 small fresh mint sprigs, to decorate

wafer cookies, to serve

1 Spread out the hazelnuts on a cookie sheet and toast under a broiler preheated to medium-hot, shaking the sheet from time to time, for about 5 minutes, until golden all over. Set aside to cool.

2 Put the chocolate into the top of a double boiler or in a heatproof bowl set over a pan of barely simmering water. Stir over low heat until melted, then remove the chocolate from the heat and cool. Put the toasted hazelnuts in a food processor and process until they are finely ground. Set aside while you whip the cream.

3 Whip the cream until it is stiff, then fold in the ground hazelnuts and set aside. Beat the egg yolks with 3 tablespoons of the sugar for 10 minutes until pale and thick.

4 Whisk the egg whites in a separate bowl until soft peaks form. Whisk in the remaining sugar, a little at a time, until the whites are stiff and glossy. Stir the cooled chocolate into the egg yolk mixture, then fold in the cream and, finally, fold in the egg whites. Divide the mixture among 6 freezerproof timbales or molds, cover with plastic wrap, and freeze for at least 8 hours or overnight until firm.

5 Transfer the parfaits to the refrigerator about 10 minutes before serving to soften slightly. Turn out onto individual serving plates, dust the tops lightly with cocoa, decorate with mint sprigs, and serve with wafer cookies.

mint-chocolate gelato

serves four

6 large eggs

¾ cup superfine sugar

1¼ cups milk

⅔ cup heavy cream

large handful of fresh mint leaves,
    rinsed and dried

2 drops green food coloring,
    optional

2 oz/55 g semisweet chocolate,
    chopped finely

1 Put the eggs and sugar into a heatproof bowl that will sit over a pan with plenty of room underneath. Using an electric mixer, beat the eggs and sugar together until they are thick and creamy.

2 Put the milk and cream in the pan and bring to a simmer, where small bubbles appear all around the edge, stirring. Pour onto the eggs, whisking constantly. Rinse the pan and put 1 inch/2.5 cm water in the bottom. Place the bowl on top, making sure the bottom does not touch the water. Turn the heat to medium–high.

3 Transfer the mixture to a pan and cook, stirring constantly with a wooden spoon, until the mixture is thick enough to coat the back of the spoon and leave a mark when you pull your finger across it.

4 Tear the mint leaves and stir them into the custard. Remove the custard from the heat. Let cool, then cover and set aside to infuse for at least 2 hours, chilling for the last 30 minutes.

5 Strain the mixture through a small nylon strainer to remove the pieces of mint. Stir in the food coloring (if using). Transfer to a freezerproof container and freeze the mixture for 1–2 hours, until frozen 1 inch/2.5 cm from the side of the container.

6 Scrape into a bowl and beat again until smooth. Stir in the chocolate pieces, smooth the top, and cover with plastic wrap or foil. Freeze until set, for up to 3 months. Soften the ice cream in the refrigerator for 20 minutes before serving.

chocolate rice dessert

serves eight

½ cup long-grain white rice

pinch of salt

2½ cups milk

½ cup granulated sugar

7 oz/200 g semisweet or
  bittersweet chocolate, chopped

4 tbsp butter, diced

1 tsp vanilla extract

2 tbsp brandy

¾ cup heavy cream

whipped cream, for piping
  (optional)

quick chocolate curls (see page
  263), to decorate (optional)

VARIATION

To mold the chocolate rice,
soften 1 envelope powdered
gelatin in about ¼ cup cold
water and heat gently until
dissolved. Stir into the chocolate
just before folding in the
cream. Pour into a rinsed
mold, let set, then unmold.

---

1 Bring a pan of water to the boil. Sprinkle in the rice and add the salt. Reduce the heat and simmer gently for 15–20 minutes until the rice is just tender. Drain the rice, rinse, and drain again.

2 Heat the milk and sugar in a large heavy-based pan over medium heat until the sugar dissolves, stirring frequently. Add the chocolate and butter to the pan and stir until melted and smooth.

3 Stir in the cooked rice and reduce the heat to low. Cover and let simmer, stirring occasionally, for 30 minutes, until the milk is absorbed and the mixture thickened. Stir in the vanilla extract and brandy. Remove from the heat and let cool to room temperature.

4 Using an electric mixer, beat the cream until soft peaks form. Stir one heaped spoonful of the cream into the chocolate rice mixture to lighten it; then fold in the remaining cream.

5 Spoon into glass serving dishes, cover, and let chill for about 2 hours. If wished, decorate with piped whipped cream and top with quick chocolate curls. Serve cold.

phyllo nests

serves four

1 tbsp unsalted butter

6 sheets phyllo pastry, about
12 x 6 inches/30 x 15 cm each

1½ oz/40 g semisweet chocolate,
broken into pieces

½ cup ricotta cheese

16 seedless green grapes, halved

24 seedless black grapes, halved

1 Put the butter into a small pan and set over low heat until melted. Remove from the heat. Preheat the oven to 375°F/190°C. Cut each sheet of phyllo pastry into 4 pieces, to give 24 rectangles, each measuring about 6 x 3 inches/15 x 7.5 cm, then stack them all on top of each other. Brush 4 shallow muffin pans with melted butter. Line 1 pan with a rectangle of phyllo pastry, brush with melted butter, and place another rectangle on top at an angle to the first, and brush it with melted butter. Continue in this way, lining each pan with 6 rectangles, each brushed with melted butter. Brush the top layers of the pastry nests with melted butter.

2 Bake in preheated oven for 7–8 minutes, until golden and crisp. Remove the pastry nests from the oven and set aside to cool in the pans.

3 Put the chocolate into the top of a double boiler or in a heatproof bowl set over a pan of barely simmering water. Stir over low heat until melted. Remove from the heat and let cool slightly. Brush the insides of the pastry shells with about half the melted chocolate. Beat the ricotta cheese until smooth, then beat in the remaining melted chocolate.

4 Divide the chocolate ricotta mixture among the pastry shells and arrange the grapes alternately around the edges. Carefully lift the filled pastry nests out of the pans and serve immediately.

chocolate & pernod creams

serves four

2 oz/55 g semisweet chocolate,
   broken into pieces
scant 1 cup milk
1¼ cup heavy cream
2 tbsp superfine sugar
1 tbsp arrowroot dissolved in 2 tbsp
   milk
3 tbsp Pernod
langues de chat cookies, or
   chocolate-tipped rolled wafers,
   to serve

1 Put the chocolate into the top of a double boiler or in a heatproof bowl set over a pan of barely simmering water. Stir over low heat until melted. Remove the pan from the heat and let cool slightly.

2 Pour the milk and cream into a pan over low heat and bring to just below boiling point, stirring occasionally. Remove the pan from the heat and then set aside.

3 Beat the sugar and the arrowroot mixture into the melted chocolate. Gradually stir in the hot milk and cream mixture, then stir in the Pernod. Return the double boiler to the heat or set the bowl over a pan of barely simmering water and cook, over low heat, for 10 minutes, stirring constantly, until thick and smooth. Remove from the heat and let cool.

4 Pour the chocolate and Pernod mixture into 4 individual serving glasses. Cover the glasses with plastic wrap and let chill for 2 hours. Serve the chocolate and Pernod creams with langues de chats cookies or chocolate-tipped rolled wafers.

small cakes & cookies

This chapter contains everyday delights for chocolate fans. You are sure to be tempted by our wonderful array of cookies and small cakes.

Make any day special with a home-made chocolate cookie to be served with coffee, as a snack or to accompany a special dessert. Although some take a little longer to make, most are quick and easy to prepare and decoration is often simple—although you can get carried away if you like!

You'll find recipes for old favorites, such as Chocolate Chip Muffins and Chocolate Chip Cookies, Chocolate Butterfly Cakes, and Chocolate Brownies. There are also new recipes for cookies and small cakes, such as Chocolate Coconut Squares or Malted Chocolate Wedges. Finally, we have given the chocolate treatment to some traditional recipes—try Chocolate Biscuits or Chocolate Chip Flapjacks.

chocolate rum babas

serves four

¾ cup strong all-purpose flour

¼ cup unsweetened cocoa

1 envelope active dry yeast

pinch of salt

1 tbsp superfine sugar

1½ oz/40 g semisweet chocolate

2 eggs

3 tbsp lukewarm milk

4 tbsp butter, melted

SYRUP

4 tbsp honey

2 tbsp water

4 tbsp rum

TO SERVE

whipped cream

unsweetened cocoa, for dusting

fresh fruit, optional

1 Lightly oil 4 individual ring pans. Sift the flour and cocoa together in a large warmed mixing bowl. Grate the chocolate and stir into the mix. Beat the eggs together in a separate bowl, add the milk and butter, and continue beating until mixed.

2 Make a well in the center of the dry ingredients and pour in the egg mixture, beating to mix to a batter. Beat for 10 minutes, ideally in a electric mixer with a dough hook. Divide the mixture between the pans—it should come halfway up the sides.

3 Place on a cookie sheet and cover with a damp dish towel. Let stand in a warm place until the mixture rises almost to the tops of the pans. Bake the rum babas in a preheated oven, 400°F/200°C, for 15 minutes.

4 To make the syrup, gently heat all of the ingredients in a small pan. Turn out the babas and place on rack placed above a tray to catch the syrup. Drizzle the syrup over the babas and let stand for at least 2 hours for the syrup to soak in. Once or twice, spoon the syrup that has dripped onto the tray over the babas.

5 Fill the center of the babas with whipped cream and sprinkle a little cocoa over the top. Serve the babas with fresh fruit, if wished.

chocolate fudge brownies

makes sixteen

7 oz/200 g low-fat soft cheese

½ tsp vanilla extract

generous 1 cup superfine sugar

2 eggs

generous ⅓ cup butter

3 tbsp unsweetened cocoa

¾ cup self-rising flour, sifted

⅓ cup chopped pecans

FUDGE FROSTING

4 tbsp butter

1 tbsp milk

⅔ cup icing confectioners' sugar

2 tbsp unsweetened cocoa

pecans, to decorate (optional)

1 Lightly grease an 8-inch/20-cm square shallow cake pan and line the bottom.

2 Beat the cheese, vanilla extract, and 5 teaspoons of superfine sugar together, then set aside.

3 Beat the eggs and remaining superfine sugar together until light and fluffy. Place the butter and cocoa in a small pan and heat gently, stirring until the butter melts and the mixture combines, then stir it into the egg mixture. Fold in the flour and nuts.

4 Pour half of the brownie mixture into the pan and smooth the top. Carefully spread the soft cheese over it, then cover it with the remaining brownie mixture. Bake in a preheated oven, 350°F/180°C, for 40–45 minutes. Cool in the pan.

5 To make the frosting, melt the butter in the milk. Stir in the confectioners' sugar and cocoa. Using a spatula spread the frosting over the brownies and decorate with pecans (if using). Let the frosting set, then cut into squares to serve.

VARIATION

Omit the cheese layer
if preferred. Use walnuts in
place of the pecans.

pain au chocolat

makes twelve

4 cups strong all-purpose flour

½ tsp salt

1 envelope active dry yeast

2 tbsp shortening

1 egg, beaten lightly

1 cup lukewarm water

¾ cup butter, softened

beaten egg, for glazing

3½ oz/100 g semisweet chocolate,
  broken into 12 squares

confectioners' sugar, for dusting

1 Lightly grease a cookie sheet with a little butter and set aside. Sift the flour and salt into a mixing bowl and stir in the yeast. Rub the shortening into the flour and yeast mixture with your fingertips. Add the egg and enough of the water to mix to a soft dough. Knead for about 10 minutes to make a smooth, elastic dough.

2 Roll out to form a 15 x 8-inch/ 38 x 20-cm rectangle. Divide the butter into 3 portions and dot one portion over two-thirds of the rectangle, leaving a small border around the edge.

3 Fold the rectangle into 3 by first folding the plain part of the dough over and then the other side. Seal the edges of the dough by pressing with a rolling pin. Give the dough a quarter turn so the sealed edges are at the top and bottom. Re-roll and fold (without adding butter), then wrap the dough and let chill in for 30 minutes.

4 Repeat steps 2 and 3 until all of the butter has been used, chilling the dough each time. Re-roll and fold twice more without butter. Let chill for a final 30 minutes.

5 Roll the dough to a 18 x 12-inch/46 x 30-cm rectangle, then trim and halve, lengthwise. Cut each half into 6 rectangles and brush with beaten egg. Place a chocolate square at one end of each rectangle and roll up to form a sausage. Press the ends together and place, seam-side down, on the cookie sheet. Cover the pain au chocolat and let rise for 40 minutes in a warm place. Brush with egg and bake in a preheated oven, 425°F/220°C, for 20–25, minutes until golden. Cool on a wire rack. Serve the pain au chocolat warm or cold.

chocolate dairy wraps

serves six

2 eggs

4 tbsp superfine sugar

⅓ cup all-purpose flour

1½ tbsp unsweetened cocoa

4 tbsp apricot jelly

⅔ cup heavy cream, whipped

confectioners' sugar, for dusting

1 Line 2 cookie sheets with pieces of baking parchment. Whisk the eggs and sugar together until the mixture is very light and fluffy and the whisk leaves a trail when lifted.

2 Sift the flour and cocoa together. Using a metal spoon or a spatula, gently fold it into the eggs and sugar in a figure-eight movement.

3 Drop rounded tablespoonfuls of the mixture onto the lined cookie sheets and spread them into oval shapes. Make sure they are well spaced apart as they will spread out during cooking.

4 Bake in a preheated oven, 425°F/220°C, for 6–8 minutes or until springy to the touch. Let cool on the cookie sheets.

5 When cold, slide the cakes onto a damp dish towel and let stand until cold. Carefully remove them from the dampened parchment. Spread the flat side of the cakes with apricot jelly, then spoon or pipe the whipped cream down the center of each one.

6 Fold the chocolate dairy wraps in half and place them on a serving plate. Sprinkle with confectioners' sugar and serve.

no-bake chocolate squares

makes sixteen

9½ oz/275 g semisweet chocolate

¾ cup butter

4 tbsp light corn syrup

2 tbsp dark rum, optional

6 oz/175 g plain cookies

1 oz/25 g toasted rice cereal

½ cup chopped walnuts or pecans

½ cup candied cherries, chopped
   coarsely

1 oz/25 g white chocolate, to
   decorate

1 Place the semisweet chocolate in a large mixing bowl with the butter, syrup, and rum (if using), and set over a pan of gently simmering water until melted, stirring until blended.

2 Break the cookies into small pieces and stir into the chocolate mixture along with the toasted rice cereal, nuts, and cherries.

3 Line a 7-inch/18-cm square cake pan with baking parchment. Pour the mixture into the pan and smooth the top, pressing down well with the back of a spoon. Let chill for 2 hours.

4 To decorate, melt the white chocolate and drizzle it over the top of the cake randomly. Let it set. To serve, carefully turn out of the pan and remove the baking parchment. Cut the cake into 16 squares.

VARIATION
Brandy or an orange-flavored liqueur can be used instead of the rum, if you prefer. Cherry brandy also works well.

chocolate butterfly cakes

makes twelve

½ cup soft margarine

½ cup superfine sugar

1¼ cups self-rising flour

2 large eggs

2 tbsp unsweetened cocoa

1 oz/25 g semisweet chocolate,
  melted

LEMON BUTTER CREAM

⅓ cup unsalted butter, softened

1⅓ cups confectioners' sugar, sifted

grated rind of ½ lemon

1 tbsp lemon juice

confectioners' sugar, for dusting

1 Place 12 individual paper cases in a shallow muffin pan. Place all of the ingredients for the cakes, except for the melted chocolate, in a large mixing bowl, and beat with an electric mixer until the mixture is just smooth. Beat in the melted chocolate, stirring until well blended.

2 Spoon equal amounts of the mixture into each paper case, filling them three-quarters full. Bake in a preheated oven, 350°F/180°C, for 15 minutes or until springy to the touch. Transfer the chocolate cakes to a wire rack and let them cool completely.

3 Meanwhile, make the lemon butter cream. Place the butter in a mixing bowl and beat until fluffy, then gradually beat in the confectioners' sugar. Beat in the lemon rind and gradually add the lemon juice, beating well.

4 When cold, cut the top off each cake using a serrated knife. Cut each cake top in half.

5 Spread or pipe the butter cream over the cut surface of each cake and push the 2 cut pieces of cake top into the frosting to form wings. Sprinkle with confectioners' sugar.

chocolate biscuits

serves four

2 cups self-rising flour, sifted

5 tbsp butter

1 tbsp superfine sugar

⅓ cup chocolate chips

about ⅔ cup milk

COOK'S TIP

To be at their best, all biscuits should be freshly baked and served warm. Split the biscuits and spread them with chocolate hazelnut spread.

1 Grease a cookie sheet. Place the flour in a mixing bowl. Cut the butter into small pieces and rub it into the flour with your fingertips until the mixture resembles fine bread crumbs.

2 Stir in the superfine sugar and chocolate chips.

3 Mix in enough of the milk to form a soft dough.

4 On a lightly floured counter, roll out the dough to form a 4 x 6-inch/10 x 15-cm rectangle, about 1-inch/2.5-cm thick. Cut the dough into 9 squares.

5 Place the biscuits, spaced well apart, on the prepared cookie sheet.

6 Brush with a little milk and bake in a preheated oven, 425°F/ 220°C, for 10–12 minutes, until risen and golden. Serve warm.

439

chocolate crispy bites

makes sixteen

WHITE CHOCOLATE LAYER

4 tbsp butter

1 tbsp light corn syrup

5½ oz/150 g white chocolate

1¾ oz/50 g toasted rice cereal

SEMISWEET CHOCOLATE LAYER

4 tbsp butter

2 tbsp light corn syrup

4½ oz/125 g semisweet chocolate,
   broken into small pieces

2¾ oz/75 g toasted rice cereal

COOK'S TIP

These bites can be made
up to 4 days ahead. Keep them
covered in the refrigerator
until ready to use.

1 Grease an 8-inch/20-cm square cake pan with butter and line with baking parchment.

2 To make the white chocolate layer, melt the butter, light corn syrup, and white chocolate in a bowl set over a pan of simmering water.

3 Remove from the heat and stir in the toasted rice cereal until it is well combined.

4 Press into the prepared pan and smooth the surface.

5 To make the semisweet chocolate layer, melt the butter, light corn syrup, and chocolate in a bowl set over a pan of simmering water.

6 Remove from the heat and stir in the rice cereal. Pour the semisweet chocolate over the hardened white chocolate layer, cool, and chill until hardened.

7 Turn the mixture out of the cake pan carefully and cut into small squares using a sharp knife.

chocolate coconut squares

makes nine

8 oz/225 g semisweet chocolate
    graham crackers

⅓ cup butter or margarine

¾ cup canned evaporated milk

1 egg, beaten

1 tsp vanilla extract

2 tbsp superfine sugar

⅓ cup self-rising flour, sifted

1⅓ cups shredded coconut

1¾ oz/50 g semisweet chocolate,
    optional

1 Grease a shallow 8-inch/20-cm square cake pan and line.

2 Crush the crackers in a plastic bag with a rolling pin or process them in a food processor.

3 Melt the butter or margarine in a pan and stir in the crushed crackers until well combined.

4 Press the mixture into the bottom of the cake pan.

5 Beat the evaporated milk, egg, vanilla, and sugar together until smooth. Stir in the flour and shredded coconut. Pour over the cracker layer and use a spatula to smooth the top.

6 Bake the coconut mixture in a preheated oven, 375°F/190°C, for 30 minutes or until the coconut topping has become firm and just golden.

7 Let cool in the cake pan for about 5 minutes, then cut into squares. Let cool completely in the pan.

8 Carefully remove the squares from the pan and place them on a board. Melt the semisweet chocolate (if using) and drizzle it over the squares to decorate them. Let the chocolate set before serving.

VARIATION

Store the squares in an
airtight container for up to
4 days. They can be frozen,
undecorated, for up to 2 months.
Thaw at room temperature.

chocolate éclairs

makes ten

DOUGH

⅔ cup water

5 tbsp butter, cut into small pieces

¾ cup strong all-purpose flour, sifted

2 eggs

CRÈME PÂTISSIÈRE

2 eggs, beaten lightly

¼ cup superfine sugar

2 tbsp cornstarch

1¼ cups milk

¼ tsp vanilla extract

FROSTING

2 tbsp butter

1 tbsp milk

1 tbsp unsweetened cocoa

½ cup confectioners' sugar

a little white chocolate, melted

1 Lightly grease a cookie sheet. Place the water in a pan, add the butter, and heat gently until the butter melts. Bring to a rolling boil, then remove the pan from the heat and add the flour in one go, beating well until the mixture leaves the sides of the pan and forms a ball. Let cool slightly, then gradually beat in the eggs to form a smooth, glossy mixture. Spoon into a large pastry bag fitted with a ½-inch/1-cm plain tip.

2 Sprinkle the cookie sheet with a little water. Pipe éclairs 3-inches/7.5-cm long, spaced well apart. Bake in a preheated oven, 400°F/200°C, for 30–35 minutes or until crisp and golden. Make a small slit in each one to let the steam escape. Cool on a wire rack.

3 Meanwhile, make the crème pâtissière. Whisk the eggs and sugar until thick and creamy, then fold in the cornstarch. Heat the milk until almost boiling and pour onto the eggs, whisking. Transfer to the pan and cook over low heat, stirring until thick. Remove the pan from the heat and stir in the vanilla extract. Cover with baking parchment and let cool.

4 To make the frosting, melt the butter with the milk in a pan, remove from the heat, and stir in the cocoa and sugar. Split the éclairs lengthwise and pipe in the crème pâtissière. Spread the frosting over the top of the éclair. Spoon over the white chocolate, swirl in, and let set. If preferred, the éclairs can be filled with plain or sweetened whipped cream.

chocolate chip muffins

makes twelve

generous ⅓ cup soft margarine

1 cup superfine sugar

2 large eggs

⅔ cup whole-milk plain yogurt

5 tbsp milk

2 cups all-purpose flour

1 tsp baking soda

1 cup semisweet chocolate chips

VARIATION

The mixture can also be used to make 6 large or 24 mini muffins. Bake mini muffins for 10 minutes or until springy to the touch.

1 Line a 12-muffin pan with paper cases.

2 Place the margarine and sugar in a mixing bowl and beat with a wooden spoon until light and fluffy. Beat in the eggs, yogurt, and milk until well combined.

3 Sift the flour and baking soda together and add to the mixture. Stir until just blended.

4 Stir in the chocolate chips, then spoon the mixture into the paper cases and bake in a preheated oven, 375°F/190°C, for 25 minutes or until a fine skewer inserted into the center comes out clean. Let the muffins cool in the pan for 5 minutes, then turn them out onto a wire rack to cool completely.

chocolate biscotti

makes sixteen

1 egg

⅓ cup superfine sugar

1 tsp vanilla extract

1 cup all-purpose flour

½ tsp baking powder

1 tsp ground cinnamon

1¾ oz/50 g semisweet chocolate, chopped coarsely

½ cup toasted slivered almonds

⅓ cup pine nuts

1 Lightly grease a large cookie sheet. Set aside while you prepare the cookie mixture.

2 Whisk the egg, sugar, and vanilla extract in a mixing bowl with an electric mixer until thick and pale—ribbons of mixture should trail from the whisk as you lift it.

3 Sift the flour, baking powder, and cinnamon into a separate bowl, then sift into the egg mixture and fold in gently. Stir in the coarsely chopped semisweet chocolate, toasted slivered almonds, and pine nuts.

4 Turn out on to a lightly floured counter and shape into a flat log, 9-inches/23-cm long and ¾-inch/1.5-cm wide. Transfer to the cookie sheet.

5 Bake in a preheated oven, 350°F/180°C, for 20–25 minutes or until golden. Remove the cookie log from the oven and let cool for 5 minutes or until firm.

6 Transfer the log to a cutting board. Using a serrated bread knife, cut the log on the diagonal into slices about ½-inch/1-cm thick and arrange them on the cookie sheet. Cook for 10–15 minutes, turning halfway through the cooking time.

7 Let cool for about 5 minutes, then transfer to a wire rack to cool.

chocolate chip tartlets

serves six

1¾ oz/50 g toasted hazelnuts

1¼ cups all-purpose flour

1 tbsp confectioners' sugar

⅓ cup soft margarine

FILLING

2 tbsp cornstarch

1 tbsp unsweetened cocoa

1 tbsp superfine sugar

1¼ cups semi-skim milk

3 tbsp chocolate and hazelnut
  spread

2½ tbsp semisweet chocolate chips

2½ tbsp milk chocolate chips

2½ tbsp white chocolate chips

1 Finely chop the nuts in a food processor. Add the flour, the 1 tablespoon of confectioners' sugar, and margarine. Process for a few seconds until the mixture resembles bread crumbs. Add 2–3 tablespoons of water and process to form a soft dough. Cover and let chill in the freezer for 10 minutes.

2 Roll out the dough and use to line six 4-inch/10-cm loose-bottomed tartlet pans. Prick the bottom of the tartlet shells with a fork and line them with loosely crumpled foil. Bake in a preheated oven, 400°F/200°C, for 15 minutes. Remove the foil and bake for another 5 minutes, until the tartlet shells are crisp and golden. Remove from the oven and let cool.

3 Make the filling. Mix the cornstarch, cocoa, and sugar together with enough milk to make a smooth paste. Stir in the remaining milk. Pour into a pan and cook gently over low heat, stirring until thickened. Stir in the chocolate hazelnut spread.

4 Mix the chocolate chips together and set aside one-quarter. Stir half of the remaining chips into the custard. Cover with damp waxed paper, let stand until almost cold, then stir in the second half of the chocolate chips. Spoon the mixture into the tartlet shells and let cool. Decorate with the reserved chips, spinkling them over the top.

chocolate orange cookies

makes thirty

⅓ cup butter, softened

⅓ cup superfine sugar

1 egg

1 tbsp milk

2 cups all-purpose flour

¼ cup unsweetened cocoa

FROSTING

1 cup confectioners' sugar, sifted

3 tbsp orange juice

a little semisweet chocolate, melted

1 Line 2 cookie sheets with baking parchment.

2 Beat the butter and sugar together until light and fluffy. Beat in the egg and milk until well combined. Sift the flour and cocoa into the mixture and gradually mix to form a soft dough. Use your fingers to incorporate the last of the flour and bring the dough together.

3 Roll out the dough on a lightly floured counter until ¼-inch/5-mm thick. Using a 2-inch/5-cm fluted round cutter, cut out as many cookies as you can. Re-roll the dough trimmings and cut out more cookies.

4 Place the cookies on the prepared cookie sheet and bake in a preheated oven, 350°F/180°C, for 10–12 minutes or until golden.

5 Let the cookies cool on the cookie sheet for a few minutes, then transfer them to a wire rack and let cool completely.

6 For the frosting, place the confectioners' sugar in a bowl and stir in enough orange juice to form a thin frosting that will coat the back of a spoon. Spread the frosting over the cookies and allow to set. Drizzle with melted chocolate. Let the chocolate set before serving.

chocolate caramel squares

makes sixteen

generous ⅓ cup soft margarine

⅓ cup light brown sugar

1 cup all-purpose flour

½ cup rolled oats

CARAMEL FILLING

2 tbsp butter

2 tbsp brown sugar

generous ¾ cup condensed milk

TOPPING

3½ oz/100 g semisweet chocolate

1 oz/25 g white chocolate, optional

1 Beat the margarine and brown sugar together in a bowl until light and fluffy. Beat in the flour and the rolled oats. Use your fingertips to bring the mixture together if necessary.

2 Press the oat mixture into the bottom of a shallow 8-inch/20-cm square cake pan.

3 Bake in a preheated oven, 350°F/180°C, for 25 minutes or until just golden and firm. Cool the mixture in the pan.

4 Place the ingredients for the caramel filling in a pan and heat gently, stirring until the sugar has dissolved and the ingredients combine. Bring slowly to a boil over very low heat, then boil very gently for 3–4 minutes, stirring constantly, until the filling has thickened.

5 Pour the caramel filling over the oat layer in the pan, smooth with a spatula, and let set.

6 Melt the semisweet chocolate and spread it over the caramel. If using the white chocolate, melt it and pipe lines of white chocolate over the semisweet chocolate. Using a toothpick, feather the white chocolate into the semisweet chocolate. Let set. Cut into squares.

COOK'S TIP

If liked, you can line the pan with baking parchment so that the oat layer can be lifted out before cutting into pieces.

malted chocolate wedges

makes sixteen

generous ⅓ cup butter

2 tbsp light corn syrup

2 tbsp malted chocolate drink

8 oz/225 g malted milk cookies

2¾ oz/75 g light or semisweet
    chocolate, broken into pieces

2 tbsp confectioners' sugar

2 tbsp milk

1 Grease a shallow 7-inch/18-cm round cake pan or tart pan and line the bottom with baking parchment.

2 Place the butter, light corn syrup, and malted chocolate drink in a small pan and heat gently, stirring all the time until the butter has melted and the mixture is well combined.

3 Crush the cookies in a plastic bag with a rolling pin, or process them in a food processor. Stir the cookie crumbs into the chocolate mixture and mix well.

4 Press the mixture into the prepared pan and then chill in the refrigerator until firm.

5 Place the chocolate pieces in a small heatproof bowl with the confectioners' sugar and the milk. Place the bowl over a pan of gently simmering water and stir gently until the chocolate melts and the mixture is thoroughly combined.

6 Spread the chocolate frosting over the cookie bottom and let set in the pan. Using a sharp knife, carefully cut the mixture into wedges to serve.

VARIATION

Add chopped pecans to
the cookie crumb mixture in
Step 3, if liked.

checkerboard cookies

makes eighteen

¾ cup butter, softened

6 tbsp confectioners' sugar

1 teaspoon vanilla extract or grated
rind of ½ orange

2¼ cups all-purpose flour

1 oz/25 g semisweet chocolate

a little beaten egg white

1 Lightly grease a cookie sheet.
Beat the butter and confectioners'
sugar in a mixing bowl until light and
fluffy. Beat in the vanilla extract or
grated orange rind.

2 Gradually beat in the flour to
form a soft dough. Use your
fingers to incorporate the last of the
flour and bring the dough together.

3 Melt the chocolate. Divide the
dough in half and beat the melted
chocolate into one half. Keeping each
half of the dough separate, cover, and
let chill for 30 minutes.

4 Roll out each piece of dough to a
rectangle measuring 3 x 8 inches/
7.5 x 20 cm and 3-cm/1½-inches thick.
Brush one piece of dough with a little
egg white and place the other on top.

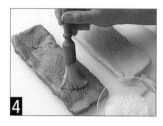

5 Cut the block of dough in half
lengthwise and turn over one
half. Brush the side of one strip with
egg white and butt the other up to it,
so that it resembles a checkerboard.

6 Cut the block into thin slices and
place each slice flat on the
prepared cookie sheet, allowing
enough room for the slices to spread
out a little during cooking.

7 Bake in a preheated oven, 350°F/
180°C, for about 10 minutes,
until just firm. Let cool on the cookie
sheets for a few minutes, before
carefully transferring to a wire rack
with a spatula. Let cool completely.

chocolate meringues

makes eight

4 egg whites

1 cup superfine sugar

1 tsp cornstarch

1½ oz/40 g semisweet chocolate

TO FINISH

3½ oz/100 g semisweet chocolate

⅔ cup heavy cream

1 tbsp confectioners' sugar

1 tbsp brandy, optional

1 Line 2 cookie sheets with baking parchment. Whisk the egg whites until standing in soft peaks, then gradually whisk in half of the sugar. Continue whisking until the mixture is very stiff and glossy.

2 Carefully fold in the remaining sugar and cornstarch. Grate the chocolate.

3 Spoon the mixture into a pastry bag fitted with a large star or plain tip. Pipe 16 large rosettes or mounds on the lined cookie sheets.

4 Bake in a preheated oven, 275°F/140°C, for about 1 hour, changing the position of the cookie sheets halfway through cooking. Without opening the oven door, turn off the oven and let the meringues cool in the oven. Once the meringues are cold, carefully peel away the baking parchment.

5 Melt the semisweet chocolate and spread it over the bottom of the meringues. Stand them upside down on a wire rack until the chocolate has set. Whip the cream, confectioners'

sugar, and brandy (if using) until the cream holds its shape. Spoon into a pastry bag and use to sandwich the meringues together in pairs. Serve.

VARIATION

To make mini meringues, use a star-shaped tip and pipe about 24 small rosettes. Bake for about 40 minutes until crisp.

mexican chocolate meringues

makes twenty five

4–5 egg whites, at room
   temperature
a pinch of salt
¼ tsp cream of tartar
¼–½ tsp vanilla extract
¾–1 cup superfine sugar
⅛–¼ tsp ground cinnamon
4 oz/115 g semisweet or
   bittersweet chocolate, grated
TO SERVE
ground cinnamon, for dusting
4 oz/115 g strawberries or other
   fruit
chocolate-flavored cream (see
   Cook's Tip)

1 Whisk the egg whites until they are foamy, then add the salt and cream of tartar and beat until very stiff. Whisk in the vanilla extract, then slowly whisk in the sugar, a small amount at a time, until the meringue is shiny and stiff. This should take about 3 minutes by hand, and under a minute if you have an electric mixer.

2 Whisk in the cinnamon and grated chocolate. Spoon mounds of about 2 tablespoons, onto an ungreased, non-stick cookie sheet. Space the mounds well apart.

3 Place in a preheated oven, 300°F/150°C, and cook for 2 hours.

4 Carefully remove from the cookie sheet. If the meringues are too moist and soft, return them to the oven to firm up and dry out more. Let them cool completely.

COOK'S TIP

To make the flavored cream, simply stir half-melted chocolate pieces into stiffly whipped cream, then chill until solid.

5 Serve the chocolate meringues dusted with cinnamon and accompanied by strawberries or other soft fruit of your choice and a little of the chocolate-flavored cream.

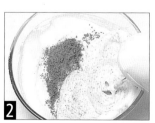

viennese chocolate fingers

makes eighteen

½ cup unsalted butter

6 tbsp confectioners' sugar

1½ cups self-rising flour, sifted

3 tbsp cornstarch

7 oz/200 g semisweet chocolate

1 Lightly grease 2 cookie sheets. Beat the butter and sugar in a mixing bowl until light and fluffy. Gradually beat in the flour and cornstarch.

2 Melt 2¾ oz/75 g of the semisweet chocolate and beat into the cookie dough.

3 Place in a pastry bag fitted with a large star tip and pipe fingers about 2-inches/5-cm long on the cookie sheets, spaced apart to allow for spreading.

4 Bake in a preheated oven, 375°F/190°C, for 12–15 minutes. Let cool slightly, then transfer to a wire rack and cool completely.

COOK'S TIP

If the cookie dough is too thick to pipe, beat in a little milk to thin it out before you place it in the pastry bag.

5 Melt the remaining chocolate and dip one end of each cookie in the chocolate, allowing the excess to drip back into the bowl.

6 Place the cookies on a sheet of baking parchment and let the chocolate set before serving.

chocolate hazelnut palmiers

makes twenty-six

TOPPING

13 oz/375 g ready-made puff pie
dough

8 tbsp chocolate hazelnut spread

½ cup chopped toasted hazelnuts

2 tbsp superfine sugar

1 Lightly grease a cookie sheet. Roll out the puff pie dough on a lightly floured counter to a rectangle about 15 x 9 inches/38 x 23 cm in size.

2 Spread the chocolate hazelnut spread over the pie dough using a spatula, then sprinkle the chopped hazelnuts over the top.

3 Roll up one long side of the pie dough to the center, then roll up the other side so that they meet in the center. Where the pieces meet, dampen the edges with a little water to join them. Using a sharp knife, cut into thin slices. Place each slice onto the prepared cookie sheet and flatten slightly with a spatula. Sprinkle the slices with the superfine sugar.

4 Bake in a preheated oven, 425°F/220°C, for 10–15 minutes, until golden. Transfer to a wire rack to cool.

VARIATION

For an extra chocolate flavor, dip the palmiers in melted semisweet chocolate to half-cover each one. Place the chocolate-dipped palmiers onto a sheet of baking parchment and let set.

rice pudding tartlets

serves six

1 package frozen unsweetened pie
  dough

4 cups milk

pinch of salt

1 vanilla bean, split, seeds removed
  and set aside

½ cup risotto or short-grain white
  rice

1 tbsp cornstarch

2 tbsp sugar

unsweetened cocoa, for dusting

melted chocolate, to decorate

GANACHE

generous ¾ cup heavy cream

1 tbsp light corn syrup

6 oz/175 g semisweet or
  bittersweet chocolate, chopped

1 tbsp unsalted butter

1 Thaw the pie dough, and then use it to line six 4-in /10-cm tart pans. Fill them with baking beans and bake blind in an oven preheated to 400°F/200°C for about 20 minutes, until the pie crust is set and golden at the edges. Transfer to a wire rack to cool.

2 To make the ganache, bring the heavy cream and corn syrup to a boil. Remove from the heat and immediately stir in the chopped chocolate. Continue stirring until melted and smooth, then beat in the butter until well combined. Spoon a 1-inch/2.5-cm thick layer into each tartlet. Set aside.

3 Bring the milk and salt to a boil in a pan. Sprinkle in the rice and return to a boil. Add the vanilla bean and seeds. Reduce the heat and let simmer gently until the rice is tender and the milk creamy.

4 Blend the cornstarch and sugar in a small bowl and add about 2 tablespoons of water to make a paste. Stir in a few spoonfuls of the rice mixture, then stir the cornstarch mixture into the rice. Bring to a boil and cook for about 1 minute, until thickened. Cool the pan in ice water, stirring until thick.

5 Spoon the rice mixture into the tartlets, filling each to the brim. Let set at room temperature. To serve the rice pudding tartlets, dust with cocoa and pipe or drizzle a little melted chocolate over each.

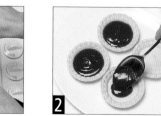

chocolate brownies

makes twelve

2 oz/55 g unsweetened pitted
    dates, chopped

2 oz/55 g no-soak prunes, chopped

6 tbsp unsweetened apple juice

4 medium eggs, beaten

2 cups brown sugar

1 tsp vanilla extract

4 tbsp lowfat drinking chocolate
    powder, plus extra for dusting

2 tbsp unsweetened cocoa

1½ cups all-purpose flour

⅓ cup semisweet chocolate chips

FROSTING

¾ cup confectioners' sugar

1–2 tsp water

1 tsp vanilla extract

COOK'S TIP

Make double the amount,
cut one of the cakes into bars,
and open-freeze, then store in
plastic bags. Take out pieces of
cake as and when you need
them—they'll take no time
at all to thaw.

1 Preheat the oven to 350°F/180°C. Grease and line a 7 x 11-inch/ 18 x 28-cm cake pan with baking parchment. Place the dates and prunes in a small pan and add the apple juice. Bring to a boil, cover, and let simmer for 10 minutes until soft. Beat to form a smooth paste, then set aside to cool.

2 Place the cooled fruit in a mixing bowl and stir in the eggs, sugar, and vanilla extract. Sift in 4 tablespoons of drinking chocolate, the cocoa, and flour, and fold in along with the semisweet chocolate chips until everything is well combined.

3 Spoon the mixture into the pan and smooth over the top. Bake in the preheated oven, for 25–30 minutes, until firm to the touch or until a skewer inserted into the center comes out clean. Cut into 12 bars and let cool in the pan for 10 minutes. Transfer to a wire rack to cool completely.

4 To make the frosting, sift the sugar into a bowl and mix with enough water and the vanilla extract to form a soft, but not too runny, frosting.

5 Drizzle the frosting over the chocolate brownies and let set. Dust with chocolate powder.

cannoli

makes twenty

3 tbsp lemon juice

3 tbsp water

1 large egg

1¾ cups all-purpose flour

1 tbsp superfine sugar

1 tsp ground allspice

pinch of salt

2 tbsp butter, softened

corn oil, for deep-frying

1 small egg white, beaten lightly

confectioners' sugar

FILLING

3¼ cups ricotta cheese, drained

4 tbsp confectioners' sugar

1 tsp vanilla extract

finely grated rind of 1 large orange

4 tbsp very finely chopped candied peel

1¾ oz/50 g semisweet chocolate, grated

pinch of ground cinnamon

2 tbsp Marsala wine or orange juice

1 Combine the lemon juice, water, and egg. Put the flour, sugar, spice, and salt into a food processor and quickly process. Add the butter, then, with the motor running, pour the egg mixture through the feed tube. Process until the mixture just forms a dough.

2 Turn the dough out onto a lightly floured counter and knead lightly. Wrap and let chill for at least 1 hour.

3 Meanwhile, make the filling. Beat the ricotta cheese until smooth. Sift in the confectioners' sugar, then beat in the remaining ingredients. Cover and let chill until required.

4 Roll out the dough on a floured counter until ¹⁄₁₆-inch/1.5-mm thick. Using a ruler, cut out 3 ½ x 3-inch/ 9 x 7.5-cm pieces, re-rolling and cutting the trimmings. The dough should make about 20 pieces.

5 Heat 2 inches/5 cm of oil in a skillet to 375°F/190°C. Roll a piece of dough around a greased cannoli mold, to just overlap the edge. Seal with egg white, pressing firmly.

Repeat with all the molds you have. Deep-fry 2 or 3 molds until the cannoli are golden, crisp, and bubbly.

6 Remove with a slotted spoon and drain on paper towels. Let cool, then carefully slide off the molds. Repeat with the remaining cannoli.

7 Store the cannoli unfilled in an airtight container for up to 2 days. Pipe in the filling no more than 30 minutes before serving to prevent the cannoli becoming soggy. Sift confectioners' sugar over the top just before serving.

chocolate & coconut cookies

makes twenty four

½ cup soft margarine

1 tsp vanilla extract

½ cup confectioners' sugar, sifted

1 cup all-purpose flour

2 tbsp unsweetened cocoa

⅔ cup shredded coconut

2 tbsp butter

3½ oz/100 g white marshmallows

⅓ cup shredded coconut

a little white chocolate, grated

1 Lightly grease a cookie sheet. Beat the margarine, vanilla extract, and confectioners' sugar together in a mixing bowl until fluffy. Sift the flour and cocoa together and beat it into the mixture with the coconut.

2 Roll rounded teaspoons of the mixture into balls and place on the prepared cookie sheet, allowing room for the cookies to spread during cooking.

3 Flatten the balls slightly and bake in a preheated oven, 350°F/ 180°C, for about 12–15 minutes, until just firm. Remove the cookies from the oven.

4 Let the chocolate and coconut cookies cool on the cookie sheet for a few minutes before carefully transferring to a wire rack. Let the cookies cool completely.

5 To make the frosting, place the butter and marshmallows in a small pan and heat gently, stirring until melted. Spread a little of the marshmallow frosting mixture over each cookie, using a knife or small spoon, and dip in the coconut. Let them set. Decorate the chocolate and coconut cookies with grated white chocolate before serving.

dutch macaroons

makes twenty

rice paper

2 egg whites

1 cup superfine sugar

1⅔ cups ground almonds

8 oz/225 g semisweet chocolate

1 Cover 2 cookie sheets with rice paper. Whisk the egg whites in a large mixing bowl until stiff, then fold in the sugar and ground almonds.

2 Place the mixture in a large pastry bag fitted with a ½-inch/1-cm plain tip and pipe fingers, about 3-inches/7.5 cm-long, allowing space between them for the mixture to spread during cooking.

3 Bake in a preheated oven, 350°F/180°C, for 15–20 minutes, until golden. Transfer to a wire rack and let cool. Remove the excess rice paper from around the edges.

4 Melt the semisweet chocolate and dip the bottom of each cookie into the chocolate. Place the macaroons on a sheet of baking parchment and let set.

COOK'S TIP

Rice paper is edible so you can just break off the excess from around the edge of the cookies. Remove it completely before dipping in the chocolate, if you prefer.

5 Drizzle any remaining chocolate over the top of the cookies (you may need to re-heat the chocolate in order to do this). Let the chocolate set before serving.

chocolate chip flapjacks

makes twelve

½ cup butter

⅓ cup superfine sugar

1 tbsp light corn syrup

4 cups rolled oats

½ cup semisweet chocolate chips

⅓ cup golden raisins

COOK'S TIP

The flapjacks will keep in
an airtight container for up
to 1 week, but they are so
delicious they are unlikely
to last that long!

1 Lightly grease a shallow
8-inch/20-cm square cake pan.

2 Place the butter, superfine sugar,
and light corn syrup in a pan and
cook over low heat, stirring until the
butter and sugar melt and the mixture
is well combined.

3 Remove the pan from the heat
and stir in the rolled oats until
they are well coated. Add the
chocolate chips and the golden raisins
and mix well.

4 Turn into the prepared pan and
press down well.

5 Bake in a preheated oven,
350°F/180°C, for 30 minutes. Let
cool slightly, then mark into fingers.
When the mixture is almost cold cut
into bars or squares and transfer to a
wire rack until cold.

chocolate chip cookies

makes eighteen

1½ cups all-purpose flour

1 tsp baking powder

½ cup soft margarine

scant ⅔ cup brown sugar

¼ cup superfine sugar

½ tsp vanilla extract

1 egg

⅔ cup semisweet chocolate chips

VARIATION

For Choc & Nut Cookies,
add ½ cup chopped hazelnuts
to the basic mixture.
For Double Choc Cookies,
beat in 1½ oz/40 g melted
semisweet chocolate.
For White Chocolate Chip
Cookies, use white chocolate
chips instead of the semisweet
chocolate chips.

1 Place all of the ingredients in a large mixing bowl and beat until they are thoroughly combined.

2 Lightly grease 2 cookie sheets. Place tablespoonfuls of the mixture onto the cookie sheets, spacing them well apart to allow for spreading during cooking.

3 Bake in a preheated oven, 375°F/190°C, for 10–12 minutes or until the cookies are golden brown.

4 Using a spatula, carefully transfer the chocolate chip cookies to a wire rack to cool completely.

millionaire's shortbread

serves four

1½ cups all-purpose flour

½ cup butter, cut into small pieces

⅓ cup brown sugar, sifted

TOPPING

4 tbsp butter

⅓ cup brown sugar

1¾ cups canned condensed milk

5½ oz/150 g light chocolate

1 Grease a 9-inch/23-cm square cake pan.

2 Sift the flour into a mixing bowl and rub in the butter with your fingertips until the mixture resembles fine bread crumbs. Add the sugar and mix to form a firm dough.

3 Press the dough into the bottom of the prepared pan and prick the bottom with a fork.

4 Bake in a preheated oven, 375°F/190°C, for 20 minutes, until lightly golden. Let cool in the pan.

5 To make the topping, place the butter, sugar, and condensed milk in a non-stick pan and cook over gentle heat, stirring constantly with a wooden spoon, until the mixture comes to a boil.

COOK'S TIP

Ensure the caramel layer is completely cool and set before coating it with the melted chocolate, otherwise they will mix together.

6 Lower the heat and cook for 4–5 minutes, until the caramel is pale golden and thick and is coming away from the sides of the pan. Pour the topping evenly over the shortbread layer and let cool.

7 When the caramel topping is firm, melt the light chocolate in a heatproof bowl set over a pan of simmering water. Spread the melted chocolate over the topping, let set in a cool place, then cut the shortbread into squares or fingers.

florentines

makes ten

4 tbsp butter

¼ cup superfine sugar

scant ¼ cup all-purpose flour, sifted

⅓ cup almonds, chopped

⅓ cup chopped candied peel

¼ cup raisins, chopped

2 tbsp chopped candied cherries

finely grated rind of ½ lemon

4½ oz/125 g semisweet chocolate,
   melted

VARIATION

Replace the semisweet chocolate
with white chocolate or, for a
dramatic effect, cover half of
the florentines in semisweet
chocolate and half in white.

---

1 Line 2 large cookie sheets with
baking parchment.

2 Heat the butter and superfine
sugar together in a small pan
until the butter has just melted and the
sugar dissolved. Remove the pan from
the heat.

3 Stir in the flour and mix well. Stir
in the chopped almonds, candied
peel, raisins, cherries, and lemon rind.
Place teaspoonfuls of the mixture well
apart on the cookie sheets.

4 Bake in a preheated oven,
350°F/180°C, for 10 minutes or
until they are lightly golden.

5 As soon as the florentines are
removed from the oven, press the
edges into neat shapes while still on
the cookie sheets, using a cookie
cutter. Let cool on the cookie sheets
until firm, then transfer to a wire rack
to cool completely.

6 Spread the melted chocolate
over the smooth side of each
florentine. As the chocolate starts to
set, mark wavy lines in it with a fork.
Let set, chocolate-side up.

lemon chocolate pinwheels

makes forty

¾ cup butter, softened

1⅓ cups superfine sugar

1 egg, beaten

3 cups all-purpose flour

1 oz/25 g semisweet chocolate,
   melted and cooled slightly

grated rind of 1 lemon

COOK'S TIP

To make rolling out easier, place
each piece of dough between
2 sheets of baking parchment.

1 Grease and flour several cookie
sheets, enough to accommodate
40 cookies comfortably.

2 Cream the butter and sugar
together in a large mixing bowl
until light and fluffy.

3 Gradually add the beaten egg to
the creamed mixture, beating well
after each addition.

4 Sift the flour into the creamed
mixture and mix thoroughly until
a soft dough forms.

5 Transfer half of the dough to
another bowl and then beat in
the cooled melted chocolate.

6 Stir the grated lemon rind into the
other half of the plain dough until
well incorporated.

7 Roll out the 2 pieces of dough on
a lightly floured surface to form
rectangles of the same size.

8 Lay the lemon dough on top of
the chocolate dough. Roll up the
dough tightly into a sausage shape,
using a sheet of baking parchment to
guide you. Let the dough chill in the
refrigerator to firm up.

9 Cut the roll into about 40 slices,
place them on the cookie sheets,
and bake in a preheated oven, 375°F/
190°C, for 10–12 minutes or until the
slices are lightly golden. Transfer the
lemon chocolate pinwheels to a wire
rack and let them cool completely
before serving.

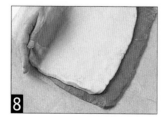

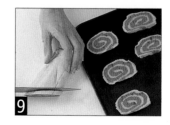

chocolate pretzels

makes thirty

generous ⅓ cup unsalted butter

½ cup superfine sugar

1 egg

2 cups all-purpose flour

¼ cup unsweetened cocoa

TO FINISH

1 tbsp butter

3½ oz/100 g semisweet chocolate

confectioners' sugar, for dusting

1 Lightly grease a cookie sheet with a little butter. Beat the butter and sugar together in a large mixing bowl until light and fluffy. Beat in the egg, ensuring all the ingredients are well combined.

2 Sift the flour and cocoa together and gradually beat into the egg mixture to form a soft dough. Use your fingers to incorporate the last of the flour and bring the dough together. Let chill for 15 minutes.

3 Break pieces from the dough and roll into thin sausage shapes about 4-inches/10-cm long and ¼-inch/6-mm thick. Carefully twist into pretzel shapes by making a circle, then twist the ends through each other to form a letter "B."

4 Place the chocolate pretzels on the prepared cookie sheet, slightly spaced apart to allow for spreading during cooking.

5 Bake in a preheated oven, 375°F/190°C, for 8–12 minutes. Let the pretzels cool slightly on the cookie sheet, then transfer them to a wire rack to cool completely.

6 Melt the butter and chocolate in a bowl set over a pan of gently simmering water, stirring to combine.

7 Dip half of each pretzel into the chocolate and allow the excess chocolate to drip back into the bowl. Place the pretzels on a sheet of baking parchment and let set.

8 When set, dust the non-chocolate-coated side of each pretzel with confectioners' sugar.

chocolate boxes

serves six

8 oz/225 g semisweet chocolate

about 8 oz/225 g bought or
ready-made semisweet or
chocolate sponge cake

2 tbsp apricot jelly

⅔ cup heavy cream

1 tbsp maple syrup

3½ oz/100 g prepared fresh fruit,
such as small strawberries,
raspberries, kiwifruit or red
currants

1 Melt the semisweet chocolate and
spread it evenly over a large sheet
of baking parchment. Let the chocolate
harden in a cool room.

2 When just set, cut the chocolate
into 2-inch/5-cm squares and
remove from the parchment. Make
sure that your hands are as cool as
possible and handle the chocolate as
little as possible.

3 Cut the cake into 2 cubes,
2 inches/5 cm across, then cut
each cube in half. Warm the apricot
jelly in a small pan and brush it over
the sides of the cake cubes. Carefully
press a chocolate square on to each
side of the cake cubes to make
4 chocolate boxes with cake at the
bottom. Let chill in the refrigerator for
20 minutes.

4 Whip the cream with the maple
syrup until just holding its shape.
Spoon or pipe a little of the mixture
into each chocolate box.

5 Decorate the top of each box with
the prepared fruit. If wished, the
fruit can be partially dipped into melted
chocolate and allowed to harden
before being placed into the boxes.

fried chocolate fingers

makes twenty four

4 eggs, beaten lightly

2½ cups milk

5 tbsp sherry

8 slices of day-old white bread,
    ½ inch/1 cm thick

4 tbsp corn oil

generous ½ cup superfine sugar

8 oz/225 g semisweet chocolate

vanilla ice cream, to serve (optional)

1 Pour the beaten eggs, milk, and sherry into a shallow dish and beat lightly to mix. Cut each slice of bread lengthwise into 3 fingers. Soak the bread fingers in the egg mixture until they are soft, then drain them on paper towels.

2 Heat the oil in a large, heavy-based skillet. Carefully add the bread fingers to the pan, in batches, and cook over medium heat for 12 minutes on each side, until golden. Using tongs, transfer the fingers to paper towels to drain.

3 When all the fingers are cooked and thoroughly drained, roll them first in the sugar and then in the grated chocolate. Pile on a warmed serving plate and serve immediately, with vanilla ice cream, if desired.

meringue fingers

makes thirty

1 egg white

¼ cup superfine sugar

1½ tsp unsweetened cocoa

5 oz/140 g semisweet chocolate,
    broken into pieces

1 Line a cookie sheet with baking parchment. Whisk the egg white until it forms soft peaks. Whisk in half the sugar and continue whisking until stiff and glossy. Fold in the remaining sugar and the cocoa.

2 Spoon the mixture into a pastry bag fitted with a ½-inch/1-cm round tip. Pipe fingers about 3-inches/7.5-cm long onto the prepared cookie sheet, spacing them at least 1-inch/2.5-cm apart. Bake in apreheated oven, 250°F/120°C for 1 hour, until completely dry. Remove from the oven and transfer to a wire rack to cool.

3 Put the chocolate into the top of a double boiler or in a heatproof bowl set over a pan of barely

simmering water. Heat, stirring constantly, until the chocolate has melted and the mixture is smooth. Remove from the heat. Cool slightly, then dip the meringue fingers into the mixture, one at a time, to half-coat them. You can either coat one end completely, leaving the other plain, or dip the fingers at an angle so half the length is coated. Place the fingers on baking parchment to set.

Candy & Drinks

There is nothing quite as nice as home-made chocolates and candy—they leave the average box of chocolates in the shade! You'll find recipes in this chapter to suit everybody's taste. Wonderful, rich, melt-in-the-mouth Italian Chocolate Truffles, Chocolate Marzipans, Nutty Chocolate Clusters, Mini Chocolate Tartlets, and rich Liqueur Chocolates—they're all here. There is even some Easy Chocolate Fudge, so there is no need to fiddle about with sugar thermometers.

Looking for something to wash it all down? We have included delightfully cool summer chocolate drinks and, for warmth and comfort on winter nights, hot drinks that will simply put instant hot chocolate to shame. Enjoy!

liqueur chocolates

COOK'S TIP

Candy cases can vary in size.
Use the smallest you can find
for this recipe.

1 Line a cookie sheet with a sheet of baking parchment. Break the semisweet chocolate into pieces, place in a bowl and set over a pan of hot water. Stir until melted. Spoon the chocolate into 20 paper candy cases, spreading up the sides with a small spoon or brush. Place upside down on the cookie sheet and let set.

2 Carefully peel away the paper cases. Place a cherry or nut in the bottom of each cup.

3 To make the filling, place the heavy cream in a mixing bowl and sift the confectioners' sugar on top. Whisk the cream until it is just holding its shape, then whisk in the liqueur to flavor it.

4 Place the cream in a pastry bag fitted with a ½-inch/1-cm plain tip and pipe a little into each chocolate case. Let chill for 20 minutes.

5 To finish, spoon the semisweet chocolate over the cream to cover it and pipe the melted white chocolate on top, swirling it into the semisweet

chocolate with a toothpick. Let harden. Alternatively, cover the cream with the melted semisweet chocolate and decorate with white chocolate curls before setting. If you prefer, place a small piece of nut or cherry on top of the cream, then cover with semisweet chocolate.

nutty chocolate clusters

makes thirty

6 oz/175 g white chocolate

3½ oz/100 g graham crackers

⅔ cup chopped macadamia nuts or
   brazil nuts

1 oz/25 g preserved ginger,
   chopped (optional)

6 oz/175 g semisweet chocolate

1 Line a cookie sheet with a sheet of baking parchment. Break the white chocolate into small pieces and melt in a large mixing bowl set over a pan of gently simmering water.

2 Break the graham crackers into small pieces. Stir the crackers into the melted chocolate with the chopped nuts and preserved ginger (if using).

3 Place heaping teaspoons of the chocolate cluster mixture onto the prepared cookie sheet.

4 Chill the chocolate cluster mixture until set, then carefully remove from the baking parchment.

5 Melt the semisweet chocolate and let it cool slightly. Dip the clusters into the chocolate, letting the excess to drip back into the bowl. Return to the cookie sheet and let chill until set.

fruit & nut fudge

makes twenty-five

9 oz/250 g semisweet chocolate

2 tbsp butter

4 tbsp canned evaporated milk

3 cups confectioners' sugar, sifted

½ cup coarsely chopped hazelnuts

⅓ cup golden raisins

VARIATION

Vary the nuts used in this recipe; try making the fudge with almonds, brazil nuts, walnuts, or pecans.

---

1 Lightly grease an 8-inch/20-cm square cake pan.

2 Break the chocolate into pieces and place it in a bowl with the butter and evaporated milk. Set the bowl over a pan of gently simmering water and stir until the chocolate and butter have melted and the ingredients are well combined.

3 Remove the bowl from the heat and gradually beat in the confectioners' sugar. Stir the hazelnuts and golden raisins into the mixture. Press the fudge into the prepared pan and smooth the top. Chill until firm.

4 Tip the fudge out onto a cutting board and cut into squares. Place in paper candy cases and let chill in the refrigerator until required.

mini chocolate tartlets

makes eighteen

1½ cups all-purpose flour

⅓ cup butter

1 tbsp superfine sugar

about 1 tbsp water

FILLING

3½ oz/100 g full-fat soft cheese

2 tbsp superfine sugar

1 small egg, beaten lightly

1¾ oz/50 g semisweet chocolate

TO DECORATE

generous ⅓ cup heavy cream

semisweet chocolate curls (see
   page 263)

unsweetened cocoa, for dusting

COOK'S TIP

The tartlets can be made up to
3 days ahead. Decorate on the
day of serving, preferably no
more than 4 hours in advance.

1 Sift the flour into a mixing bowl. Cut the butter into small pieces and rub in until the mixture resembles fine bread crumbs. Stir in the sugar. Add enough water to mix to a soft dough, then cover with plastic wrap and let chill for 15 minutes.

2 Roll out the dough on a lightly floured counter and use to line 18 mini tartlet pans or mini muffin pans. Prick the tartlet shells with a toothpick.

3 Beat the full-fat soft cheese and the sugar together. Beat in the egg. Melt the chocolate and beat it into the mixture. Spoon into the tartlet shells and bake in a preheated oven, 375°F/190°C, for 15 minutes, until the dough is crisp and the soft cheese and chocolate filling set. Place the pans on a wire rack to cool completely.

4 Chill the tartlets. Whip the cream until it is just holding its shape. Place the cream in a pastry bag fitted with a star tip and pipe rosettes of whipped cream on top of the chocolate tartlets. Decorate with chocolate curls and finish with a dusting of cocoa.

rocky road bites

makes eighteen

FILLING

4½ oz/125 g light chocolate

2½ oz/50 g mini multi-colored
   marshmallows

¼ cup chopped walnuts

1 oz/25 g no-soak dried apricots,
   chopped

VARIATION

If you cannot find mini
marshmallows, use large
ones and chop them before
mixing them into the
melted chocolate.

---

1 Line a cookie sheet with baking
   parchment and set aside.

2 Break the chocolate into small
   pieces and place in a large mixing
bowl. Set the bowl over a pan of
simmering water and stir until the
chocolate has melted.

3 Stir in the marshmallows, walnuts,
   and apricots, and toss in the
melted chocolate until well covered.

4 Place heaping teaspoons of the
   marshmallow mixture onto the
prepared cookie sheet.

5 Let chill in the refrigerator until
   the candy is set.

6 Once they are set, carefully
   remove the rocky road bites from
the baking parchment.

7 Place in paper candy cases to
   serve, if wished.

chocolate mascarpone cups

makes twenty

3½ oz/100 g semisweet chocolate

FILLING

3½ oz/100 g light or semisweet
  chocolate

¼ tsp vanilla extract

7 oz/200 g mascarpone cheese

unsweetened cocoa, for dusting

VARIATION

Mascarpone is a rich Italian
soft cheese made from fresh
cream, so it has a high fat
content. Its delicate flavor
blends well with chocolate.

1 Line a cookie sheet with a sheet of baking parchment. Break the semisweet chocolate into pieces, place in a bowl and set over a pan of hot water. Stir until melted. Spoon the chocolate into 20 paper candy cases, spreading up the sides with a small spoon or brush. Place the chocolate cups upside down on the cookie sheet and let set.

2 When set, carefully peel away the paper cases.

3 To make the filling, melt the chocolate. Place the mascarpone cheese in a bowl and beat in the vanilla extract and melted chocolate until well combined. Let the mixture chill in the refrigerator, beating occasionally until firm enough to pipe.

4 Place the mascarpone filling in a pastry bag fitted with a star tip and pipe the mixture into the cups. Decorate with a dusting of cocoa.

rum truffles

5½ oz/125 g semisweet chocolate

small piece of butter

2 tbsp rum

½ cup shredded coconut

3½ oz/100 g cake crumbs

6 tbsp confectioners' sugar

2 tbsp unsweetened cocoa

COOK'S TIP

Make sure the chocolate is cut into even sized pieces. This way, you will ensure that it all melts at the same rate.

1 Break the chocolate into pieces and place in a bowl with the butter. Set the bowl over a pan of gently simmering water, stir until melted and combined.

2 Remove from the heat and beat in the rum. Stir in the shredded coconut, cake crumbs, and two-thirds of the confectioners' sugar. Beat until combined. Add a little extra rum if the mixture is stiff.

3 Roll the mixture into small balls and place them on a sheet of baking parchment. Chill until firm.

4 Strain the remaining confectioners' sugar onto a large plate. Sift the cocoa onto another plate. Roll half of the truffles in the confectioners' sugar until thoroughly coated and roll the remaining rum truffles in the cocoa.

5 Place the truffles in paper candy cases and let chill in the refrigerator until required.

VARIATION

Make the truffles with white chocolate and replace the rum with coconut-flavored liqueur or milk. Roll them in unsweetened cocoa or dip in melted light chocolate.

mini chocolate cones

makes ten

2¾ oz/75 g semisweet chocolate

generous ⅓ cup heavy cream

1 tbsp confectioners' sugar

1 tbsp crème de menthe

chocolate-coated coffee beans, to

decorate (optional)

1 Cut 10 circles, 3 inches/7.5 cm across, out of baking parchment. Shape each circle into a cone shape and secure with sticky tape.

2 Break the chocolate into pieces, place in a bowl and set over a pan of hot water. Stir until melted. Using a small brush, coat the inside of each cone with the melted chocolate.

3 Brush a second layer of chocolate on the inside of the cones and let chill until set. Carefully peel away the baking parchment.

4 Place the cream, confectioners' sugar, and crème de menthe in a mixing bowl and whip until just holding its shape. Place the flavored cream in a pastry bag fitted with a star tip and carefully pipe the mixture into the chocolate cones.

5 Decorate the filled mini chocolate cones with chocolate-coated coffee beans (if using) and let chill in the refrigerator until required.

collettes

makes twenty

3½ oz/100 g white chocolate

FILLING

5½ oz/150 g orange-flavored
semisweet chocolate

⅔ cup heavy cream

2 tbsp confectioners' sugar

COOK'S TIP

If they do not hold their
shape well, use 2 cases to make
a double thickness mold. Foil
cases are firmer, so use these if
you can find them.

1 Line a cookie sheet with baking parchment. Break the white chocolate into pieces, place in a bowl, and set over a pan of hot water. Stir until melted. Spoon the melted chocolate into 20 paper candy cases, spreading up the sides with a small spoon or brush. Place upside down on the prepared cookie sheet and let set.

2 When the chocolate has set, peel away the paper cases.

3 To make the filling, melt the orange-flavored chocolate and place in a mixing bowl with the heavy cream and the confectioners' sugar. Beat until smooth. Chill until the mixture becomes firm enough to pipe, stirring occasionally.

4 Place the filling in a pastry bag fitted with a star tip and pipe a little into each candy case. Chill the collettes until required.

chocolate marzipans

makes thirty

1 lb/450 g marzipan

⅓ cup very finely chopped candied cherries

1 oz/25 g preserved ginger, chopped very finely

1¾ oz/50 g no-soak dried apricots, very finely chopped 12 oz/350 g semisweet chocolate

1 oz/25 g white chocolate confectioners' sugar, to dust

1 Line a cookie sheet with baking parchment. Divide the marzipan into 3 balls and knead each ball to soften it.

2 Work the candied cherries into one portion of the marzipan by kneading on a counter lightly dusted with confectioners' sugar.

3 Do the same with the preserved ginger and another portion of marzipan, and then the apricots and the third portion of marzipan.

4 Form each flavored portion of marzipan into small balls, keeping the different flavors separate.

5 Break the semisweet chocolate into pieces, place in a bowl, and set over a pan of hot water. Stir until melted. Dip one of each flavored ball of marzipan into the chocolate by spiking each one with a toothpick, letting the excess chocolate to drip back into the bowl.

6 Place the balls in clusters made up of the 3 flavors on the cookie sheet. Repeat with the remaining marzipan balls. Chill until set.

7 Melt the white chocolate and drizzle a little over the tops of each cluster of marzipan balls. Chill until hardened, then remove from the baking parchment and dust the marzipan with sugar to serve.

VARIATION

Coat the marzipan balls in white or light chocolate and drizzle with semisweet chocolate, if you prefer.

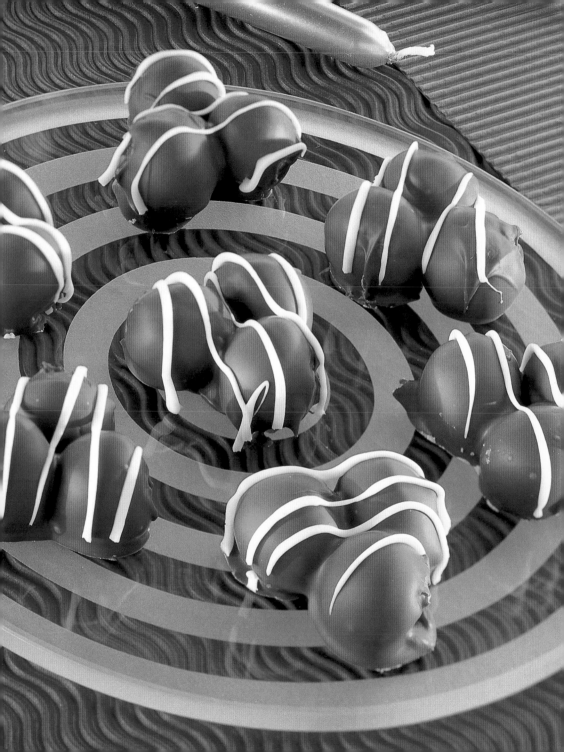

mini florentines

makes forty

⅓ cup butter

⅓ cup superfine sugar

2 tbsp golden raisins or raisins

2 tbsp chopped candied cherries

2 tbsp chopped candied ginger

1 oz/25 g sunflower seeds

¾ cup slivered almonds

2 tbsp heavy cream

6 oz/175 g semisweet chocolate

1 Grease and flour 2 cookie sheets or line with baking parchment.

2 Place the butter in a small pan and heat gently until melted. Add the sugar, stir until dissolved, then bring the mixture to a boil. Remove from the heat and stir in the golden raisins or raisins, cherries, ginger, sunflower seeds, and almonds. Mix well, then beat in the cream.

3 Place small teaspoons of the fruit and nut mixture onto the prepared cookie sheet, allowing plenty of space for the mixture to spread. Bake in a preheated oven, at 350°F/180°C, for 10–12 minutes or until light golden in color.

4 Remove from the oven and, while still hot, use a circular cookie cutter to pull in the edges to form perfect circles. Let cool and go crisp before removing from the cookie sheet.

5 Break the chocolate into pieces, place in a bowl over a pan of hot water, and stir until melted. Spread most of the chocolate onto a sheet of baking parchment. When the chocolate is on the point of setting, carefully place the cookies flat-side down on the chocolate and let harden completely.

6 Cut around the florentines and remove from the baking parchment. Spread a little more chocolate on the coated side of the florentines and use a fork to mark waves in the chocolate. Let set. Arrange the florentines on a plate (or in a presentation box for a gift) with alternate sides facing upward. Keep the florentines cool.

easy chocolate fudge

makes twenty-five pieces

1 lb 2 oz/500 g semisweet
   chocolate
⅓ cup unsalted butter
1¾ cups canned condensed milk
½ tsp vanilla extract

1 Lightly grease an 8-inch/20-cm
  square cake pan.

2 Break the chocolate into pieces
  and place in a large pan with the
butter and condensed milk.

3 Heat gently, stirring until the
  chocolate and butter melts and
the mixture is smooth. Do not let the
mixture boil.

4 Remove from the heat. Beat in
  the vanilla extract, then beat the
mixture for a few minutes until
thickened. Pour it into the prepared
pan and smooth the top.

5 Chill the mixture in the
  refrigerator until firm.

6 Tip the fudge out onto a large
  cutting board and cut into
squares to serve.

COOK'S TIP

Store the fudge in an airtight
container in a cool, dry place for
up to 1 month. Do not freeze.

chocolate cherries

12 candied cherries

2 tbsp rum or brandy

9 oz/250 g marzipan

5½ oz/125 g semisweet chocolate

extra light, semisweet, or white
  chocolate, to decorate (optional)

VARIATION

Flatten the marzipan and use it
to mold around the cherries to
cover them, then dip in the
chocolate as in main recipe.

1 Line a cookie sheet with a sheet of baking parchment.

2 Cut the candied cherries in half and place in a small bowl. Add the rum or brandy and stir to coat. Let the cherries soak for at least 1 hour, stirring occasionally.

3 Divide the marzipan into 24 pieces and roll each piece into a ball. Press half a cherry into the top of each marzipan ball.

4 Break the chocolate into pieces, place in a bowl, and set over a pan of hot water. Stir until melted.

5 Dip each candy into the melted chocolate using a toothpick, allowing the excess to drip back into the bowl. Place the coated cherries on the baking parchment and chill until set.

6 If wished, melt a little extra chocolate and drizzle it over the top of the coated cherries. Let set.

italian chocolate truffles

makes twenty four

6 oz/175 g semisweet chocolate

2 tbsp Amaretto liqueur or orange-
    flavored liqueur

3 tbsp unsalted butter

4 tbsp confectioners' sugar

½ cup ground almonds

1¾ oz/50 g grated chocolate

VARIATION

The almond-flavored liqueur
gives these truffles an authentic
Italian flavor. The original almond
liqueur, Amaretto di Saronno,
comes from Saronno in Italy.

1 Melt the semisweet chocolate with the liqueur in a bowl set over a pan of hot water, stirring until well combined.

2 Add the butter and stir until it has melted. Stir in the confectioners' sugar and the ground almonds.

3 Let the mixture stand in a cool place until it is firm enough to roll into 24 balls.

4 Place the grated chocolate on a plate and roll the truffles in the chocolate to coat them.

5 Place the truffles in paper candy cases and let chill.

white chocolate truffles

makes twenty

2 tbsp unsalted butter

5 tbsp heavy cream

8 oz/225 g good-quality Swiss
   white chocolate

1 tbsp orange-flavored liqueur,
   optional

TO FINISH

3½ oz/100 g white chocolate

1 Line a jelly roll pan with a sheet of baking parchment.

2 Place the butter and cream in a small pan and bring slowly to a boil, stirring constantly. Boil the mixture for 1 minute, then remove the pan from the heat.

3 Break the chocolate into pieces and add to the cream. Stir until melted, then beat in the orange-flavored liqueur (if using).

4 Pour into the prepared pan and chill for about 2 hours, until firm.

5 Break off pieces of the truffle mixture and roll them into balls. Chill for another 30 minutes before finishing the truffles.

6 To finish, melt the white chocolate in a bowl set over a pan of gently simmering water. Dip the balls in the chocolate, allowing the excess to drip back into the bowl. Place on non-stick baking parchment, swirl the chocolate with the tines of a fork, and let harden.

7 For an effective decoration, and a pleasing color contrast, drizzle a little melted semisweet chocolate over the truffles if wished and then let them set before serving.

chocolate eggnog

serves four

8 egg yolks

1 cup sugar

4 cups milk

8 oz/225 g semisweet chocolate

⅔ cup dark rum

1 Beat the egg yolks with the sugar until thickened.

2 Pour the milk into a large pan. Grate the chocolate and add it to the milk. Bring to a boil, then remove from the heat and gradually beat in the egg yolk mixture. Stir in the rum and pour into heatproof glasses.

hot brandy chocolate

serves four

4 cups milk

4 oz/115 g semisweet chocolate,
   broken into pieces

2 tbsp sugar

5 tbsp brandy

TO DECORATE

6 tbsp whipped cream

4 tsp unsweetened cocoa, sifted

1 Pour the milk into a pan and bring to a boil, then remove from the heat. Place the chocolate in a small pan and add 2 tablespoons of the hot milk. Stir over low heat until the chocolate has melted. Stir the chocolate mixture into the remaining milk and add the sugar.

2 Stir in the brandy and pour into 4 heatproof glasses. Top each with a swirl of whipped cream and sprinkle with a little sifted cocoa.

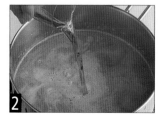

cold chocolate drinks

serves two

CHOCOLATE MILK SHAKE

2 cups ice-cold milk

3 tbsp drinking chocolate powder

3 scoops chocolate ice cream

unsweetened cocoa, for dusting

CHOCOLATE ICE CREAM SODA

5 tbsp Glossy Chocolate Sauce (see
page 360)

soda water

2 scoops chocolate ice cream

heavy cream, whipped

semisweet or light chocolate, grated

1 To make the chocolate milk shake, pour half of the ice-cold milk in a blender.

2 Add the drinking chocolate powder to the blender and 1 scoop of the chocolate ice cream. Blend until frothy and well mixed. Stir in the remaining milk.

3 Place the remaining 2 scoops of chocolate ice cream in 2 tall serving glasses and carefully pour the chocolate milk over the ice scoops of chocolate cream.

4 Sprinkle a little cocoa over the top of each drink and serve immediately.

5 To make the chocolate ice cream soda, divide the Glossy Chocolate Sauce between 2 glasses.

6 Add a little soda water to each glass and stir to combine the sauce and soda water. Place a scoop of ice cream in each glass and top up with more of the soda water.

7 Place a dollop of whipped heavy cream on the top, if liked, and sprinkle with a little grated semisweet or light chocolate.

COOK'S TIP

Served in a tall glass, a
milk shake or an ice cream
soda makes a delicious
snack in a drink. Serve with
straws, if wished.

INDEX